Women in Russia

A New Era in Russian Feminism

Edited by
ANASTASIA POSADSKAYA
and Others at the
MOSCOW GENDER CENTRE

Translated by
Kate Clark

Originated by
Ruth Steele

VERSO

London · New York

First published by Verso 1994
© Moscow Gender Centre 1994
Translation © Verso 1994
All rights reserved

Verso
UK: 6 Meard Street, London W1V 3HR
USA: 29 West 35th Street, New York, NY 10001–2291

Verso is the imprint of New Left Books

ISBN 0–86091–487–9
ISBN 0–86091–657–X (pbk)

British Library Cataloguing in Publication Data
A catalogue record for this book is available from the British Library

Library of Congress Cataloging-in-Publication Data
Women in Russia : a new era in Russian feminism / edited by Anastasia Posadskaya ;
    translated by Kate Clark.
    p.   cm.
  Includes bibliographical references.
    ISBN 0–86091–487–9. — ISBN 0–86091–657–X (pbk.)
    1. Feminism—Russia (Federation) 2. Women—Russia (Federation)—Social
conditions. 3. Russia (Federation)—Social conditions.
  I. Posadskaya, Anastasia.
HQ1665.15.W66   1994
305.42'0947——dc20   94–17273
                                                                                            CIP

Typeset by Type Study, Scarborough
Printed and bound in Finland by
Werner Söderström OY

Contents

Acknowledgements   vii

Translator's Preface   ix

Introduction   1

1   Women as the Objects and Motive Force of Change in Our Time
  Anastasia Posadskaya   8

2   What Does Our New Democracy Offer Society?
  Tatiana Klimenkova   14

3   The Mythology of Women's Emancipation in the USSR as the Foundation for a Policy of Discrimination
  Olga Voronina   37

4   No Longer Totalitarianism, But Not Yet Democracy: The Emergence of an Independent Women's Movement in Russia
  Valentina Konstantinova   57

5   What Does the Future Hold? (Some Thoughts on the Prospects for Women's Employment)
  Yelena Mezentseva   74

6   Women in the Labour Market: Yesterday, Today and Tomorrow
  Zoya Khotkina   85

7   Equal Opportunities or Protectionist Measures? The
    Choice Facing Women
    Yelena Mezentseva   109

8   The Mythology of Womanhood in Contemporary
    'Soviet' Culture
    Olga Lipovskaya   123

9   Virgin Mary or Mary Magdalene? The Construction
    and Reconstruction of Sex during the Perestroika
    Period
    Olga Voronina   135

10 The Lesbian Subculture: The Historical Roots of
    Lesbianism in the Former USSR
    Olga Zhuk   146

11 Feminism in Russia: Debates from the Past
    Svetlana Aivazova   154

12 A Feminist Critique of Policy, Legislation and Social
    Consciousness in Post-socialist Russia
    Anastasia Posadskaya   164

APPENDIX   Self-Portrait of a Russian Feminist
           An Interview with Anastasia Posadskaya   183

Notes on the Contributors   202

Acknowledgements

The Centre for Gender Studies has several people to thank for this book. It was just before the First Independent Women's Forum in Dubna – in March 1991 – that we first met Ruth Steele, who was running a joint publishing enterprise called Inter-Verso which had recently been set up. Shortly after the Forum, Ruth suggested to us that we should write this book. The idea appealed to us immediately – no specialist works had ever been written by Russian women attempting to evaluate their own 'perestroika' experience. There had been interviews and a few separate articles by Russian women in Western books about the woman question – but not an entire book by Russian experts. Now, a few years on, after many problems and unforeseen complications, the book has come out. Ruth worked hard to achieve this, encouraging us, writing letters to the publishing house in London, helping to get the manuscripts to them – and she was always there on our side, which was so important to us. All our contributors are deeply indebted to Ruth; in fact the book would have been impossible without her. We are also grateful to Hilary Pilkington of the University of Birmingham, who did the initial Reader's Report for Verso, and whose comments were invaluable to us in preparing our essays for publication. We would like to express our particular appreciation to Katrina vanden Heuvel for her encouragement and support in preparing this English edition. Lastly, our special thanks go to Kate Clark, who translated the book. Kate has shown incredible professionalism, persistence and goodwill in working on our difficult texts.

Translator's Preface

In early 1990 I attended a meeting of the newly formed Centre for Gender Studies. There were about thirty women crowded into a small room on one of the upper corridors of the Institute for Research into Socio-Economic Problems of the Population near Profsoyuznaya Metro station. It was informal, and very exciting, because the Russian women who spoke were so enthusiastic, so determined, so optimistic that they could make a useful contribution to feminist studies, now that they had at last won the right to set up their own research Centre for Gender Studies. From those small beginnings, the Moscow Gender Centre has flourished and grown in influence. It has organized two Independent Women's Forums, which have had considerable resonance both inside Russia and in the West. From an initial staff of five, it has expanded to fifteen researchers, has a Library and database, and has set up a women's information network. And it is carrying on important gender research which does not go unnoticed, despite the increasing patriarchalism characteristic of the present post-socialist period in Russia. The interview with Anastasia, published as an appendix to this collection, evokes the context in which the Gender Centre began its work.

Back in 1985, one of the very first interviews I did as a journalist in Moscow was with a woman judge at the Soviet Women's Committee. I can still remember the astonishment I felt when, in answer to my question about sex crimes, she told me that there were no such crimes in the USSR and that she, as a judge, had never had to deal with any cases of this kind. I have often wondered how she could tell me such a barefaced lie – she a judge, of all people. But this was just before perestroika began, before the April Plenum 1985 when Mikhail Gorbachev set out the planks of his new reform process. In a way, though, that interview, hypocritical though it was on the judge's part, epitomizes the state of women's equality under Soviet socialism. On the one hand, women *did* have equality in law, and there *were* women in all the professions, some of which – like the judiciary – still remain virtually closed to women in Britain, for instance. And yet, as readers will see in this book, much of what had been gained legally remained a formality, and women in the USSR were very far from achieving real sex equality.

As the contributors point out, even when glasnost began lifting the veil from so many of society's problems, the woman question was strangely absent. It was as if there was a tacit agreement between all – reformers and conservatives alike – that this question didn't need to be addressed. And then came the breakthrough – the famous article which appeared in the CPSU's theoretical journal *Kommunist* in April 1989, written by one of the contributors to this book, Anastasia Posadskaya, and two women closely associated with the foundation of the Gender Centre, Natalia Zakharova and Natalia Rimashevskaya. Only shortly before that I had had a heated discussion with the deputy editor of that journal, Otto Lacis, about the lack of women's equality in the Soviet Union and the need, as I saw it, for an independent women's liberation movement. And here at last was a serious, extremely well-documented paper proving just how far the stated aims of women's equality in socialist society had diverged from the reality. It is hard to put yourself back into those times – so much had already changed in the glasnost era, yet so little had changed as regards the woman question. It was exhilarating to see that at last there were women who were prepared to defy the all-pervasive patriarchal attitudes of the time, and raise anew the woman question from a distinct, refreshingly feminist perspective.

Prevailing patriarchal attitudes were typified by Karem Rash's deeply sexist feature in the Party newspaper *Pravda* only a few weeks before the *Kommunist* article. Referred to by more than one of the contributors to this book, the feature blamed women for all the ills of society. I remember being so enraged by the sneering tone of the piece that I sent a protest letter to *Pravda*'s editor, Viktor Afanasiev. Rooting among my journalist files recently, I found this letter. It reads:

As a working woman journalist, I was insulted by the offensive tone of the piece, as I presume must have been very many Soviet women workers. . . . I would have expected that your paper would have ensured that an article on such a subject would have given a more serious analysis of the problem and at least not contained the offensive tone which unfortunately characterized it. Especially since the Communist Party's policy as determined by its 27th Congress and 19th Party Conference is one of encouraging promotion of women to leading posts both within the Party and in the economy.

And there we have it again: the contradiction between the formally proclaimed (promotion of women in all spheres) and the reality (absence of women in decision-making bodies, women segregated into feminized areas of low-paid production, women's double burden of work and domestic chores).

That's why I agree wholeheartedly with the Independent Women's Forum which, in a statement issued at the start of the December 1993 parliamentary election campaign, stressed the importance of the women's movement remaining *independent*. If there is one thing that has been proved by the entire period since the 1917 Revolution – which first enacted equal rights for women – it is surely the need for *independent* campaigns and movements which can take up particular issues and lobby for them.

In its statement, the Independent Women's Forum criticized the elections as 'undemocratic', for various reasons including the lack of time to campaign, and the risk of violence to those who raised awkward issues. However, the Forum (which has emerged out of the national forums organized by the Gender Centre) felt that it was essential to take part in, not to boycott, those parliamentary elections, the first held under Boris Yeltsin's Presidency. Thus the Forum called on members to support all women candidates from whatever party. They were not prepared to call on their supporters to back candidates of any party in particular. As they point out in their pre-election statement: 'Many blocs do not even include in their pre-election campaign programmes the need to improve the social status of women and guarantee equal opportunities.' The Forum called on women to make up their own minds whom they should support, and play an active role in raising consciousness about women's issues, helping to promote women candidates and organizing women's voter groups: 'It is not we who accept the ideology of the blocs and parties to which we belong: on the contrary, *we* are taking *our* ideology into these blocs.'

One section of the women's movement which did organize as a party for those elections was the new Women of Russia. Set up on the basis of the old Soviet Women's Committee (now Russian Women's Union), Women of Russia won over 8 per cent of the vote. Many feminists are wary of its political stance and fearful of the danger of being manipulated, as the women's movement was in the past. When Yekaterina Lakhova, Yeltsin's former adviser on women and the family, approached the Independent Forum to join the Russian Women's Union (which became part of the Women of Russia electoral bloc), the Forum declined, preferring to retain its independence though expressing willingness to work with Women of Russia at local level to support women candidates. The relatively high vote Women of Russia obtained in those elections

shows that the potential for a strong women's movement exists at the
present time. The 8 per cent vote did seem to express general female
dissatisfaction over falling living standards for many women – especially
pensioners and young women with children – and disillusionment with
most political parties. Clearly women's issues are a force to be reckoned
with in the future.

Readers may want to know what role the contributors to this book
played in the December 1993 elections to the new State Duma. Several
women active in the Gender Centre and Independent Women's Forum
decided to stand as candidates. Anastasia Posadskaya and Olga Lipovskaya stood for the bloc led by Grigori Yavlinksky, who had been
Mikhail Gorbachev's economic adviser during the late perestroika
period. This centrist bloc, which stood for less harsh economic reforms
than the Gaidar government's shock therapy, gained slightly fewer votes
than Women of Russia. Other Independent Forum members supported
other parties or blocs which did not manage to get the required number of
signatures to pass the first stage – like the Preobrazheniye group, of which
our contributor Tatiana Klimenkova was a candidate; or Otechestvo
(Fatherland), an alliance supported by women connected with the
defence industry and various left groups including the Socialist Party of
Working People (incidentally, the only Russian party with a woman
leader: Lyudmila Vartazarova). No Independent Women's Forum
candidates were elected.

The independent women's movement will continue to play an important role, whether its people are inside or outside Parliament. The
Independent Women's Forum statement issued in October 1993 declares
its outright opposition to the government's parliamentary bill 'Protection
of the Family, Motherhood, Fatherhood and Childhood', for instance,
considering it likely to entrench women's inferior status rather than do
anything to improve their position in present-day Russian society. By
submitting position papers on draft legislation and bringing a feminist
perspective to bear on the woman question, the IWF may in time be able
to exert considerable influence.

The situation for very many women in Russia today is critical; in 1992
women comprised 73.5 per cent of unemployed people with higher
education, and 78.3 per cent of all unemployed with secondary specialized education. In Moscow 81.7 per cent of registered unemployed
constitute office workers, and of these 80.9 per cent are women. Of the
unemployed, 43.5 per cent are between 30 and 45 years of age and 36.0
per cent are between 45 and 55.

The Gender Centre and Independent Women's Forum are at present
working jointly with Women of Russia to prevent abortion becoming
fee-paying – a proposal contained in draft legislation on health in the

Russian Federation. Three hundred thousand abortions are carried out annually on girls under eighteen. 'In a situation where the state has virtually stopped buying in contraceptives, the threat to free abortion is all the more dreadful,' Anastasia Posadskaya commented.

The Centre for Gender Studies has come a long way in these four years. It has matured, and spread its wings far beyond the confines of Russia. It aims to develop into a fully fledged Institute of the Academy of Sciences, so that it can undertake much-needed research into a wider range of women's issues than is possible at present. 'In my opinion, the most important goal the women's movement must strive for is social visibility,' Anastasia Posadskaya told the Second Independent Women's Forum. To put all the 'enormous number of women's organizations' she mentioned in her opening address to that Forum in contact with each other, the Gender Centre has set up a Women's Information Network, one of whose aims is to support journalists prepared to speak up against discrimination of women and against sexism in the media.

It will not be easy. The present time in Russia is especially difficult for feminists. But this book is proof of the pressing need for such research to continue – and proof too, if any were needed, that the academics of the Gender Centre, together with other feminists unconnected with the Centre, are well equipped to undertake this task in the years ahead.

KATE CLARK
London, 1 June 1994

Introduction

Almost three years have gone by since this book was first conceived. During that time huge changes have taken place, not only in Russia but throughout the world. We were pleased that the August 1991 putsch failed, and looked forward to a new period of real, positive change. Have our hopes been realized? The USSR has ceased to exist, and its collapse is stained with the blood of its citizens. A frightening wave of nationalism and racism has swept across the former socialist camp. East–West confrontation has taken a new shape, which culminated in the war in the Persian Gulf. Again we see the 're-partition of the world', as in the First and Second World Wars, and every day we witness thousands of new victims of this. And we are gradually realizing that this is both a time of great hopes and one of great trials. This is why we cannot afford to keep on waiting, and why, when we were setting up one of the first independent women's organizations, we called it 'NeZhDI' (Don't Wait). We women should not wait; we must act. We cannot depend on someone else to better our situation on our behalf. We ourselves have to think about what changes we want and work for them ourselves, whatever the circumstances.

Democracy without women is not real democracy. This was our slogan when we went out onto the streets to demonstrate our solidarity with the people of Lithuania on 20 January 1991, and later on in support of Yeltsin and the democrats. When the first Independent Women's Forum opened in Dubna, in March 1991, the White House in Moscow was surrounded by tanks. The worst scenario, we thought, would be if the military or the Communists took power. The putsch of August 1991 saw perhaps even more women than men out on the streets defending parliament and democracy. Calls were broadcast by megaphone telling women to go

1

home to their families and their children, but they stayed put, arguing with the soldiers perched on their tanks, and urging them not to support the putschists. Some of these women were old enough to be the soldiers' mothers; others were young women. Once the putsch was over, and awards handed out, President Yeltsin appointed a new government and sent out his trusted people to be regional governors. Not a single woman was among them.

I think we can say that there have been a number of stages in our critique of our society. When I say 'our critique', I mean the group of women who had for several years been doing research on the woman question in the USSR and who, in April 1988, decided to form the 'Lotus' group (League for Emancipation from Sexual Stereotypes): Olga Voronina, Valentina Konstantinova, Natasha Zakharova and myself – Anastasia Posadskaya). Lotus soon grew much larger, becoming the nucleus of the Centre for Gender Studies, and took part in joint events like the First and Second Independent Women's Forums in Dubna. This book represents an unashamedly feminist critique of society. Our readers will be able to make up their own minds whether or not we are right in what we say. The focus of our critique is a thorough feminist examination of the social schemes introduced in Russia (socialism, perestroika, democratization, the market system) from the point of view of their gender programmes.

At first, it was important to us to see how we differed from the prevailing view of society; what it was that we understood that they did not. The freedom we gained enabled us to say aloud what up until then had been impossible: that in Russia the woman question had *not* been settled; that sex equality under socialism was merely symbolic; that our society was in fact full of sexual stereotypes; and that our Communist leaders were bent on sending women back to the home. In the years from 1985 to 1989 the focus of our critique was Soviet socialism's gender programme, at a time when criticism of socialism as a system was widespread in the USSR. Our criticisms of past and present societies looked at such issues as:

- the so-called achievements of socialism in settling the woman question;
- gender stereotypes;
- the policy of returning women to the home;
- the way women are reflected in the mass media;
- the official women's organizations (*zhensoviety*) and their 'ruling body', the Soviet Women's Committee;
- the way economists, demographers and politicians in all periods of reform (including perestroika) have viewed the 'woman question' as something that can be manipulated to suit the prevailing ideology;
- the ideology of social protectionism with regard to women;

- the concept that it is possible to liberate women as a sex without liberating the individual;
- the political economy of socialism, which excluded and marginalized whole areas of female labour.

Our criticism led us to conclude that:

- No real gender emancipation had been achieved, and relations of gender inequality beyond the framework of the family were reproduced throughout society.
- All attempts to liberate the sex without liberating the individual are doomed to failure.
- Just as there is a 'woman question', so there is a 'man question'. Therefore gender liberation is a two-way process, and this should find reflection in any feminist programme of reforms.

The second stage of our criticism, in 1990–91, focused on the gender programme of perestroika. From about the spring of 1989 it became quite clear that perestroika was basically a male project, and that not only the Communists, but also the democrats had turned their backs on women. The country's move to a market economy only served to confirm that the concepts of the democrats who had succeeded Gorbachev in power were no different from those expounded by Gorbachev in 1987. There is an interesting point here, which might become decisive in future political struggle: it was actually the Communists, and the left-wing parties and movements formed by communists (like, for instance, the Party of Labour), who first understood that a more flexible stand on women's issues was needed. The last CPSU draft programme, published just before the August 1991 putsch, contained a clear strategy designed to bring women much more fully into the reform process. But it was too late. *Pravda* was by that time hardly read by anybody except political scientists, mainly those in other countries, and people mostly regarded Communist Party programmes as bearing little relevance to real life or to the actual intentions of their authors, in a country where socialism was on the way out.

The main conclusion we drew was that in fact all democratic political movements, parties and groups, within the framework of opposition ideology (opposition to the fundamental postulates of the socialist doctrine), had in the main a very poor and naïve understanding of women's issues. Most of them had no women's programme, and their personal views amounted to the same old theory about the need to 'return women to the home and give them a rest from socialism'.

Turning from ideology to the reality of perestroika, we observed a

whole number of asymmetrical gender consequences of the changes
taking place.

- In politics, women are being squeezed out of legislative and executive
  power.
- In the economy, we are seeing increased discrimination against women
  in terms of wages, getting jobs, career promotion and redundancies.
  What we are witnessing is the feminization of poverty, and an increase
  in job segregation.
- Legislation is now oriented towards measures making it easier for
  women to stop working, not those helping to integrate women into the
  new economic structures.
- We are also seeing an intensification of propaganda which propagates
  patriarchal relations between the sexes – the so-called ideology of
  women's 'natural mission' – and at the same time a massive
  exploitation of sexuality through the commercialization of the female
  body.

All this leads to the following conclusions:

- Perestroika, though in itself intended to augment the sphere of
  individual freedoms (the movement towards political and economic
  pluralism), represented a period of post-socialist patriarchal renaissance – which, incidentally, is typical of all the former socialist
  countries.
- The attempt at liberating the individual without liberating the female
  sex is just as pointless as the socialist project of liberating the sex
  without liberating the individual.

Turning to our present critique of the gender programme of the
post-perestroika period from 1991 onwards, the main conclusion that can
be drawn is that, at the macro-level, the same tendencies remain as in the
preceding period. What is more, if we consider the areas of legislation,
employment, education and culture as a whole, we can see that the
negative tendencies noted earlier have, as we foresaw, become more
marked.

At the first Forum, held in Dubna from 29 to 31 March 1991, our main
concern was to show that a women's independent voice did exist in the
country; that women were setting up their own new organizations and
initiatives, unlike the previous situation, when such organizations were
set up on orders from above; and to foment the awareness that
'democracy without women is not real democracy'. The Forum's final
document, drawn up by the women who had attended, spoke of the many

forms of discrimination against women both during the period of state
socialism and during the perestroika years.

The second Forum, whose slogan was 'From Problems to Strategies',
concentrated on the need for specific actions; the need to take decisions
which would change the situation; and to work for policies and public
awareness which would take women's problems on board, not as
secondary problems which would automatically be solved once the
situation as a whole improved, but rather as an essential and inalienable
component of the entire process of social change. In putting the emphasis
on working out strategies, we envisaged multiple levels of operation: at
the level of state policy (we invited representatives of the state authorities
and members of parliament); at the level of the separate regions and
cities; of the different branches and sectors of the economy; of factories
and institutes and local authorities. It was an attempt to see ourselves and
our problems as part of the global female social spectrum, with a right to
our own voice in the making of the new world order.

When we were preparing for the Forum we were often asked whether it
had any political orientation. Today, when not a single political party or
group has a proper, workable programme, for improving the social status
of women; when women are practically excluded from the processes of
political decision-making at all levels of power; when all illusions about
the automatic improvement of the social position of women during the
periods of socialism, perestroika and post-perestroika have been
shattered, it would be a mistake to rely on any particular political force.
What women have to learn is how to use the existing political structures to
achieve the aims of their social programme. It is unfortunately true that
the many years during which women's social activity was politically
manipulated have led to women rejecting all politics as something
unworthy of their efforts. But we must be clear: we cannot bring about
radical change in the macro-social situation unless we do enter politics.
We must work out how to overcome the internal and external resistances
relating to women's stereotypical unsuitability as politicians. The
question of how to go about changing these structures once we have
infiltrated them is a quite different matter; how we can turn them into a
tool for solving social problems, not for fulfilling individual personal or
political ambitions. We need to create a new kind of political culture and
political activist: ethically integrated policies conducted by people intent
not on acquiring and holding on to power at all costs, but on solving social
problems. The situation at present is such that there can be no talk of such
policies. We can see how dubious means of political struggle are used not
only by representatives of opposing groups, but even by politicians of the
same persuasion. We did not write the rules of the political game, but we
have to realize that unless we do change them we cannot expect that the

presence of more women in the power structures will of itself bring about change. This conclusion is illustrated by the example of the socialist period, when women occupied one-third of all parliamentary seats, and yet power remained totalitarian. This does not however mean that we should not examine our problems from a political standpoint. We are not against politics as such, we are simply against that sort of politics.

We are often asked why we call our Forum 'independent' – independent from what and whom? After all, one single political party no longer holds a monopoly: the entire situation is different from when our first Forum was held. I am of the firm conviction that the word *independence* as applied to the women's movement in our country (and perhaps in other post-totalitarian countries too) is essential to an understanding of the movement's essence. After decades of political manipulation, when the women's movement was an integral part of the totalitarian state system, women have finally decided to get themselves organized and discuss the issues that concern them. They have decided to tell society that there is discrimination against women, and that they understand its consequences and are prepared to take action to change the situation. It is particularly important that the independent women's movement does not attempt to speak for *all* women; nor is it assuming the role of an all-Russian women's organization. What we are is an open tribune for any women's organization and for any woman who is seeking her own answer to the 'woman question'.

We are often asked whether we are addressing our concern about the position of women to the government, to Parliament, to the political parties, or to men in general. My reply may seem somewhat banal, but in fact we are mainly addressing ourselves. Because unless we are ourselves aware that our problems are not simply women's problems, but problems for society as a whole which have to be solved politically, we shall never reach the level at which they can be solved: the level of social action.

In the event, we cannot help but see that the situation is beginning to change. We see that political parties and movements are gradually waking up, and that it is becoming the fashion to have a woman speaker or chairperson; a women's fraction or women's section in a party's programme. Unfortunately, in a country with no tradition of an independent women's movement, this fashion might well result in replacing one kind of political manipulation with a different kind. We must be aware of this danger and not permit any party or any movement to construct its policies and win our votes by the use of political manipulation of women's problems. Only the sort of political structure which in practice really draws women into the decision-making process can count on women's support.

Unfortunately, most women's problems remain in the shade, outside the realm of heated political debate. One topic which certainly deserves journalists' attention is the widespread infringement of elderly women's rights in the process of housing privatization. Our Centre has received many letters asking for help from elderly women living on their own, saying that they are being terrorized and threatened; that they fear for their lives but have nowhere else to go. We have tried to help, but to our amazement not one of the newspapers we contacted was prepared to send a reporter to look into these women's plight. You may be thinking, why are you referring only to women, surely this affects men too? That is true, but the vast majority of elderly, infirm people living on their own in this country are women, so this is in fact primarily a women's problem. If I were a journalist, I would set up an association of journalists (both women and men) against sex discrimination in the mass media. The newly emerging women's movement badly needs support from journalists; it needs intelligent, in-depth articles which go some way towards destroying the negative stereotypes about the women's movement and feminism, rather than reinforcing them as is so often the case.

The most positive thing about the changes taking place today is that the independent women's movement continues to develop, despite everything. It seeks new forms of coordinated action, and tries to understand the processes taking place to work out a collective answer to the 'woman question'. We have held two forums in Dubna; a women's information network called ZhISET has been set up; and the Forum's regional women's organizations are becoming more and more active. Four seminars organized by the Forum's political section have been held in Zhukovsky, and a third Forum is planned. Our economic section held its first seminar in May 1993. With the help of the German women's organization Frauenstiftung a Women's Information Centre is being created, which will consist of a library, archives, and a database. The Independent Women's Forum is becoming an open, public women's organization which will bring women together, not divide them. It will help to bring women's problems out of the shade and into the forefront of society's attention. It will work to prepare, promote and support women parliamentary and local government candidates. It is not that women lack initiative, or that they are reconciled to their situation: new women's organizations, women's companies and mutual support groups are springing up all the time. The problem is that there is little contact among them, as yet we have no means of keeping people informed about their activity. However I am sure that the future belongs to the independent women's movement which is working to foster in Russia's newly emerging civil society the understanding that 'democracy without women is not real democracy'.

ANASTASIA POSADSKAYA
September 1993

Women as the Objects and Motive Force of Change in Our Time

Anastasia Posadskaya

I would like to outline my understanding of the history and current state of the 'woman question' in Russia. In pre-revolutionary Russia there were two groups principally concerned with the woman question: the social democrats, who envisaged it as part of the overall social revolution, and feminists – or the 'equal rights girls', as they were called – who had their own agenda on the woman question, independent of the overall social transformation, and who demanded equal rights for women in all walks of life. After the Revolution, which put an end to political pluralism, the Bolsheviks acted swiftly to merge the 'woman question' into their overall strategy for social transformation. Feminism was classed as a bourgeois, alien movement, and for many years ceased to exist. A Marxist-Leninist strategy for solving the woman question gradually took shape. The main plank of this strategy was that women would play a full part in industry, while the state would assume the burden of childcare and education, provide the necessary services, and promote new relations between the sexes. In practice, the main emphasis in implementing this strategy was on getting women to work outside the home – the other components were never fully implemented. It is doubtful whether the Bolshevik Party's male leadership was ever really sincere in proclaiming its intention to promote new relations between the sexes. That inspired and passionate advocate of the principle of new relations, Alexandra Kollontai, soon received strict instructions to bring women's emancipation back into the approved Party framework.

By the early 1930s, the Party's *zhenotdely* (women's departments) were closed down and the woman question was pronounced resolved. The question, of course, had not been resolved, but this action spelled the end of any possibility of evaluating the actual state of affairs comprehensively and in an unprejudiced manner; a situation that proved typical of all other social questions. Three decades of rhetoric about 'great achievements' followed, during which one of the harshest crimes against women was perpetrated – the prohibition of legal abortion. The woman question resurfaced in (mainly academic) political debate only in the early sixties, during the political thaw of the Khrushchev years. The rehabilitation of Western sociology in the USSR paved the way for overcoming structural functionalism, which had held sway for two decades. But structural functionalism was immediately absorbed into the armoury of the new Soviet Marxist–Leninist sociology as one of the key theories for interpreting the situation of women and the family. The structural functionalist theory of women stressed women's three roles: worker, mother and housewife. And it still dominates approaches to the 'woman question' today.

Now let us sum up the results of socialism's method of liberating women. Firstly, the quantitative indicators. We must emphasize that official statistics do not permit an exhaustive analysis of the position of women, since they conceal more than they reveal about the true situation. Therefore, my data are the result of the sociological research that for the last three decades has served as a substitute for non-existent national statistics. Let us examine the indicator that for many years was considered the chief criterion as to whether the woman question had been solved: how many women work outside the home. Until recently this was one of the highest indices in the world. It is now falling, however, owing to the effects of market reforms, and Russia has now been overtaken by Sweden. The proportion of women within the employed population is subject to large fluctuations: during periods of reform to streamline the economy, the proportion of women goes down; during periods of intensive development, it goes up. From 1970 to 1989 the proportion of women in the employed population remained at about 51 per cent; preliminary data for 1990 indicate that it has fallen to 48 per cent. What do these figures mean? In my opinion, these employment figures for women do not in themselves prove that women have achieved emancipation. Neither the women's movement nor women themselves were the motivating force behind the changes in employment levels. On the contrary, these fluctuations reflected the authorities' pragmatic approach towards women as a useful tool. Women's labour-power was a means, a resource used to solve the problem of economic growth: the authorities alternately introduce the ideology of sex equality and the ideology of women's 'natural mission', depending on what suits them at the time. What lies behind these quantitative indices? Statistics show that in the scale for grading industrial skills, women are on average two to three grades lower than men; women are segregated into low-paid, low-prestige jobs with poor working conditions – 'women's jobs' – which means that although women's general level of education is higher than men's, in both specialized secondary and higher education, they are unable to put their education to use in a managerial capacity.

Perhaps women have achieved more within the family? Yes indeed, if a second working shift is considered an achievement. The distribution of labour in the family according to sex has not changed: as in the past, women are trapped in the traditional sphere of their 'natural' duties.

Thus we see that in the seventy years of rule that called itself Soviet and socialist, the woman question was by no means settled. In fact, a system of patriarchal relations permeated society as a whole. Discrimination against women was carefully concealed by the absence (or fabrication) of statistics. The women's movement was unable to instigate social change. Feminism was not one of the social movements rehabilitated in the sixties: indeed, studies of feminism were conducted with the sole aim of criticizing the object of study.

The main result of the policy towards women in the decades preceding perestroika was total apathy among women: an inability to engage in political struggle or organize themselves politically; a lack of experience in promoting themselves in public affairs; and many hidden problems dismissed as private or personal, such as wife-beating and child abuse, increasing violence and the impossibility of displaying an alternative sexual orientation, etc. Perestroika's transformation of society did not act as a stimulus for an independent women's movement.

Women during Perestroika

The official line on women has changed at least three times since 1985. In fact, official policy oscillates between two basic approaches: the politicization and depoliticization of women. One example of the politicization approach was when, in 1986, orders came 'from above' to set up a nationwide network of *zhensoviety* (women's councils) under the auspices of the politically reliable Soviet Women's Committee. Sociological research indicates that women themselves did not feel that the *zhensoviety* expressed their interests, but saw them mainly as a food-distribution network at a time when shopping for food was becoming increasingly difficult. However, those individual *zhensoviety* which took an independent stand, formulated their own objectives and investigated ways to achieve them did prepare the ground for a new women's movement independent of officialdom.

Gorbachev's infamous appeal for women 'to return to their purely womanly mission' found little support from women or from the professionals involved in drawing up the draft State Programme for Improving the Position of Women and Protection of the Family, Maternity and Childhood. Despite its patriarchal title, this document affirms the principle that the family should be separate and independent from government legislation and programmes. The essence of this approach is that it is not the state but people themselves, men and women, who should decide the balance between 'family' and 'work', in accordance with personal preference, not sex-role stereotypes. Thus it follows that all state allowances for working people with family responsibilities should be paid not directly to women, but to the family. It was this approach, compounded by labour legislation to protect women at work as well as legislation which provided maternity benefits, that reinforced the traditional notion that domestic duties were women's concern, a notion increasingly at odds with women's employment outside the home. The new State Duma must ensure that the new programme fits in with this new approach. But however progressive the conception underlying the state programme, it remains, as before, a programme *for* women, not one conceived *by* women themselves. Even now it is quite clear that the programme is inadequately financed, which makes it unlikely that its objectives will be met. However, no programme can help women unless they help themselves. In fact, this attitude towards women puts them in a socially inferior category and, in my opinion, degrades them. For decades we have been hearing about 'assistance for mothers' and 'protection of mothers and children', yet there has been no real change or improvement. It was precisely these attitudes that moulded and fed the stereotype about women as inferior members of Russian society. We are not social outcasts, we do not want to go around with outstretched hands or demand special entitlements and privileges; we do want politicians to take our interests into account when distributing the public wealth we have helped to create. Then we ourselves will work out what to do with it.

I believe that women should understand that no one ever has liberated us and no one ever will liberate us, unless we do it ourselves. We must free ourselves from our silence, stereotypes and political manipulation. Only a revolution of morals and ideology can transform women from the objects of a policy formulated by others into the driving force of social change.

The Independent Women's Movement

Do the prerequisites for such a transformation exist at present? What obstacles need to be overcome? What strategy needs to be formulated?

The independent women's forums held in Dubna in 1991 and 1992 helped to provide answers to these questions, addressing key issues for women.

Women and the economy

Today's economic reality highlights the problem of women's unemployment. Now it is clear to all, even to the Soviet Women's Committee, that protectionist, 'protective' ideology results in women being regarded as unprofitable employees who are a burden on enterprises and firms because of their various entitlements and privileges. Where there is a mixed workforce, management first tries to get rid of women. In women-only workforces, women with small children are the first to go. Among those who came to our forum were many who have managed to find their own solution to the problem of unemployment: they have started businesses of their own, formed associations of businesswomen and opened business schools. They have been able to find a suitable alternative to routine, low-paid (and often unhealthy) work. But I think we shall be the poorer if these women do not bring to the business world different values and a fresh understanding and approach to management. It is to be hoped that they will not blindly copy the aggressive male business model, but will create women's businesses that will conduct their affairs in a more civilized manner. This is one of the most promising ways in which women will become a more important force in society.

Women and politics

The important thing is that a women's movement exists and is here to stay. Women's groups and organizations differ in their aims, their size and ways of working. It is very tempting to try to unite them all under one umbrella. Is this really necessary? After decades of being 'united' from above, I think women have developed quite a strong resistance to this sort of unification. Before its disbandment following the August 1991 coup, the Communist Party belatedly manifested a new interest in the 'woman question': the Party wanted to coopt new people and new ideas, in an attempt to retain power and control. They wanted women's organizations to unite: without any advance notice the Party planned to announce at virtually closed meetings of politically 'reliable' women that a new women's organization, open to other women's associations, groups and individuals was being set up.

If it is true that the Communist Party was the first to understand that it had to use all the political levers and material resources at its disposal to win over women, most of the democratic parties still naïvely believe that campaign promises to grant women a shorter working day can substitute for an overall policy on women's issues. Deciding on behalf of women that what women need is 'a bit more rest', they think democratic changes are possible without women's active participation. In fact this attitude can only result in a huge political loss for the democrats that will hinder our fledgling democracy.

Women, the family and sexuality

The distribution of labour in the family by sex, which essentially entails the exploitation of female labour, was not discovered by perestroika. But it is only recently that we have become aware of the ugly phenomenon of wife-beating in the family. It is only one of a number of other hidden female tragedies about which women keep silent. I will mention just some of these: the far higher level of rape than officially recorded: rape of female students and workers in our infamous dormitories; sexual harassment and coercion by colleagues or fellow-students, particularly by senior men in the office. Sexual coercion exists in our prisons and places of detention. Our post-totalitarian society still remains totalitarian in its consciousness, which finds expression in the attitude to individuals who exhibit signs of an alternative sexual orientation. Sexual orientation is an issue for both men and women, but it is men who are subject to prosecution for homosexuality. The heterosexual majority has no grounds – if it wants to call itself civilized – to deny people the right to choose their partner. We could make millions of our compatriots happy – all those who are forced to hide and suppress their mutual feelings – if we were to rid ourselves of these traces of Stalinism and collective arrogance.

How will the emerging independent women's movement develop? It will surely take the form of informal groups of women, in which they can discuss their problems and be listened to and heard. Such groups will be able to relay our opinion about social issues to the world at large. Second, the movement will cooperate with existing structures with the aim of making them more humanistic and humane. Third, it will organize its own independent structures, which will uphold the goals and values of the women's movement. The support of a sympathetic mass media, their understanding and willingness to cooperate, and the creation of women's own programmes, newspapers and magazines are all prerequisites for transforming women from the silent majority into an active driving force in society.

2

What Does Our New Democracy Offer Society?

Tatiana Klimenkova

Russian society is going through a difficult period in its history. The old methods of administration by decree are disintegrating. All of society welcomed these positive changes at the start of the reforms, but though they began so well, the reforms so far have not lived up to expectations, often producing quite different results from those we had hoped for. The destruction of the socialist economic system and the disbanding of the Communist Party have not changed the situation. Power-seeking and the threat of a return to repression once again rear their ugly heads. We all know that throughout the country there has been a sharp increase recently in the number of rapes and other crimes of a sexual nature, organized mafia crime is growing, and the latest phase of nationalism has already resulted in countless deaths. Are these not indications of a struggle for power? Undoubtedly, though perhaps they are obscured by the restrictions imposed by political censorship. We do not yet know what is more important in shaping the kind of power we have – the normal, overt kind or the more hidden, indirect kind. Perhaps the fundamental problem of our present restructuring is not economic or political in the narrow sense, but cultural?

Once we begin to analyse the cultural situation in Russia we see that until recently a very clearly defined cultural style ruled our lives almost completely, a style which included engaging in historic global exploits, and the full-scale reorganization of both nature and human relationships. The main focus of this drive was on organizing industrial production and technological development, but recently we have begun to see a rejection of the politics and ethics of preceding decades, and enthusiasm for technology has become discredited. There has been a shift towards a new world view, and the emergence of new social and political forces has brought forth a new ideology. Social criticism is no longer the prerogative only of philosophers, sociologists and political scientists, but of the public in general. The social strata which have appeared are imbued with 'cultural pessimism' – people who refuse to believe in the possibility of society's planning for the future, or the possibility of improving the way we live by means of global decisions or grandiose revolutionary schemes. The 1980s brought about a new social orientation whose essence was the commercialization of all areas of our social life. New 'business imperatives' have appeared. There has thus been a certain change, which is generally known as the transition from a modernist to a postmodernist cultural project.[1] Russian postmodernism, however, has a number of distinctive characteristics. The first is that it uses economic terminology and utilizes the discourse of the transition from socialism to capitalism. Let me explain what I mean. If we are to believe the political assessments which are currently prevalent, Russia's main problem at the moment is to establish a market economy and introduce a capitalist economic system. Our mass media drum this view into our consciousness by constant repetition. But it is becoming more and more clear to those of us who live in Russia that the 'business imperatives' I mentioned earlier operate here in a peculiar fashion. Before commercialization even had time to set in, it migrated from business to science and culture, while the so-called 'market approach' very often operates in Russia according not to the logic of economics but to a totally different logic.

It appears that this country is going through a period of looking for the means to express the new crisis, but this realization is in the 'Procrustean bed' of economic terminology (which, of course, is not accidental). It is not surprising, therefore, that market reforms have had practically no success: in fact economic problems are not really being tackled at all. The economy functions, but instead of proceeding from what needs to be done, it acts as a signifying system in which other issues are represented.[2]

At the start of perestroika, when the new politicians characterized the situation as being one of crisis, this assessment was (in my view) more ideological than anything else. The external signs of crisis were still not evident in the country at that time. It is a different matter now, when the political forces currently in power have succeeded in turning the situation into a crisis. For them, this crisis is a necessary and basic part of the postmodern condition, since they can carry out their tasks only in a situation that is what may be called an 'allegory of deconstruction'. During the following exposition I shall try to expand my ideas on this in a more systematic way. First, however, I should like to clarify my understanding of postmodern theory and warn against simplistic interpretation.

Postmodernism is sometimes regarded simply as a current of

philosophical thought. But in this case its main affirmation – the refusal
to look beyond the signs for the reality they supposedly represent – is
lost. Postmodernism stresses the process of metaphorical signifying activity, which is endlessly self-referential, and for which 'reality' is only a
part of the process of signification. Strictly speaking, we cannot evaluate
postmodernist thought as cognitive, since thinking is realized in concepts, whereas postmodernism does not recognize any such specific cognitive mode of conduct. Instead, it operates through a specific activity of
deconstruction which, however, cannot be called 'irrational' – on the
contrary, it is highly rational, which is why it finds meaning in the actual
play of the market. Let us recall that according to intellectual approaches prevalent before postmodernism, structures of reality were
said to be reproduced through structures of mental activity; postmodernism has lost this epistemological optimism.

The maximum result that can be expected of the usual conceptual
theoretical approach is critical analysis. And it must be said that there
has been a great deal of critical investigation recently of the fundamentals of culture both in the West and in Russia. Thus the 1960s and
70s in Russia saw theoretical criticism, from different approaches, of the
fundamentals of socialism. This was a time when censorship was not an
obstacle to discussing quite a wide spectrum of problems, especially
when analysing and comparing the views of Western thinkers. As a
result, philosophical and sociological literature, and that of economics
and political science, already offered a broad spectrum of theoretical
arguments whose content was essentially critical of the various aspects
of Soviet socialist thought. But what was required was not really intellectual criticism, but the destruction of the very foundations of these dis-
ciplines.

During the 1980s, various political forces emerged in Russia which
were in critical opposition to socialism, including groups from the nascent business circles and the intelligentsia. But only one political force,
the fundamentalists, contained within itself the capacity for deconstructive opposition. Only they, it seems, were able to organize a truly decen-
tring opposition to the Soviet modernist cultural style. The
fundamentalists made widespread use of democratic phraseology – in
fact they declared themselves to be the sole conveyors of democratic
ideas in Russia.[3]

Thus it seems that the second feature of postmodernism in Russia is
its 'fundamentalist' nature. Who are these fundamentalists? They represent different groups who have banded together not for some social
purpose, such as to support private property, but because they agree on
cultural policy: they all claim to be the defenders of tradition. Why were
'fundamentalists' the means of the deconstruction of modernist cultural

norms in Russia? Because they opposed not modernism itself, but the underlying concept that legitimized it – what could be termed humankind's optimistic historic aspiration.

It would be quite natural to consider the 'fundamentalists' as a political force of the right. Their programmes are in favour of limiting the financing of social benefits: expanding the private sector of the economy into medicine and healthcare, encouragement of fee-paying and home-based education; increasing the importance of the Church (with their strange interpretation of religiosity – 'church by television'); and so on. Ideologically they stand for restoring the authority of tradition. All these features – and many more besides – make their social policies similar to the usual policies of right-wing parties. However, I do not think it would be correct to characterize them as a conventional right-wing group, nor would it be accurate to describe them as ultra-populists: such an evaluation belongs to the modernist cultural framework – both populism and the opposition of 'right' and 'left' belong to political life in the modernist era.

The democratic upsurge which has gripped the entire country since the late 1980s has taken a very strange form. On the one hand, this was a definite longing for liberation – yet for many people, democratization has meant a sharp fall not only in living standards but in overall social status, and women have been especially affected. But because of the widespread desire for the liberation of society from so many fetters of the past, the term 'democracy' is still used, despite the glaring contradictions. There is a certain degree of social consensus as to where our problems are, which is why harsh measures leading to unemployment and inflation (for instance) are nevertheless supported and considered democratic. However, it is obvious that problems are piling up in every single sphere of life.

Certain cultural technologies are at work which create motivation. They have such a rapid effect on the population that people do not have a chance to work out their own interests for themselves. People are already convinced about something even before they understand what it is that they should be convinced about. Thus people internalize what is presented to them as being in their own interests. They understand the issue of democratization in whichever way it is presented to them – for instance, by the largely pro-fundamentalist mass media. Thus people's actual understanding of democracy is shaped in conformity with fundamentalist views.

In what sense, then, does Russian fundamentalism go beyond the bounds of traditional politics? It claims to speak in the name of Nature itself. It sees its main task as saving that nature which was violated during the socialist period.[4] As we know, the question of sources was one of the most vexed and important for modernist theory, where almost any subject under discussion was explained by reference to its origins. Postmodernism refuses to work with the terminology of origins. Nor can Nature be fully understood in the conventional way – that is, it is not a substitute for the term 'source of origin'. Russian fundamentalists would probably agree with the postmodernist theory about the impossibility of finding the true origin of anything; they support the view that nothing has an origin. But this point of view does not necessarily presuppose an absence of origin: it is possible to acknowledge a recurrence that never begins and never ends. That is, in fact, the position taken by a number of cultural texts which, though from different eras, bear a similarity to each other. The recurrence of such texts throughout the ages explains 'Nature', as our 'fundamentalists' understand it. By advocating an 'everlasting return' to traditional values, they ultimately adopt a quasi-religious position. But the essence of this Nature is in no way connected with human reality, and so this Nature has no need for a transcendental God or a religious relationship.

It would appear that the fundamentalists do their moralizing in the name of this quasi-religious position, and subsequently apply their own evaluations of events in the distant and near past. Here their favourite objects are the discursive practices of the post-revolutionary years: the fundamentalist-minded mass media often arbitrarily place these 'broken' pieces of discourse next to each other (in the best traditions of postmodernism). Moreover, they do not worry that their 'game' at times appears contradictory or that it bears no relation to common sense.

Behind all this stands a doctrine which essentially upholds the traditional culture. At the present time this can no longer prolong its existence, as it used to do, by cultural consensus. Traditional culture can now only reproduce its existence through mechanisms or technologies which were not formerly the object of special attention, but which are now becoming visible and being questioned. It would therefore be extremely dangerous to read the cultural text of perestroika directly, without taking into account the postmodern 'signifying practices' which were always present.

This extension of traditional culture through the deconstructive potential of postmodernist methods has given rise to the strange phenomenon of 'Westernization'. It would be naïve to interpret the Westernization now taking place in Russia as an assimilation of the lessons of Western democracy – as it might seem at first sight. In fact, a totally different process is going on. A new ideological system is being promoted in Russia today, according to which two distinct notions are contrasted: a 'good' Western one, and a 'bad' Eastern one. The 'Western' type is linked with a self-regulating economy, and the 'Eastern' with totalitarianism. While the West considers it fundamental to organize life in a rational way, and values are given only secondary importance, Russia has acted in the opposite way – that is, the values and ideals of socialism were given priority over real economic needs: a historical catastrophe took place in Russia in 1917, as a result of which market initiative was crushed by the aims of socialism. Market initiative was replaced by a compulsory exchange that was artificially organized through administrative channels. The fundamentalists proceed from the premise that socialist principles replaced private initiative by the collectivist way of life, and freedom was replaced by despotism.

At first glance it would seem that such a scheme is untenable simply because of its primitivism; however, we know that it has gained currency in our country and that it is highly influential. This is because it fulfils a function quite different from what it seems. In present-day Russia 'Westernization' and the very word 'West' have a signification which works in the way we have indicated. In the public consciousness they stand in for imaginary fantasies which actually bear no relation to the real Western world; rather, they indicate the real state of consciousness in Russian society today.

One of the main representations of this fantasy about the West in the public mind is the symbol 'America'. America signifies something like a porno-paradise, although it is known that the real America is a country with quite puritanical morals. But here the logic of the 'West–East' model is of greater importance than the actual state of affairs, and as a result, America (as the leading power in the Western world) functions for Russians as the homeland of pornographic freedom and pleasure. It is not surprising that a film festival held in Moscow ran under the name of 'Sex on the Screens of America'. Many Russians view such festivals as the incarnation of shameless pleasure. Westernization of this kind is a forced process. In this sense it shares the fate of other components of 'fundamentalist Nature'.[5]

I have already explained that the events relating to our current reforms express a crisis not of the economy but of culture. To define this theory more precisely, I would argue that this is primarily a crisis of gender. First, I shall point out that the strange 'textual–political' activity of our postmodernists is aimed at removing from everyday use everything that could in any way show this country's crisis to be really one of gender. Naturally, this concerns feminism, through which optic gender has primarily been viewed.

Feminists have shown quite clearly that traditional culture, relying on rational values, ascribed rational activity only to men. 'Male' and 'female' are contrasted: 'male' belongs to the world of reason; 'female' to that of the senses. Traditional culture regards men as creators and achievers, and women as custodians of the values of homeliness and sympathy. In engaging in his rational activity, man's mission is to fulfil his basic civilizing task – to develop an interest in knowledge. Woman is seen only in her sexual capacity; whereas man is not only one of the participants in the historical process, but the sole representative of humanity as a whole, who is called upon to speak in humanity's name. This means, of course, that he can pass his own interests off as the common interest. Thus feminists believe that traditional culture erects boundaries that narrow the possibilities of its being analysed. The so-called 'woman question' thus finds itself outside the boundaries of traditional theoretical description. There is nothing surprising in the fact that the 'woman question', in its traditional interpretation, is considered trivial and uninteresting; it is of insufficient theoretical interest, since the 'woman's' point of view questions precisely this traditional, theoretical and abstract interest. For the 'women's point of view' to be analysed would require enlarging the boundaries of research, taking into account time, which is 'beyond the bounds of theory', its relation to particular life-conditions and the 'indirect involvement' of individual groups. Clearly feminists are opposed to postmodernist analysis, but their objective is not to restore the traditional cultural base, but to develop a positive alternative. Thus the struggle between these currents is not a coincidence, but a matter of principle. The fact that a false image of feminism is now being created in the public consciousness is of course the result of a definite political strategy.

Our mass media print all sorts of articles against feminism without ever giving any information about the content of feminist theory. Despite the total absence of knowledge of the feminist perspective, it has become normal to rage against feminist 'stupidity' and 'aggressiveness' – the usual features the mass media ascribe to feminism are man-hating and lesbianism. It does not even occur to the Russian reading public that feminism might provide fertile soil for an alternative cultural formation.

The gender approach deals precisely with this alternative. Sexual differences are not simply anatomical, but one of the ways through which culture expresses itself. A particular cultural functioning can be discovered in sexual relations – for example, in processes of speech practice, which reflect this cultural work. So it is not surprising that 'male' and 'female' are not only words, but cultural matrices which we shall understand here in the broad sense – as a means of analysis and description of a particular situation.[6] Gender, strictly speaking, is a product not of social, but of cultural activity, since it is culture which allocates and constitutes such specific objects as bodies. The organization of the regime of the body differs from social mechanisms – it is power operating on a micro-level.[7] In this sense, gender relations in present-day Russia are a clear example of these micro-technologies of power: this aspect of discussion is now prohibited. The problem of relations between the sexes is now discussed ad nauseam, but not from structural gender positions. This prohibition, of course, facilitates the promotion and defence of some groups' interests at the expense of others. It works by replacing gender problems by sexual ones, saying that sexuality is purely physiological. Thus, sex now plays the role of a means by which discussion of gender relations is made taboo; that is, it fulfils a particular political function, which is not in itself surprising, since sex has always had a political function. This particular cultural 'reinforcement' has now appeared in the current Russian situation.

Journalism, for example, is not merely a means for transmitting information, but constitutes a real 'fourth power', whose main political effect is not only to influence, but also to manipulate public opinion. The postmodern condition presents wonderful opportunities for this since it enables the media to wield influence by other than overt means. Its deconstructive questioning of cultural foundations means that it is directly implicated in the circuit of 'bio-power'.

It would therefore be naïve to accept in good faith what the media say about Russia at last having had a 'sexual revolution'. They assert that, since pornography was banned under socialism, now that the era of democracy has dawned, pornography has become an expression of freedom; under socialism, it was not possible to talk about 'dirty' things, but now it is. The reality is that today's mass media are not talking *about* 'dirty things', nor *about* pornography – it is the manner of presentation that is pornographic.[8] This approach guarantees Russian journalism direct access to individuals – they have discovered that symbolism has a direct relation to power. Many journalists are now using their ability to launch new social technologies to generate primitive, worthless and lumpen strata of the population, whom it will be easy to manipulate by creating in them a debased type of sexuality. A 'sexual revolution' of this type does not, of course, set itself the aim of sexual emancipation! It is simply laughable, in my opinion, to compare it with the West's 'sexual revolution' of the sixties, since at that time an attempt – however naïve – was being made in Western countries to liberate individuals through sex, whereas in today's Russia nothing of the kind is taking place. On the contrary, the fundamentalists' intention – and the mass media in particular – is quite clear: they seek to sexually 're-educate' the entire population. *Moskovsky Komsomolets*, for instance, told its young readers in March 1991: 'Whether or not you feel like it, you ought to do IT [meaning, of course, sexual intercourse] no less than three hundred times a year.' Similarly in one issue in 1989, *Pravda* described the sexual positions a bride should adopt. Countless 'sex education' manuals are devoted to one thing alone: giving advice to men on how to get the crudest possible pleasure from the sexual act. Sexuality itself is always understood in the same way: as men's natural right deliberately to degrade women through sex. This interpretation of sex seems so obvious to our mass media that it is not discussed at all, but it is absolutely crucial to an understanding of the state of affairs in contemporary Russia. It is this that is now determining the main model other cultural practices should follow. In all this advice to men on what their role should be in the sexual act, pleasure is always described as something excessive, something that goes beyond the boundaries of the normal. Women are not taken into account at all. They have to accept that, although they comprise over half the population, all this 'democratization' is not for them.

I mentioned earlier that, according to the Russian postmodern conception of 'Westernization', a schema is functioning whereby the rational, pragmatic West is placed in opposition to the totalitarian East, which is more morals-oriented. But it would be incorrect to think that the 'West' is understood as a successful system merely because it represents market economies. I have already shown that the West is viewed in Russia as a symbol of the resolution of purely Russian problems: the main thing is not the market itself, but what is symbolized by it, which is that activity in market terms equals the ability to break the law in order to achieve power. 'Market' terminology obscures the essential problem of power. It is only a system of symbols that channels this activity and provides the opportunity of articulating itself in the sphere of human relationships. The essence of this process is the enforced criminalization of the male gender.[9]

Conversely, the concept 'East' is seen as predominantly female; it is understood not only as totalitarian and collectivist, but also as value-tinged, intuitive (as distinct from rational), and therefore linked with emotionalism – the quality that characterizes women, according to conventional wisdom. It thus becomes clear that women fall into a situation of double discrimination. They are discriminated against in the usual way as women, but also as outsiders within the framework of this 'West–East' model – which of course in no way corresponds to reality. Russian women are neither weak nor unskilled, but they now carry an extremely heavy burden. They work for a pittance and manage to keep their families going in a practically impossible situation. Nevertheless, the cultural norm operates in accordance with the model indicated and only sees in women what it wants to see. Now even the word 'woman' is being used more and more to signify not real beings of the female sex but a scantily clad, tartish painted doll – i.e., a popular male fantasy.

This particular type of discrimination makes it impossible for women to express their own interests. What institutional means prevent this? Before perestroika, Russia had various kinds of women's organization. It is true, of course, that these were not so much organizations *of* women as *for* women. But still, some form of organization, albeit very weak, did exist. Now all means of women organizing at a national level have been destroyed. Women have no institutional channels through which their interests can be expressed. The only body left that expresses women's opinions is the Ministry of Social Protection. In other words, women are represented from the institutional point of view in only one capacity – as social invalids. This is no mere coincidence, but the result of a definite cultural strategy.

So that women understand that they *must* appear weak, mechanisms are being set up to support what is culturally apparent. One of these mechanisms, it seems to me, is the system of so-called entitlements. According to current legislation, women are entitled to a number of maternity benefits. This is a highly complex and contradictory system. Entitlements are paid very irregularly, and yet on the ideological plane this system operates very well. The press is constantly exploiting this situation to create a damaging image of women.[10] How was it possible to destroy the mechanism by which women's interests were represented to the national government? Because the basis which legitimated it was destroyed. The 'fundamentalists' replaced the former legitimation, based on egalitarian principles, by a different one of universal postmodernist performance. People are merely the medium through which the signifying process is carried out. This was the situation in which the fundamentalists launched the attack against women's rights on all fronts. From perestroika's beginnings a number of leading political figures made clear their positive attitude to the conventional division between male and female roles. Both Mikhail Gorbachev and Boris Yeltsin spoke to this effect on several occasions in official and unofficial speeches,[11] and nearly all representatives of government circles held the same point of view.

During the first period of perestroika, the attack on women's rights began in a light-hearted, even jocular manner, but then the pressure began. At first the mass media ran articles about how happy American housewives were and how contented they were with their lives. Then they started to write about how the main thing for women is to have long legs and a narrow waist, and those who do not agree with this opinion are simply envious of beautiful women. Then it turned out that both women and the workplace suffer from women working outside the home, that 'women are not fit to work' (this in a country where over half the industrial output was at that time produced by women!). However, in a postmodern situation, people do not set themselves the task of making words fit reality. What is important here is something else: to defend the

conventional order of Nature, according to which women are supposed to
be weak and feel out of place everywhere except in the home. As *Pravda*
wrote: 'Women think they are welcome at work. Alas, our mothers knew
the salutary [!] wisdom, that women are not especially wanted anywhere
in the world.'[12]

The pages of all our newspapers have been full of this kind of
moralizing during recent years.[13] Their aim has been to create in women a
feeling of being second-class citizens. According to these notions,
working women should feel guilty about working, and ashamed of taking
any interest in their work, since this interest betrays an 'active' – i.e.,
unfeminine – attitude to life. Let us recall what, according to my
hypothesis, the 'female' spectrum of post-Soviet understanding of gender
actually is. It seems to me that it is a social technology that links women
with all that is emotional, with trustfulness and a belief in 'ideals'. This
puts women in an especially difficult position now, since these qualities
are precisely the butt of the postmodernist ideology which favours
aggressive activism. Women 'should' be passive, which means they
should also symbolize all the other characteristics that this latest ideology
finds unattractive. So, in the model of West–East opposition – where the
former is understood as the norm and the latter as the deviation – women
are put in the position of a politically marginal group.

In an interview published in *Moskovsky Komsomolets* (18 August
1989), one of perestroika's leading younger politicians, Sergei Stanke-
vich, expressed the following opinion about political activity:

> JOURNALIST: 'A politician should be a leader, a ruler, a boss . . . and leadership
> is, I think, an occupation for men alone.'
> STANKEVICH: 'I agree with you about that.'
> JOURNALIST: 'If we try to define politics, we can see why political affairs are a
> man's domain.'
> STANKEVICH: 'It is a matter of principle. If we think of humanity as one big
> family, then women in this system are responsible for stability and continuity,
> whereas men are responsible for seeking solutions, taking risks, moving
> forward, experimenting. . . . Women can never play a primary or even an
> equal role in politics.'

Pravda attempted to develop this view in an article that claimed that
men should also take the moral lead, while women should 'take a back
seat'. The author barefacedly advocates that women's wages be paid to
their husbands! Fundamentalist aspirations were expressed even more
precisely by a member of the former Presidential Council, the writer,
Valentin Rasputin, when he declared: 'women should give sustenance to
the people'. What is interesting here is that he of course knows what
women *ought* to do; and second, that it is not that she should 'feed' (in

Russian, *nakormit'*), but 'give sustenance to' (*okormit'*), so it is clearly a question of something greater than mere feeding. Third, 'women' are contrasted with 'the people' (this is obvious from the very structure of the sentence); consequently what is meant by 'people' is all who are 'non-women'. It is thus clear that it is in 'the people's' – or men's – interest to gain unlimited access to female energy.

The West–East model plays an important role in implementing gender policies in Russia, but the sphere of its influence is wider than the phenomena examined above. There is another more complex model for analysing the workings of culture. The various fragments of social reality are now starting to be examined from the logic of this model, and these then have a reverse effect on the formation of gender strategies. It is interesting to interpret the national problem according to this model. The nature of this dichotomy is put in such a traditional way,[14] that it takes the classical nation-state as the norm – that is, the situation where a particular nation has a particular government which looks after its interests and builds up the nation's wealth, even by means of expanding its territory at the expense of neighbouring states. Here the main object of disputes and the main interest is that 'surface' space which extends outwards in linear fashion from the metropolitan centre of the empire.

This interpretation, however, does not take into account certain special features of Russia's present national situation and its reflection in events of the recent past. After all, the methods by which industrialization was carried out in the West and in Russia were very different. The West industrialized within relatively egalitarian societies, in which an abstract recognition of equality between separate individuals prevailed. Russia's industrialization was carried out, as we know, on the principle of 'emancipation of classes'. In a country such as Russia, where enterprises were communal rather than privately owned, industrialization did not have the same meaning as in Western countries. It was more of a common aspiration and a drive for new norms of social and historical life.

As E. Nadtochy has rightly observed, the ideology of sacrificial effort stood behind this aspiration, which was closely related to a particular conception of the sexes. Of course, the overall direction of the movement of history continued to be male-dominated, but the particular interpretation of this doctrine was in fact quite distinctive. The 'male' predominated here not so much due to overtly displayed attributes of power as to his functional place which consisted of the privileged right to the main type of sacrifice, that is, the right to disseminate his meanings in the 'feminine other' in exchange for voluntary and unpaid receipt of certain levels of female symbolic life. This strategy of constructing gender technologies was based on a high degree of cultural sublimation, inextricably linked with the conditions of symbolic exchange. This exchange took place on the 'sacred–utopian' symbolic plane and was meant to link together all those taking part in this 'historic mission' in a single act.[15] The exchange taking place in this 'sex act' was not between two individuals of the opposite sex, since it was enacted on the symbolic level and was possible only due to the existence of a communal collective.[16] Our people did not represent a collective whole because individual members had come together in the sex act (copulated); on the contrary, they were able to come together in the sex act only because they already felt that they belonged to a communal (copulated) collective.[17]

This collective of the 'nation' was created to sacrifice itself in 'heroic deeds'. The economic functions performed by this united 'work collective' were full of symbolic content. The symbolic note and its semantic nuance are here seen at their most important when solving purely economic tasks. It must be noted that these points were deliberately taken into account when economic policy programmes were being drawn up to construct the praxis of 'socialist construction'. The main issue at stake in our economy was to produce not more essential goods or surplus-value, but to ensure that these goods were produced at the same rate. This correlation of rates produced by collective effort was the primary aim of our economic activity. Economic life consisted of a number of heterogeneous group efforts performed by collectives. These were calculated not so much to produce a direct result as to highlight a particular function of labour in the construction of the overall communal body. For each body was made up of small heterogeneous collectives existing in isolation, connected with each other only through feedback about the overall rate of 'socialist competition'. Accordingly, those who lagged behind had to be 'taken in tow', 'pulled along' to keep up with the general pace. Individuals were not so much 'transcendental subjects' with their 'arbitrariness of imagination' as members of work collectives.[18] Of course, this ordering of people's lives operated within both the female and male gender regimes. Russia's understanding of gender is not as closely related to the sexual proper as it is in the Western paradigm. Russia can be likened to one big family, in which all members are linked to one another by a highly specific relationship – not one based on blood kinship, but one expressed in productive economic activity.

It would be interesting to trace the development of mental stages in the process of individual socialization. It is possible that the Russian people's 'childlike quality' could be explained not merely by under-development but by the fact that conditions of life and relationships between children and adults in these collectives are somewhat different from those in the West. This might explain the open nature of the Russian *ethnos*;[19] the desire for an existence based on its special 'relationship' with other nations (*ethnos*), the desire to support our existence not so much through the organization of social interaction, as through links at the level of cultural micro-components of a joint organization of bodies; our constant self-doubt with regard to other nations. Perhaps the Russian *ethnos* is capable of perpetuating itself because it breaks spatial restrictions – that is, it has broken precisely that which groups traditional states together in economic unity. It is possible that the policy of mass resettlement of peoples served to reinforce this particular historical feature of Russia.

But in this sense, the understanding of Russia as a 'metropolis' and the other republics as 'colonies' is extremely classical and traditional. When the media in the Baltic states call the Russians colonizers operating according to the Western model, it sounds very false to the Russian ear since, as I have tried to show, the issue is not at all one of Great Russian chauvinism. The oft-repeated theory about the 'collapse of Empire' (according to the Eastern model) sounds just as false, since to talk about collapse of Empire there must have been an empire in the first place. The Russian *ethnos* even now seems to be outside the terms of that model. For the Russian *ethnos* the meaning assigned to it is of a quite different semantic order than what the West accepts as paradigmatic.

One of the key cultural patterns for Russia (relating to standardizing 'female' symbols) is the figurative image of the Earth. The symbolic function of the Earth has been part of the Russian world-view in a quite special way, since it is not simply the object of economic activity, but virtually the reason for that activity. The land has been a key issue for the last two centuries. At the time of the abolition of serfdom, the crucial question was: how can the Earth, which belongs not to people but to God, be divided among people? It is not as simple as it might seem to contest this view. It is no coincidence that Russia was the birthplace of Nikolai Fyodorov, whose doctrine of radical Christianity contended that as a result of humanity's historic work resurrection of the fathers in the flesh is possible. The emergence of this doctrine was conceivable only because of a particular attitude to the Earth's symbolic role. This ancient and sacred relationship with the Earth is encapsulated in the definition familiar to any Soviet person: 'Mother Earth is damp.' The 'female' connotation of this symbol is clear. The Earth is represented in this way in the works of many Russian writers, including Andrei Platonov. Platonov sensed perfectly the ambivalent destroying/giving birth aspects of the Earth's symbolism. This symbolism was incomprehensible to Platonov's contemporary critics, who regarded his works simply as a manifestation of anti-Sovietism. The Earth is not merely a spatial category, but one of the most fundamental ones. But the symbolic concept of the Earth surpasses its spatial concept: Mother Earth points to its temporal origin in the collective memory, rather than place of birth. Formulations of this kind are an example of a particular gender *ekstasis* that exists in the people's collective memory and is one of the most stable components of the 'political unconscious' which was shared equally by both the Christian and non-Christian nations that comprised the former Soviet Union.[20]

What is now taking place is not a legitimation crisis as such, but rather a fading of the people's cultural memory of revolutionary events. However, the *mechanisms* by which the people's 'political unconscious' works have not faded. I do not believe that these operational mechanisms of the collective memory have been in any way obliterated from the contemporary cultural situation inside the former Soviet Union. The arguments of our theorists – that the unity of peoples in the former USSR was a lie – do not sound convincing. Deprived of mutual support, our people are experiencing profound cultural upheavals, which are constantly being covered up by 'economic explanations'.

Serious research on the workings of our country's cultural memory is required, regardless of whether this is to anyone's liking or not. The politicians who have come to power placate themselves by saying that the 1917 Revolution was foisted on the country by the Bolsheviks; that the 'coin stood on its edge' (i.e., it was a most unlikely occurrence). But, if we take a more impartial look, we will see that this is not so. The revolution had an extremely solid foundation in the depths of this *ethnos*, and this has yet to be analysed. Otherwise, it would not have had such historic import that it could operate as the fundamental matrix of subsequent historical development. Mere coincidence could not have provided the historical foundations to make the Revolution such a rich symbolic event. Whether we like it or not, this event has already served as a source of popular memory, which transformed the real chain of historical changes that took place at that time – however harsh the sufferings – into a special, isolated event and endowed it with a specific 'quasi-property'. This consists in being the source,[21] moving to the level of collective fantasy and working out common methods of action.[22]

I have already stated that the gendered approach in the economy produced not only a clear policy of sex discrimination, but a wider spectrum of the cultural formation and regulation of bodies. Any process of forming body matrices is of indirect importance for the gender situation. It would be inappropriate, in my view, to discuss the coming together of peoples in our country only on the traditional economic or political plane, which is what many new parties are constantly trying to do.[23]

I should like to stress that this is not simply a national crisis, but something of a far more all-embracing nature, since we understand the matrices 'masculine' and 'feminine' to apply to all aspects of culture. It is indeed the function of legitimation which is, in my view, the key feature

of these matrices. And the fact that they play an indirect role in the
formation of such important areas of social life as national relations,
politics and power should therefore be taken into account from the
outset.

Unfortunately, the 'sexual proper' is not as clear as we would have
liked, but we are beginning to see the way it takes shape through
circumstances that at first glance seem unconnected. We are thus enabled
to use such a broadened interpretation of the socio-cultural function of
gender in our understanding of the diverse means of historical behaviour
of different peoples. Most importantly, we can study those nations
outside Western models. This primarily concerns those nations which,
owing to different circumstances, have not accepted in their classical form
one of the main Western *a priori* principles – the market economy, which
is woven into the very fabric of Western culture.

The present-day Russian situation offers us a perfect example. Our
country has demonstrated that it was capable of developing considerable
scientific and economic potential, while preserving our distinct culture. It
has exploited its own resources and found its own means of carrying out
industrialization. However, with the advent of the 'technotronic era' of
microchips and computers it began to fall sharply behind, and the
country's economic mechanism degenerated. To analyse this situation
adequately, we must again compare overall trends in the historical
destinies of Russia and the West and examine their differences. We must
first of all point out that both the modernist and the postmodernist
cultural project turned out to be our common fate, but in different
versions.

Both in this country and in the West the modernist style was based on
expanding industry and technology, which required a huge army of
labourers. These had to be not slaves or serfs but a mass of educated,
active workers who continually improved their qualifications. In the West
this was done by introducing a new and egalitarian gender paradigm,
which began long before modernism came on to the scene. As far back as
the eighteenth century, classical views on the correlation of sexual roles
began to be undermined, and this continued throughout the next century.
This change provided the opportunity for constructing a new gender
paradigm in which women obtained more opportunities to play a role in
public life, which, in turn, paved the way for their role in industrialization. It must be stressed that the modernist project would not have been
consolidated had it not been constructed on the basis of a substratum of
'egalitarian' gender views.

In the West, egalitarianism was understood as the potential equality of
individuals. In practice, such views on equality proved unrealistic, since
they only operated in the abstract. On the one hand, the modernist

project embraced all individuals, but this occurred on a highly universalized plane. This meant that only those who were able to take advantage of this abstract concept – i.e., men – were able to reap the benefits. On the other hand, according to the content of the principle itself (assertion of equality) it served as a slogan, although it could not, of course, truly change the essence of inequality.[24]

Russian modernist ideas about equality, as I have attempted to illustrate, were totally different. They were based on the priority not of the individual body, but on the communal, which only later 'split into two' according to strict rules. These particular features of the gender paradigm were clearly reinforced by the entire symbolic structure of the USSR's cultural life. The spiritual climate imposed on Soviet women the 'duty' of taking pride in the basic principles of the Constitution on equality. In fact, these ensured not so much the equality of women in the Western sense, but a social technology for constructing the communal body.[25]

Thus, the gender doctrines of the West and of Russia differ substantially. The former is based on abstract rationality and on individualism; while the latter refers directly to the corporeal level of cultural symbolism, which here functions almost directly, practically avoiding complex transmission links and social disturbances. Modernist gender strategy saw as its goal neither the achievement of real equality nor the creation of an 'androgynous' individual – modernism did not of course require such an individual. What it did need was a huge influx of workers, and the gender concession of liberating women from the home was, of course, a forced measure that arose from this need. Nevertheless, the modernist era shattered the centuries-old idea that women's role in the family is dictated by Nature and therefore women are simply incapable of holding down jobs. Experience has shown that women possess ample qualities to enable them to cope with the demands of work outside the home. It has become evident that the withdrawal of women into the private world of the family was not caused by nature but was the result of a particular method of social organization. Once this method of organization changed, women were able to cross the public/private boundary, which is one of the fundamental dichotomies of contemporary society. However, though women have crossed this boundary, they have not changed our culture as such. This has proved incapable of reassessing its basic principles, and has soon begun to revert; under the flag of postmodernism it has returned to the pre-modernist, not modernist, construction of corporeality.

The final problem for postmodernism in general – and for the Russian version in particular – has turned out to be a key one. In asserting the anti-organizational understanding of the biological domain, postmodernism transfers the problem of 'body' to the plane of specific 'political history'. This is formed from a number of artificial constructs, often of a fictitious, performative type, whose essential condition is activity, even aggressiveness. The 'performance' of perestroika started from the fact that 'angry men' were claiming a special place in history. Since all the places in the country's political spectrum had already been apportioned, they had to organize an aggressive campaign to free a special 'locus of power' for themselves. As I have already mentioned, women began to be labelled second-rate, scatterbrained and inadequate. For almost a decade not a day has gone by without the mass media doing everything possible to create a negative image of women, not allowing them to forget for one moment that they are irrelevant. The media do not hesitate to use methods long since outlawed, and frequently resort to exaggeration and juggling the facts.[26]

An equally forceful campaign has been organized within the mass media with the aim of 'raising the authority of men'. It has been performed in a purely postmodernist key (though media people themselves have no idea of this, of course, since the theory of postmodernism is unfamiliar to all but a narrow circle of people in Russia today). 'Raising the authority of men' meant first of all consolidating their patriarchal role in society. Men's position of power is proclaimed lawful; granted them as a birthright, by 'nature itself'. All this has been done in the name of democracy, yet no one appears to care that the new political parties' rules demand the right of the 'individual' to develop, while they demand that women 'return to the home'. Nor does anyone seem concerned about the growth of fascist groups.[27]

The new political forces do not seem to realize that by putting men in a 'lawful' position of power, they are not only departing from the elementary requirements of democracy, but are also doing men a great disservice. In the guise of highlighting the importance of 'genuine male qualities', men are in fact being subjected to very strict regimentation, as the range of possibilities for their own behaviour is narrowed.[28] The social roles being offered them are often, in practice, most unattractive – 'business activity' in our today's conditions is at best semi-criminal. As for rape, to which men are gradually being urged, this is also a criminal offence. We can see very clearly now in this country how right feminism is to say that rape is not only an illegal act, but a social institution of the patriarchal culture: the number of rapes has increased tenfold in some regions. The present interpretation of sexuality, which we have already discussed, plays an important role in consolidating the legitimation of male power.

All this fits only too well into the context of the postmodern era. I have already mentioned that one of the main postmodernist tendencies is a de-regimentation of the body. In a situation of gender asymmetry, this aim is realized by constructing special actively ironic sets of assumptions about the female body and female identity. This is exactly the situation we now have in this country, where the female body has become an object of constant derision, intended to arouse a certain sort of pleasure. Women's bodies are deliberately viewed as something shameful and therefore as an object of ridicule par excellence. This explains the countless indecent features, comic sketches and cartoons on this theme, in which men appear playing with the sexual organs of women standing or lying before them, or which simply show the female sexual organs as a substitution for the real woman. One television interview, for example, featured a fully-dressed male journalist interviewing a completely naked woman. This also accounts for the multitude of porn shows, exhibitions and contests. Another extreme of the 'ironic construction' of the female body is the ridiculing of teenage girls. Moscow television, for example, frequently shows a naked young girl, on whose buttocks the word 'heifer' appears, painted in red.

Another favourite postmodernist method is exaggeration. This can be seen in the emphatic activism of the 'aesthetic' position. In the modern Russian variant, this emphasis often takes the form of sinister exaggeration. People are accustomed to listening reverently to the hallowed call of symbolic architectonics of historical meaning; thus the postmodernist imperative is revealed in its horrifying gravity. The principle of aestheticism is transformed into one of suicide, by an attack of 'struggle with history'. Activism unleashed by the postmodernist movement sets in motion the frightening machine of war and apologism for all kinds of destruction. The performance of violence played out on our streets at night gains strength and is played up by the press. Most papers publish this sort of material several times a week. The following excerpt is taken from *Moskovsky Komsomolets* (31 March 1990):

> Seven murders this week, fourteen people with grievous bodily harm. . . . A youngster nearly kills his own uncle by knifing him in the stomach. . . . Elderly woman killed – she was found in her flat. . . . A man was beaten to death, he died without gaining consciousness. . . . Youth murdered rival with knife, then jumped through window. . . . Came across a find in a goods train – a woman's head and legs. . . . Old woman born in 1918 raped. . . . Son raped mother. . . . Ten-year-old kills little boy. . .

Such reports are non-stop – on the radio, on television, and in papers selling millions of copies. A particularly significant effect is obtained, of course, if the two postmodernist tendencies are linked – the ironic construction of the female body and the performance of violence. The descriptions are intricate, and spicy details openly savoured. In reports like 'Woman's Head Found on Rubbish Tip', the story will tell in great detail how the female body was cut up. Rape cases where some instrument was used will be described in great detail. Half a page will describe, for example, the gas-mask the rapist put on the young girl before raping her.

The postmodernist style is now the cultural destiny both of the West and of Russia. Whatever the result may have been for Western countries of being drawn into the chaos, for Russia it has turned out to be disastrous. Swept up in the current of postmodernist elements, Russia has lost faith in itself and its political rulers, seduced by the simplicity of the West–East model. Russians have ceased to realize their specific national idiosyncrasy, and no longer know how to distinguish between legitimizing matrices and cultural norms. And although questioning of foundations is of course important, not only postmodernist ways of doing this are valid. The 'inadvertent postmodernism' of Russia is a caricature of this approach.[29] The use of the 'naïve' West–East model to understand the state of affairs in Russia is quite useful: there is the seductiveness of its aesthetic simplicity, the clarity and easily explicable technique of separating 'theirs' from 'ours' and the opportunity of thus developing performative contexts of culture. Over almost a decade, journalists, writers and 'experts' (sociologists, political and social scientists) have actively exploited this model; by repeating it dozens of times per day, they have drummed it into the heads of the people. The result is a vacuum, and therefore it has become impossible to discuss any alternative schemes.

However, the problem is more that of being alert to the processes of legitimation that are taking place at the points where cultural norms do not 'fit'. It is obvious that we cannot merely discuss this at a theoretical level. It is not so much the concepts but the resultant traumas bodies have suffered from these 'cultural technologies' that we need to analyse. Can postmodernism take society beyond the sphere of universal performance? We do not see such a possibility, at least not for Russia at present.

Our country's present grave situation demonstrates that the responsibility of re-examining the legitimating foundations of culture is a very serious and responsible one. It is also extremely urgent, since it is not enough to talk of the 'historical costs' of our current crisis. The millions of refugees within the former Soviet Union, the tens of millions of old people going hungry, the young people who are being corrupted, those killed in nationalistic pogroms, the victims of crime on the streets and the whole suffering nation – can anyone escape the 'costs'? Are the costs justified? To what end, and who benefits? Is it merely for the sake of a new 'process of signification'?

Notes

1. One often hears claims that Russia and the West are different, but they also have something in common. In this case, I think, the difference can be understood in terms of each society's experience of socialism or capitalism, and their similarity in terms of our common destiny in passing from a modernist to a postmodernist cultural phase.

2. It is extremely difficult at the present, in my opinion, to establish the crisis of socialism as being purely economic (unless, of course, one unreservedly identifies socialism with the bureaucracy, as our mass media do for their own ideological ends).

3. By fundamentalism we do not mean religious fundamentalism alone. At the present time fundamentalist views in our country are supported by a broad coalition of social forces which bear no direct relation to religion, and although the Church's current activity is also tinged with fundamentalism, this is not its distinctive feature.

4. Here we can foresee objections of a theoretical nature: it could be said that we do not have the right to ascribe to this doctrine views concerning Nature and politics because postmodernism does not recognize either. However we shall follow the logic of this doctrine later.

5. A lot of people protest about programmes in languages they do not understand, especially about showing American children's films. (Nothing is ever done to prepare adults or children for these programmes, and this is not accidental – violence operates in this case as a means of signification for Western society, and the language of films is thus seen as immaterial.)

6. To help clarify concepts, let us recall that the gender approach develops through comparison with conventional social sciences, such as for example, classical sociology. We know that traditional sociological theories developed in conditions either of abstract rational discussion, or of empirical descriptive ideas. Both bear the imprint of masculinist orientation (including the very dichotomy of the empirical and the theoretical). Even if we try to construct, in the name of sociology, an unconventional doctrine, the difficulty still persists, because the subject of sociology is *society*, whereas the subject of the gender approach is *culture*. Society is always organized not only according to legal, political and other rules, but also according to body canons. In this sense, however, the common definition of gender as a social reality, or as socialized sex, is perhaps not quite correct.

7. The French philosopher Michel Foucault set out a methodological approach to analysing this. He proposed undertaking research into the conditions which create the unspoken of a particular speech discourse. If a particular culture is discursively produced, in ways that cannot be articulated in speech, then the functioning of the body is equally enmeshed in the prohibitions of 'bio-power'.

8. In the West pornography appeals to a fairly limited group of 'sick' people; but in today's postmodernist Russian conditions, the mass media are trying to make the whole of Russian society 'sick' through pornography.

9. It is the done thing in Russia nowadays to think that a man should be 'active'; but no matter how active he is, he is somehow not considered a 'real man' unless he breaks the law.

10. The bill now being drafted 'On protection of the family, motherhood, fatherhood and children' states that women with children under 14 should (!) have a working week of not more than thirty-five hours. The disastrous result of this 'entitlement' is quite evident. No enterprise, either state-owned or private, is going to want workers of this kind, of course. This law will in fact throw women out of the production process altogether.

11. For example, their joint appearance on a Soviet–American television hook-up on 4 September 1991. During the programme, a woman expressed her concern about the unfavourable position of women in the Soviet Union. To her question on what the prospects for improvement were, Gorbachev replied: 'Our main concern is for children, women and invalids.' Yeltsin, for his part, offered to do what he could to return women to the home.

12. *Pravda*, 22 February 1989.

13. The ideological nature of this orchestrated campaign against women's rights is quite evident. It will not be difficult for future historians to record its main features from countless newspaper articles.

14. This scheme which is taking root in the public consciousness greatly impoverishes the understanding not only of Russia, but of the West too.

15. This should not be confused with contemporary social technologies intended to order performance.

16. Specific historical conditions – like the massive construction projects of the BAM type, etc. – constantly required new sacrifices.

17. *Translator's note*: This is a pun in Russian on the words 'communal' and 'copulated', which have different meanings, but sound the same – a fact that is not, of course, coincidental.

18. This differs from contemporary postmodernist technologies for organizing perform-ance. This procedure is of course strongly connected with the traditional one. But this traditionality itself relates to a kind unlike the classical traditions of Western rationality. It must be noted that Russia after 1917 was able to organize its economy only because, in spite of all its super-revolutionariness, it provided a means of subsistence for many people who did not fit in with the new way of life (this was done by creating a new folklore, by developing a pseudo-classical style in art and so on). This in turn indicates that the revolutionary events of that time were compatible with this type of traditionalism.

19. *Translator's note*: The author uses the Greek word to signify a geopolitical concept: that which unites people who have shared a common historical, political and social past.

20. The power of symbols like this to energize people has not yet been properly assessed. In a certain sense, the symbol of the Revolution also works according to the same image. The Great October Revolution itself, taken not as the simple event but as a fantasy and a part of the political imagery of contemporary culture, was the well-known 'Motherland of the whole of progressive humanity' which was called upon to be the 'Motherland for all'. People all over the world, hearing the sacred connotations of these ideas, responded to their signifying flow. This tragic and in many ways senseless attempt to start afresh, to forge a new link in the time-chain will remain henceforth an inexplicable temptation to establish a new spirituality, and create a new legitimating space which will allow the construction of new models of cultural activity.

21. Moreover, a source not in the sense of timeless transcendentalist *a priori*, but a source of Utopia, situated in an essentially open temporal dimension.

22. This is not to deny that it was a situation involving suffering and bloodshed. But by no means every experience of mass suffering can claim such a fundamental status. For example, the earthquake and civil war in Armenia did not become the basis for creating a new consensus, although politicians and the mass media tried hard to channel events along these lines.

23. The traditional understanding of the relationship between 'centre' and 'periphery' is at present leading to nationalism: the nations on the 'periphery' want to 'cleanse' their peoples of relations with others. But in so doing, they take away their 'micro-components' and transform them into traditionally understood nation-state unity. This is the reason for so much discussion in the media and at conferences of the problem of Ukrainian, Kazakh, Tatar, Moldovan, Lithuanian, etc., identity. In essence, their aim amounts to simplifying the understanding of *ethnos* and traditionalizing the way it came together. The periphery is trying to reduce this identity to the level of straightforward generalization – i.e., to reduce it to what is 'characteristic' for the nation in question, and then give the world the benefits of this (which is what follows from the name 'identity'). The fact that various peoples are thus deprived of 'cross-fertilization' at the same time deprives them of their ritual-mystical stratum. Their transfer to the spatial-linear level immediately brings in the war machine and opposing territorial claims. We can therefore see why it is that 'liberated' nations have started to impose their ethnic regimes on others and introduce various kinds of repression against 'aliens' living on their territory. Although in the abstract this situation certainly has the meaning of 'questioning foundations', in the conditions of Russia's traditionalist consciousness this postmodernist 'call of time' turns 'questioning' into performance with a real sub-machinegun in hand!

24. It is no coincidence that even the understanding of the general principle of equality is based here on the idea of brotherhood among people. The word 'brotherhood' is, of course, used as a collective category, but would the slogan 'All men are brothers' have the same

meaning if we replaced it by 'All people are sisters', as one feminist suggested? It would certainly not.

25. It must be stressed that the Western model cannot simply be reversed in order to obtain an Eastern model, since they work on different planes. The Russian model of gender-formation takes place in the sphere of legitimation, and questioning of the dominant cultural schemas.

26. Here is an example from a news broadcast early in January 1992: 'As a result of flooding, all women and children were evacuated, whilst the adult population stayed behind to do battle with the elements.' And this text was read by a female newsreader!

27. The democratic *Nyezavisimaya Gazeta* (Independent Gazette) ran an interview 14 November 1991 with the Fascist Party chairman, in which he declared that all the country's ills stemmed from the fact that women have too much freedom. He assured readers that when the Fascists came to power, they would restore order. 'Fascism is a male doctrine', he said, echoing Hitler's words, 'and male rule must prevail.'

28. Men are removed from the sphere of the family and forced into a social order in which political anxiety and economic chaos reign, in an atmosphere where the truth is often obscured.

29. We know that chaos and ruin are an inalienable part of postmodernist style. Russia is a more than adequate expression of the 'classic' postmodernist landscape. It is obvious that a situation in which the very foundations of culture are put in doubt may result in various kinds of disorganization. It is also clear that in some of its manifestations, this situation may to a certain extent resemble pluralism and bear some similarity to democratization. However, it seems that the process of destroying foundations has not yet engendered new social and political opportunities for society. Russia's present situation proves that the process of deconstruction does not automatically lead to consolidating democratic norms of communal life. There has been an alarming increase recently in mutual intolerance, more and more people are acquiring arms (not for hunting purposes) and safeguards of basic human rights have weakened. The country has one-and-a-half million refugees, and the right to work, holidays, housing and personal safety have been much undermined as compared with the preceding decade.

3

The Mythology of Women's Emancipation in the USSR as the Foundation for a Policy of Discrimination

Olga Voronina

The position of women in our country is one of the most crucial, yet contradictory, social issues. It is not only that it affects the greater part of the population, 53 per cent of which is female. The reason it has become so crucial is due to the way the 'Soviet experiment in solving the woman question', as it is called, was carried out. In fact, this experiment in settling the woman question turned out to be one of the most refined social mystifications that came into being in the society of so-called actually existing socialism. With regard to other social myths (that ours is a society of social justice and equality, the triumph of proletarian internationalism, etc.), there was always a hidden scepticism, which at times was transformed into open criticism of the system by those commonly branded dissidents. However, the myth about women's equality in the Soviet Union was never actually questioned.[1] Even today, when many of the practices and values of our former life are being reappraised, when it has become obvious that there is no social equality and justice, politicians and journalists vie with each other in enumerating the most pressing social issues and calling for assistance to the various groups of the population whose political and social interests have been infringed – but women are not on the list. It is of course generally recognized that women are overburdened by domestic concerns and that something needs to be done about this: at times the authorities have called for an 'expansion of the network of services to the population', but it has never been achieved. Now more and more often we hear a different kind of call – to return women to 'their purely womanly mission'.[2]

Attempts by younger social scientists to focus the attention of colleagues and society as a whole on the need to demystify the state's present ideology and policy concerning women are usually ignored by politicians and most specialists; they face a concerted attack by unqualified opponents of the very idea of women's liberation.[3] The primary leitmotiv of this very moderate criticism of the Soviet practice in dealing with the woman question, now adeptly reinforced by speeches of certain politicians and journalists, is an alleged over-emancipation, the 'cost' of emancipation, which is the supposed cause of the difficulties women face.

The very use of such phrases as 'cost of emancipation' reveals the speakers' own particular ideological stand. After all, emancipation signifies liberation (the term was originally used in Roman law to describe the process by which adult sons of the head of the family – the patriarch – and his slaves were released from his legal guardianship and his power). Later, in the nineteenth century, the term was used to designate the liberation of women from the power of men (fathers and husbands), a power that allotted women a subordinate place in the social and familial hierarchy. It is this aspect of the emancipation process, I believe, that provokes such irate resistance from present-day opponents of women's independence. This is why they treat the concept with scorn, and portray in a purely negative light the alleged over-emancipation – an expression that is essentially meaningless and inhumane. For how can one possibly define a cut-off point, a 'ceiling' on the degree of liberation of one person from the power of another? It is possible only if you already know for certain that one of them should wield power and the other should be subordinate. The bases for subordination or holding power in traditional Western cultures are sex, age, and nationality (race), by which criteria the central power figure turns out to be the white, middle-aged man.

The inhumanity of racism or discrimination by nationality, sexism and ageism are increasingly being subjected to fundamental criticism from a number of modern Western humanists. Once we have declared our adherence to general human values, we must also learn that fundamental among these are freedom of the individual and human rights (irrespective of sex).

As far as the 'cost' of emancipation is concerned, it is clear that effect has replaced cause, and the real state of affairs has been falsified.[4] To substantiate this, I should like to give a brief outline of the fundamental characteristics of the position of women in society,[5] and the reader may decide whether this should be termed over-emancipation or over-discrimination.

Formal equal rights for men and women, enshrined in the constitution and in a number of other laws, certainly do not ensure equal rights in practice. The UN Convention on the Elimination of All Forms of

Discrimination against Women which was ratified by the USSR, never did become law in Russia and serves only as an elegant addendum to our system's humanitarian image in foreign policy.[6] The principle of equality is certainly infringed in the workplace, where professional discrimination and segregation of women is widespread. The former can be seen in the fact that in practically all areas of activity, women are excluded from decision-making and experience far greater difficulties in their work and careers, compared with men – i.e., in practice, only horizontal career moves exist for women; vertical promotion to the highest echelons of power is a male prerogative. Among professional men, for example, 48 per cent are managers at some level; whereas only 2 per cent of professional women are in managerial positions. However, when there are staff cuts of any kind, the 'ladies first' principle operates with depressing regularity: thus figures of the Institute for Socioeconomic Problems of the Population at the USSR Academy of Sciences, and the USSR Government's Goskomtrud (State Committee for Employment), show that in 1989, 80 per cent of the job losses caused by cuts in managerial staff affected women.

Women are segregated at their places of work through the creation of areas of 'women's professions', or 'women's jobs' inside 'male' professions. What is special about this sort of female work is that it lacks prestige and is low-paid.

One of the consequences of workplace discrimination and segregation has been the considerable gap in pay between 'female' and 'male' labour: on average throughout the country pay for female labour is 30 per cent less than for male. It is not unusual for men and women to receive different wages for the same job, the pretext being that 'men are the breadwinners'. Most surprising is the fact that neither the moral and social injustice of this situation nor its illegality provokes any protest.

We come across constant discrimination against women in the field of education, where women are either not accepted at all, or only in very limited quotas, by 'prestigious' universities or institutes – those which open up access to key posts in the power structure. There is another less obvious but very widespread practice of hidden discrimination against girls, whom schools gradually orient towards 'women's' jobs, scaring them away from a number of 'male' jobs with the threat that they might lose their femininity. Moreover, this orientation of girls begins in childhood, when they are taught that the main thing for women is the family and family responsibilities, not knowledge, education and a job; this of course cannot but distort young girls' values.

Women as a social group are virtually isolated from politics. On the one hand, it is considered that they do not have any special political and social interests distinct from those of men; on the other hand, men are fully convinced that politics is not a matter for women. So here too what we come up against is the suppression of women's interests rather than 'over-emancipation'.

One hardly likes to mention that women are overworked in the family and the home, so often is this theme raised (though without yielding concrete results) whenever women and 'their' problems are discussed. The entire, so-called 'woman question' in this country is essentially reduced to everyday life and family squabbles. And since this is the case, all these 'women's problems' acquire a special status, affecting only the 'fair sex'. But here, I believe, lies one of the main mechanisms by which traditional patriarchal ideology is reproduced. By rigidly tying women only to children, family and everyday life, and by linking the family's well-being with the woman alone, society reinforces powerful socio-sexual stratification: the home is the place for women and the world is home for men. There have been different periods and different ideological campaigns concerning the family in the history of the Soviet Union: sometimes the attempt was made to reject the family or at least reconstruct it along communist lines (in the 1920s), sometimes the laws by which the family functions and survives were simply ignored (from the early thirties up to the mid sixties), or it was 'consolidated' (from the sixties on). But in all these very different campaigns, the family sphere of life was identified with all that was female, and was counterposed to general social and state issues. Whether acting 'in the interests of the family' or against it, the Soviet state always claimed the right to be the highest authority with regard to the family, thus reproducing the masculinist hierarchy of what is private and what is public; what is female and what male; who is in command and who subordinate. Within the framework of masculinist ideology the family is always a means of suppression of women's individuality and the subordination of their interests to those of all other members of the family. The personal becomes in practice the political, since it is in the family and through the family, by reproducing the ideology of women's mission in life and the myth of the sanctity of motherhood, or domestic gynocide,[7] that women are alienated from the realms of power.

We must say a few words about a relatively new phenomenon – discrimination against women in the public consciousness (more can be found on this in Chapter 9 below). This occurs when 'truly feminine' qualities are contrasted to general human qualities and values, and a negative image of women is created, identifying them with gender and sex alone. The current debasement of women in the mass media and mass culture not only goes unpunished, but is not even recognized by this society even as it attempts to become democratic.

But the most interesting thing is that the programme of humanistic and democratic transformation of society does not even include changes in the position of women, for the myth that women have already been liberated under socialism has proved too deeply rooted in public and private consciousness. In my research I have long been interested in how this came about, and how it became possible to talk of the liberation of women in a country where they have been subject to the harshest exploitation. Women, after all, were the 'internal slaves' of socialism; for many years our economy was dependent on their cheap labour, and it still depends on it today. Families as an institution of reproduction of the workforce depend on the utilization and appropriation of unpaid female labour within the family, as does the patriarchal state that consumes this labour.

I do not believe it is possible to understand or explain the problems that have surfaced using the Marxist model of analysis typical of Soviet science. We need a new perspective, a new language to analyse the whole complex of problems concerning women's position in society and the discrimination they face, and this perspective must be a feminist one. It would be extremely interesting, of course, to present a feminist analysis of the whole range of Marxist views on the emancipation of women. But since it is impossible to do that within the confines of one article, I should like to highlight some of the basic tenets that in fact determined the Soviet state's social policy with regard to women.

Women, and the Marxist State

Discrimination against women is defined, in Marxist terms, as one particular example of the discrimination and oppression of the human being in a social and economic system based on class antagonisms. Social oppression can only be overcome through the revolutionary transformation of society as a result of class struggle. After the socialist revolution has been achieved, bringing about social and economic transformations and changes in civic law, and once a new society has developed, the question of discrimination against women will be resolved of its own accord. In a society which is free from the contradictions between labour and capital, from private property and the oppression it engenders, there is no social basis for oppression and repression, nor will there be in the future.

According to this model, the main reasons for the oppression of women are property and class contradictions. It is true that Engels in *Origin of the Family, Private Property and the State*, Bebel in his book *Women and Socialism*, and Kollontai in her many works all spoke about the social and economic dependence of women on men and the hierarchy of the sexes in society, but they always linked these exclusively with the property relations prevailing in society. Marxism's pivotal sociological concept of the contradiction between labour and capital in antagonistic formations might have been useful for constructing the theory of how civilization developed, and it enabled much of what happened in the course of history to be explained and interrelated. But the class approach became a monopoly within the framework of Marxist analysis of social events.

This was evidenced – as regards the position of women – by the fact that Engels's notion that society was stratified according to sex, explicit in his study on the origin of the family, remained in the background. Moreover, many features of his analysis turned out to be extremely weak, ambiguous and not well argued; they were accepted *a priori* for reasons of ideological adherence to class theory. For example, when Engels writes of the accumulation of wealth and property in the hands of men, which led ultimately to their domination of women, he says that in primitive society there was social equality between the sexes, and parentage was matrilineal. And suddenly, with the appearance of private property, the division of labour between the sexes led to the formation of the monogamous family for the transfer of property to blood-line sons, and led to women's economic dependence upon men. Simultaneously, class delineations began to form. It has never been clear to me why it is precisely at this moment that the division of labour according to sex acquires such decisive importance. After all, 'the first division of labour is that between man and woman for child breeding', as Engels wrote in *The Origin of the Family, Private Property and the State*.[8] This was the first act in history that created a system of division of labour, which led to the development of society. And if before the emergence of private property, society was matriarchal and matrilineal, then how was it that property did not concentrate in women's hands? Perhaps its concentration in men's hands was an attempt (and a very successful one) to take away from women their power and their central status in society, which was determined by their ability to give birth to new members of society? It seems to me that this leaves much to be explained. There is a strange power game being played around the category of sex and these subjects should not be discarded just like that, even for the sake of purity of class analysis. I can give several other examples of how Engels in another work (*The Condition of the Working Class in England*), as well as Bebel and Kollontai, at times come close to the problem of sexual hierarchy in society and the sexual stratification of society – and then immediately pull back. The male explanation for discrimination against women as merely due to the fact that men have owned property does of course give a certain scholastic solidity to Marxist social theory. But apart from the confusion over the effect of private property on the kind of relations between men and women in primitive society, a number of further questions arise.[9] Was the *transfer* of property to his son really so important to primitive man? And what was more important in this action – the transfer of *property*? Or the certainty of a *blood relationship* with his heir? Or the *sex* of the child/heir? Or perhaps it is worth thinking about another aspect, noted by Marx in passing:

> With the division of labour, in which 'all these contradictions are implicit and which in its turn is based on the natural division of labour in the family and the separation of society into individual families opposed to one another, is given simultaneously the *distribution*, and indeed the *unequal* distribution, both quantitative and qualitative, of labour and its products, hence property: the nucleus, the first form of which lies in the family, where wife and children are the slaves of the husband. This latent slavery in the family, though still very crude, is the first property, but even at this early stage it corresponds perfectly to the definition of modern economists who call it the power of disposing of the labour-power of others. Division of labour and private property are, moreover, identical expressions: in the one the same thing is affirmed with reference to activity as is affirmed in the other with reference to the product of the activity.[10]

Here I think we should turn our attention to the following idea: slavery in the family (i.e., women and children are slaves of men) is the first form of property; that is, the first possibility of using others' labour-power. Was not the creation of the monogamous family a condition for the accumulation of private property in the hands of men, who managed to remove children from the power of the mother and turn them all into their slaves? and into their property? It seems to me that such aggressive behaviour is much closer to the historical truth than primitive man's altruistic desire to transfer property to his son.

Perhaps in the final analysis it is not of great importance whether it was the accumulation of property in the hands of men that resulted in the enslavement of women and children in the family, or the other way around: the primary act of aggression facilitated the accumulation of property, which finally resulted in the consolidation of male power, not only in the family but in society as a whole. It is much more important to recognize that the formation of the patriarchal family, in which women, children and slaves became the property of men, signalled only the beginning of a system of patriarchal social structures. But whereas slavery as a means of organizing social production in time died out, the slavery of women in the family exists as it has done for centuries: within the family and through the family, even the poorest man continues to appropriate, like those before him, a considerable portion of the labour, time and energy of women (mothers, wives, sisters and daughters, who fetch and carry for men and boys). The relationship between power and property is therefore not only vertical (or related to 'class', in Marxist terminology), but horizontal (or socio-sexual): at every social level, in each stratum and class, the hierarchy of power goes directly from the man as the subject of this power to the woman (women) as the object of this power. This situation is multiplied by means of established social structures and cultural norms, and every person is 'plugged into' this system according to his or her sex and almost independently of personal preference.

This socio-sexual stratification of society gives rise to the familiar social antagonism between men and women. It will take more than the demise of vertical property relations between the classes (the subject of Marxist analysis) to eliminate this antagonism. It will only disappear when those horizontal relations of male ownership over the labour-power of women are eradicated; when masculinist ideology and the patriarchal principle of social organization are overcome. Cutting off parallel lines of analysis – as Marxist theorists did concerning the woman question – not only impoverishes the purely theoretical search for the truth, but, since this concerns a social problem, must result inevitably in distortions in social policies and practice.

By giving the class approach priority in analysing discrimination against women, the women workers' movement for liberation was subordinated to the proletarian movement for social revolution, which would supposedly solve all problems. The development of an independent women's movement in Russia at the turn of the century and the struggle for special rights for women (not for the transformation of society as a whole) were considered by Lenin, Bebel and Kollontai as a 'purely bourgeois venture', serving to divert the mass of women away from the revolutionary struggle. Thus a wedge was driven – lasting nearly a century – between so-called 'bourgeois feminism' and the women workers' movement (which subsequently – once again to denigrate the bourgeois movement – began to be deemed 'democratic'). There is no doubt that not only was the women workers' movement democratic, but so was the struggle of 'middle-class' sectors, which leaders of the Communist movement were too quick to describe as 'bourgeois' (and therefore 'no good' in the terms of that period).

In my view, the feminist attempt to single out specifically female interests and consequently to understand the particular features of women's position in a traditionally patriarchal society was of unquestionable value. To deny the objective formation of specific female social interests (formed, in fact, by the patriarchal nature of the very society that turned women into a marginalized group), deprives the women's movement of its essence and its own character.

Moreover, I do not believe that a class analysis of sex discrimination really is a viable approach, if we recall Lenin's definition:

By 'classes' we mean large groups of people distinguished from one another by their status in an historically-determined system of social production, by the proportion of the means of wealth production they possess, by the part they play in the social organisation of labour, and by the kind and the quantity of socially produced wealth they have at their disposal. In a class society there are groups of men who, by virtue of their favoured position in the social order, can appropriate the results of the labour of other groups.[11]

If we compare this definition with the actual social and economic position of women in different historical epochs, it quickly becomes apparent that social class is a concept that describes the status of various groups of men within 'male' society. In virtually all epochs women were ousted from the system of 'male' social production into the 'female' domestic sphere. Women played no part in property relations or in the distribution and appropriation of social production. It may therefore be said that social class is a masculinist concept, quite suitable for describing the masculinist structure of society, but not at all suitable for understanding the situation into which women have been placed by society. That definition begins to work in analysing the social position of women only if we think of both the vertical (i.e., existing between the various strata of society) and the horizontal (i.e., socio-sexual, existing within any social stratum) stratification of society. But if we understand 'groups of people' to be not only workers or capitalists, but men or women (i.e., if we extend the definition to cover not only the male part of humanity), then it will be a matter not of social, but of 'biological' classes, as the radical feminists called them in their time. They arrived at this concept from certain statements by Marx and Engels (for example, 'the first class antagonism which appears in history coincides with the development of the antagonism between man and woman in mono-gamian marriage, and the first class oppression with that of the female sex by the male'[12]). True, the idea of 'biological classes' is not, in my opinion, very useful for analysis, and it has distinctly aggressive anti-male overtones. However, the essence of the problem is not to expose a specific enemy (men) and reverse the power structure (i.e., that women should start ruling men). We need to understand which social and cultural factors fostered the masculinist ideology and patriarchal organization of society and, once we have assessed the negative consequences of this – not only for women, but for men and for society as a whole (and there is a great deal of feminist literature on this) – we must chart the prospects for getting out of the crisis. The concept of 'biological classes', popular in the 1970s, has now safely receded into the background.

The ideology of subordinating women's interests and social role to class interests displays other manifestations of typically masculinist culture. Here the male proletarian movement commandeers a number of women's sovereign rights: I have in mind their definition of the aims of the women's movement, their representation of this segment of the population's interests in society, the subordination of the movement to 'global' social aims in the male understanding of this (revolution, industrialization, building the country's defence potential, etc.).

This masculinist rejection of the independent status of women's issues, their subordination to global class aims, and the fact that the ideology of the women's movement was engulfed by class and Party ideologies can be traced throughout our entire seventy-year history. Party control over the women's movement – either overt or covert – existed for many years. For example, the widespread network of *zhenotdely* (women's departments) that appeared after 1918 functioned under Party organizations. Then in 1929, Stalin declared that their tasks had been fulfilled, and on his orders the *zhenotdely* were abolished. But in 1931 the *zhensektory* (women's sections) were set up in agitation and propaganda departments in the various Party committees. But whereas in the decade of their existence, the *zhenotdely* had gradually become mass cultural and educational organizations that at times even took on the role of defending civil rights, the *zhensektory* were organs of control and propaganda. They were supposed to demonstrate that the women's movement had not been abolished or dismantled by the state. The numerous conferences of women stakhanovites,[13] front-rank women workers in industry and agriculture, and wives of male stakhanovites[14] were called to demonstrate the birth of the new, free woman in the USSR. Party officials drew up lengthy special instructions and orders on how to conduct even these purely formal conferences: 'Model work-plan for a delegate meeting of women kolkhoz[15] workers' (1932), or 'Programme for Meetings of Female Delegates' (1932), and so on.

It is quite clear, however, that in the 1930s a new stage had begun in the masculinist assault on the women's movement. Previously the idea of women's emancipation was still included in the overall democratic transformations of society. But from the 1930s right up to Stalin's death, women's equality took the form of active participation alongside and on a par with men in industrialization, collectivization and other arenas of socialist construction.

There can be no doubt that working outside the home and being paid for their labour is one of the main conditions for women's emancipation, since such labour gives women economic independence, widens their social horizons, and helps to develop self-confidence and freedom of personality; the right to work is an inalienable right. However, women's working outside the home can be transformed from an important means of liberation into a very powerful instrument for their enslavement. This occurs when people are alienated from the results of their labour, when labour ceases to be voluntary and becomes forced. That was precisely what occurred in our country.

The process of drawing large numbers of women into the workplace was a result of the need to provide labour for industrialization – a decision put into effect in what was formerly a peasant country, devastated by war and famine. The forced collectivization and mass dispossession of the kulaks[16] that was carried out so soon after a protracted civil war, completed the destruction of the family structures that had traditionally given material support to family members. Large numbers of women found themselves without a roof or support and were forced to go out to earn a wage. However, to edge their way into the existing male employment structure, women had to agree to any and all conditions – and more often than not this was heavy, low-prestige and low-paid work, which men avoided.

Being forced to seek employment outside the home was made even worse by the traditional patriarchal ideology that viewed women as second-class citizens. These masculinist views did not disappear with time, and not only because there was no cultural policy to combat sexism or discrimination against women in the public consciousness. In my opinion, there was an additional factor at work here: in a poor, hungry, totalitarian state, the struggle to make a living forces people to go to any lengths to push past rivals for power, privileges or material wealth. People start looking for an enemy on any grounds: Party membership or lack of it, social origin, nationality or sex. In a totalitarian state, a rightless person can only assert himself at the expense of those weaker than himself – so the cultural stereotype of the 'weaker sex' becomes a godsend. Therefore our society's extreme sexism in relation to women goes hand in hand with the idea that they have supposedly been given 'equal rights'. Women are needed by the state as workers and this guarantees their access to professions and education, and ensures the formal proclamation of equal rights under the law. But since the hierarchical nature of our society is supplemented by a traditional sexual hierarchy, women find themselves pushed into the background, deprived of a voice and in practice isolated from the decision-making process. Job discrimination, segregation and unequal pay are the natural consequences.

Did Perestroika Do Anything for Women?

Mikhail Gorbachev, the Party and state leader who initiated political and economic reforms in 1985, had a very traditional approach to the problem of women's social status. The first confirmation of this was his proposal at the 27th Party Congress to revive the *zhensoviety* under CPSU leadership. Nearly a quarter of a million *zhensoviety* were set up throughout the country in 1987, the vast majority of which functioned under Party factory committees. The Soviet Women's Committee, which assumed the administrative functions, published its 'Regulations on *Zhensoviety*', which carried the note that they 'unite all Soviet women in the interests of building Communism . . . they function under CPSU guidance . . .'[17]

The women's organizations set up in the perestroika period were put under Party control and their activity regimented. Of course this does not mean that Party committees were always meddling in *zhensoviet* activities, or that the CPSU Central Committee controlled every step the Soviet Women's Committee took (although in the latter case, there was actually quite strict control). But the Party's main aim in this situation was achieved: by setting up *zhensoviety* as a part of the official political domain and by assuming the leadership, the Party immediately diffused them as a potential real social and political force to something merely nominal. And we can say today that the Party was successful: the majority of *zhensoviety* proved to be incapable of functioning and died a quiet death. As far as the Soviet Women's Committee is concerned, it continues to pretend that it is engaged in serious work, stresses its importance as an administrative centre for the women's movement and claims that it represents the interests of Soviet women. In fact its activity, even before the dissolution of the Soviet Union, was practically nil.

The second pronouncement which Gorbachev made reflecting his views on women is, I think, well known throughout the world. I am referring to his book *Perestroika*, where he calls for women to return to 'their purely womanly mission'.[18] This position in fact laid the foundation for state policy towards women during the perestroika period.

Direct confirmation of the CPSU's extremely patriarchal position (during the period when it was the leading force in our society) can be seen in its attitude towards the promotion of women to top political posts. Of the 100 People's Deputies from the Party, only 11 were women. In 1990, only 6 per cent of Central Committee members were women, even though at that time about 30 per cent of Party members were women.[19] It was not until 1990 that a woman became a member of the Politburo of the CPSU Central Committee,[20] and then in a typical 'women's post' – Galina Semyonova was made chair of a Central Committee commission on women.

In the parliamentary elections of 1989, which were in principle more democratic than previous elections, women lost out: 15.7 per cent, or 352 out of a total of 2,250 deputies, were women; in the USSR Supreme Soviet, 18.5 per cent of deputies were women.[21] It goes without saying that, just as before, the main leadership posts among deputies were filled exclusively by men. There were no women in the USSR Cabinet of Ministers. It was the same picture in the governments of the republics. By the end of the 1980s, women comprised only 5.6 per cent of top managers (although 61 per cent of specialists are women). Thus, though they comprise 53 per cent of the population of the country and 51 per cent of those employed in the national economy, women are in fact absent from all levels of decision-making and exercise of power.[22]

As we can see, our government continues to see women more as a resource for production and reproduction than as independent individuals who can and should possess the whole range of human rights. This tendency became even more noticeable during perestroika and the democratization of Soviet society. All the so-called measures for improving the position of women that were discussed and passed during those years were in fact aimed at reinforcing women's traditional family roles and keeping women in the role of social cripple and political outsider by means of policies of 'entitlements' and allowances. The 1990 State Programme for Improving the Position of Women and Protection of the Family, Motherhood and Childhood is a prime example of this. The main emphasis in this document is on the 'protection' of mothers, but there is not a word about measures to help promote women to decision-making levels, or about shielding women from the unemployment that has already become a reality for them.[23]

Women have, however, been playing a more active part in the last few years in the new political parties, popular movements and organizations. I should like to mention here some important points about women's political activity:

1. Of all the socio-political movements, women most favour Memorial,[24] the Greens, the Transnational Party (about 30 per cent of its members are women), the Christian Democratic Union of Russia, the Blue Movement 'for human ecology' (not to be confused with the 'blues'[25]), and the Committee for Social Protection. About half the membership of these organizations is made up of women. Thus it seems that women prefer to belong to parties or political organizations that stand for the restoration of violated justice, for the conservation of nature and protection of humankind, and for non-violent methods of social change.

2. Not one of the political parties in which women play a part assumes the role of representing and defending the interests of women. Even in

political organizations where women make up between one-third and one-half of the membership, their particular interests are in no way reflected in the programmes. None of the new political parties has a plan to involve women in political life, and not one of them yet plans to adhere to the principle that women should be equally represented alongside men at decision-making levels. Our democrats are quite happy to use women in the old conservative way – to carry out the work.

3. The programmes of most of the new democratic movements either say nothing about women's issues or put forward demands for the care and protection of mothers – the custodians of the home. Moreover, they stress that the 'upbringing of future generations is the honourable civic duty of mothers'. The only demands for real equal rights for women are to be found in the Programme of the Estonian Popular Front, the Declaration of Interfront in Latvia and the Manifesto of the Committee for the Liberation of Russia. But even these contain no programmes of action to achieve this objective.

4. There are practically no special women's political parties fighting for the interests of women in the social, economic and political spheres. The Women's Party in the city of Tomsk in Siberia, or the United Women's Party in Leningrad cannot yet be considered serious political organizations, because they are too small, do not have the backing of the broad masses of women and have no clear political programmes.

This brief survey would not be complete without mentioning the rather unusual founding of an 'inter-nationality coordinating centre' called 'Woman', set up by an engineer named Yevgeny Pilshchikov, whose main aim is to train a woman for the post of president of the country and then conduct an election campaign on her behalf. Despite its initial attraction, the idea is mechanistic and altogether masculinist in nature, since it involves the purely mechanical selection of women to be trained by 'intelligent men'. Pilshchikov is convinced that certain 'special features' of the female psyche will guarantee the emergence of a new type of president, who will be able to stabilize the political situation and consolidate society on the basis of national concord, preservation of the family and renewal of the Soviet Union. There is no question here of women's interests being represented. Perhaps that is why the idea has not found support among women.

Although women continue to feel alienated from the issues of 'major politics', some hopeful changes can be seen in the realm of public life. I should like to say a few words here about the growth of informal women's organizations – i.e. organizations independent from state and party structures. And here I would agree with the Soviet researcher Valentina Konstantinova of the Centre for Gender Studies who separates the organizations into democratic, feminist and conservative categories. In the first category she puts the Committee of Soldiers' Mothers (they support the depoliticization of the army and alternative national service), the Inter-regional Political Club in the town of Zhukovsky in Moscow Region, the Committee for Equal Opportunities at a car plant in the town of Naberezhnye Chelny, and the Independent Women's Democratic Initiative – NeZhDI.

Feminist initiatives include Olga Lipovskaya's *Women's Readings* magazine, SAFO – the Free Association of Feminist Organizations – led by Natalia Filippova in Moscow, Lotus – a group of women scholars who are calling for the development of women's, gender and feminist studies as part of Soviet scholarship and who also work with the broad mass of women in order to involve them in the struggle for their rights.

Women's organizations of the conservative type are represented by the Soviet Women's Committee, the Russian Women's Union and the system of *zhensoviety*. These have recently adopted new names like 'Union of Moscow Women's Organizations', and so on. Apart from these, the movement of women 'Towards a Socialist Future for our Children', the United Women's Party (Leningrad) and various religious and nationalistic women's groups belong in this conservative category.

Women's organizations, even those working towards the same goal, are often isolated and know little about each other. To help overcome this, in March 1991 members of the Lotus group, SAFO and colleagues from the Centre for Gender Studies held the First Independent Women's Forum in the city of Dubna in Moscow Region. The forum's motto was 'Democracy without Women is not Democracy', and it set out to review the strength of women's organizations. Representatives from forty-eight women's organizations from different parts of the country took part. The meetings were attended by the women's press, women researchers and women who had not yet joined any organization but who felt the need to fight for their rights – about two hundred women in all. Topics discussed were: 'Women and Politics', 'Problems of the Independent Women's Movement', 'Women and the Market Economy', 'Women's Businesses', 'Discrimination against Women in a Patriarchal Culture' and 'Violence against Women'. At the forum, it was decided to set up a Women's Information Network and to continue joint cooperation. As one of the organizers of the forum, I hope that our work will in fact serve to develop and consolidate the independent women's movement in our country.

Factors Obstructing Women's Public Activity

I should like to distinguish several kinds of factors.

   1. First, the traditionally accepted assumption in our culture is that the

most important thing in a woman's life is her family and children. This assumption, so typical of patriarchal culture, acquired a particular nuance in Russia. If we examine how the role of women was interpreted in Russian religious and philosophical thought of earlier centuries, we will see that the concepts of what is female and feminine in Russia are inseparable from the concepts of spirituality and principles of national unity. Elements of 'Russian spirituality' include a certain ascetic passivity, a renunciation of worldly things, and self-sacrifice for the benefit of others. For women this takes the form of sacrificing themselves for the sake of the family, and bowing to the traditions and authority of the men in the family. Even today this conviction (supported by Russian nationalists) holds that this is a fundamental tradition of Russian culture and that women's emancipation and an active public life undermine the foundations of Russian consciousness. Examples of this can be found in the novels by such well-known writers as Vasily Belov and Valentin Rasputin and in statements by Alexander Solzhenitsyn and many others. The line that a woman's mission is the family is drilled into children practically from birth. Yet in a society where women have for many years been going out to work on an equal footing with men, life itself ought to have eradicated this stereotype of the womanly mission. This is not happening, because society continues to propagate patriarchal cultural norms regarding women. As a result, a certain paradoxical consciousness comes into being whereby the idea of emancipation is only acceptable insofar as it does not hinder women from following their innate mission. These cultural directives contribute to the continuance of women's belief that the main thing in life is their family. These stereotypes also enable the state to continue failing to provide adequate domestic services for the population. They allow the state to spend less on public services and on manufacturing essential kitchen and domestic equipment.

2. The second factor, therefore, that stands in the way of women becoming more active in society is the manner in which family life and domestic labour are organized. Sociologists have calculated that in the early 1980s women in this country spent on average eighty hours a week on housework, whereas for men the figure was around twenty hours. Public services and amenities in Moscow, supposedly better off in this respect than other cities, provide only a fraction of all domestic work done in the city. But the situation has become even worse in recent years, as a result of the economic crisis and breakdown in the state economy.

3. The third factor hindering the development of women's social activity, I believe, is the state's policy towards women. Despite the principle of equal rights for men and women which was announced in the early years of the Soviet regime, neither Party ideology nor state policy

has ever sought genuine women's liberation – i.e. truly giving women equal opportunities with men in all spheres of life. Slogans about emancipation have always been subordinated to the tasks of specific ideological campaigns or economic programmes. For the Bolsheviks, the woman question was always part of the overall strategy of social transformation, and the women's movement – under Party control – was subordinated to the general strategy of solving the woman question. The strategy's main feature was to involve women in work outside the home (since a fast-growing economy needed – and still needs – cheap female labour). The two other principles of Marxist-Leninist theory on solving the woman question – namely, the socialization of children and propaganda about new family relations – were never put into practice. With time the image of the woman worker was transformed into the image of a woman who combined the roles of worker, mother and housewife. This combination of roles exemplifies the functional approach towards women – quite convenient for the state, which simply shifts the emphasis within this set of roles to suit a particular social and economic situation. If the state needs labour, then the role of women as workers is brought to the fore; if an economic slump occurs, the state resuscitates its ideology of the womanly mission and calls on women to go back to the home. This was what happened during the perestroika years.

Let us look at the state Programme for Improving the Position of Women and Protection of the Family, Motherhood and Childhood – a programme intended for the 1990s. Quite apart from the typical name and structure of the programme, the tasks it sets are notable for their traditionalism and patriarchalism. The programme sets itself the task of 'linking together the interests of women, family and society': the first section is devoted to the fundamentals of state family policy; the second to the fundamentals of state policy on improving the position of women, and here the main accent is on the 'protection' of women, on the various entitlements and allowances, in short, on all that makes it easier for women to look after the family and children; the third section deals with the main planks of state policy for safeguarding the health of mothers and children. But the programme contains nothing on measures to liberate women from traditional stereotypes, or measures at state level to help women reach the echelons of decision-making. When the programme was being discussed in the USSR Cabinet of Ministers, Prime Minister Valentin Pavlov stressed that 'this programme will help to fortify the nation's physical and moral health and enhance the stabilizing role of the family as society's primary unit and the family's importance in people's spiritual development.' The only thing that is not clear to me is why this remarkable programme should be called 'Programme for the Improvement of the Position of *Women* . . .'

As we can see, our government continues to consider women an appendage to the family, not as independent individuals. Thus all measures to improve the position of women aim to anchor them even more firmly to their traditional family roles. At work, through the policy of giving them entitlements and allowances, they tend to put women in the position of social outcasts and shop-floor outsiders. But since this kind of policy has absolutely no authority at the international level, the state is playing a double game. On the one hand, it signs all the international agreements and supports all the international initiatives on women's liberation. And on the other hand, in the area of internal policies, it not only advances directly opposed priorities, but even fails to acquaint the population with state policy on women at the international level. This is what happened, for instance, with the United Nations Convention on the Elimination of All Forms of Discrimination against Women. It was signed and ratified by the USSR more than ten years ago. But the convention's text was not translated into Russian until 1989 and was published in the *USSR Ministry of Foreign Affairs Bulletin*, which has a very limited readership. The public at large simply has no idea what the convention contains, even though, according to the USSR constitution, all international agreements signed and ratified by the government and parliament are law in our country.

With this sort of attitude by the authorities towards equal rights and towards the convention that establishes these rights, it is hardly surprising that practically none of the convention's articles are being put into practice. Official state statistics continue to conceal, rather than disclose, the real position of Soviet women. Public awareness continues to be manipulated and patriarchal stereotypes disseminated through the state's mass media. Transmission of patriarchal culture and its stereotypes through the mass media is yet another factor preventing women from becoming more active in public affairs.

Conclusions

I have highlighted several problems and left out much that is beyond the framework of this article, as I wanted to get away from the traditional analysis of the position of women in our country and deal mainly with those issues that were formerly outside acceptable discourse.

In conclusion I should like to offer my own answer to the question as to why the Soviet experiment in solving the woman question was not successful. It did not succeed because the ideology, policy and practice of liberation were masculinist and the objective was not in fact women's emancipation but the continuation of discrimination and suppression of women. The objection might be raised that much of what has been said here applies to men as well: the repression of the individual, lack of rights, alienation from the political process and from the results of one's labour.

The patriarchal system standardizes people according to their sex, ascribes and prescribes certain 'sexual' parameters of conduct, thinking and being. This also affects men: like women, they cannot free themselves of their sexual stereotypes, and they often feel more realized as a sex than as individuals. There is another aspect: sexual conditioning takes away freedom, even for one who has been 'lucky' and is on the upper rung of the sexual hierarchy. No one can be free while repressing others.

Notes

1. In the late 1970s, members of the Leningrad 'Maria' group took the first step towards stripping Russia's ideology of the myth of male and female equality by their publication of the book *Women and Russia*. But even the articles of this anthology exhibit a marked eclecticism of feminist and patriarchal views.

2. M.S. Gorbachev, *Perestroika: New Thinking for Our Country and the World* (London 1987), p. 117.

3. One of the clearest examples of the second tendency was the publication of an article in *Pravda* by a then little-known provincial physical education instructor, K. Rash. What was most striking was not so much Rash's overtly woman-hating tone ('Both production and the family suffer by women going out to work. Working women mean the disintegration of the family. It would be better if husbands received their wives' wages instead'), as the stand this Party publication took. Not only did they not commission a specialist to write the article, but an ideologue of the 'strong arm' and 'male principles' (for Rash, 'male' is a synonym for 'militaristic'), but the editorial board even turned a blind eye to the distortion of Lenin's ideas on female professional employment which Rash stooped to in order to prove the validity of his views. K. Rash, 'Dearer Than Any Kingdom', *Pravda*, 22 February 1989.

4. A masculinist bias is evident in the term 'cost of emancipation'. Masculinism is described by the British author Arthur Brittan as an 'ideology which justifies and considers as natural male domination'. A. Brittan, *Masculinity and Power* (Oxford 1989), p. 4. The use of masculinist terms and concepts prevents objective analysis of the real problems that accompany, and are sometimes brought out by, the process of women's liberation.

5. More details on this are to be found in O.A. Voronina, 'Zhenshchina v muzhskom obshestve', *Sotsiol. issled.*, no. 2, 1988, pp. 104–10; and in N. Zakharova, A. Posadskaya and N. Rimashevskaya, 'Kak my reshayem zhenskiy vopros', *Kommunist*, no. 4, 1989, pp. 56–65.

6. The actual text of the convention was not made public in our country, since it was only published in Russian in 1989 and then not in a mass-circulation journal, but in the bulletin of the USSR foreign ministry (*Vestnik MID SSSR*, no. 16, 1989).

7. Andrea Dworkin's neologism 'gynocide' sounds like 'genocide', but it is formed from the Greek *gune* – woman. A. Dworkin, *Woman hating* (New York 1974).

8. K. Marx and F. Engels, *Selected Works* (London 1950), vol. II, p. 205.

9. Incidentally, various ethnographic studies demonstrate the absence of any linear dependence between property and the social status of men and women.

10. 'The German Ideology', p. 31, in *Marx, Engels, Lenin: On Historical Materialism. A Collection* (Moscow 1972).

11. V.I. Lenin, *The Great Initiative* (Glasgow 1920), p. 15.

12. K. Marx and F. Engels, *Selected Works* (London 1950), vol. II, p. 205.

13. *Translator's note*: 'stakhanovites' – a movement to boost productivity levels, named after miner Aleksei Stakhanov, who, in 1935, mined 102 tons of coal in one shift, instead of the usual 7.

14. The conferences of stakhonovite wives were particularly interesting: these women were offered a complete set of ideological clichés to help inspire their husbands to labour-feats and shame those failing to keep up.

15. *Translator's note*: 'kolkhoz' – abbreviated term meaning collective farm.

16. *Translator's note*: 'kulak': a well-off peasant employing hired labour.

17. 'Regulations on Women's Councils' (Moscow 1987), p. 1.

18. M.S. Gorbachev, *Perestroika: New Thinking for our Country and the World* (London 1987), p. 117.

19. *Argumenty i Fakty*, no. 5, 1990, p. 6. I would like to add a few words here about the system of women's professions, which during the perestroika years continued to reproduce traditional Soviet masculinist ideology. Thus, for example, women in 'male' areas of employment are normally used for heavy, monotonous, routine, low-prestige and low-paid work. So-called 'female' jobs were created under the influence of the gender stereotypes which influence whether a job is considered 'prestigious' and affect the wage level for it. Practically all jobs and specializations which society thinks of as 'female' are characterized by low wages compared with those thought of as 'male'. The average differential is 30 per cent in favour of men.

20. *Translator's note*: Though in October 1988 Aleksandra Biryukova had been made a candidate member of the Politburo.

21. *Women in the USSR. Stat. Materialy* (Finansy i Statistika, Moscow 1990), p. 21.

22. *Ibid.*, p. 27.

23. According to the preliminary data of Z.A. Khotkina (Centre for Gender Studies) unemployment among women is five times greater than among men.

24. *Translator's note*: 'Memorial' – a society set up in 1988 to campaign for a monument and research centre in memory of the victims of Stalinism.

25. *Translator's note*: 'blues' – homosexuals.

4

No Longer Totalitarianism, But Not Yet Democracy: The Emergence of an Independent Women's Movement in Russia

Valentina Konstantinova

This bird is learning to fly/Soaring on the wings of her song/If sometimes she flies a bit too high/It's 'cause she was in a cage for so long. . . ./'You know my freedom is not something you can give me/I must take it for myself if I want to be free/I've got to trust my own wings if I want to learn to fly/In this cage I'll never sing, I've got to find the sky.'
R. Taubb, Song about a Caged Bird[1]

Russian women like myself have not yet learnt to fly. We lack confidence and our everyday struggle for mere survival prevents our taking off. We are faced with the question: Do we really want freedom? Are we prepared to make sacrifices for the sake of freedom in order to do our bit in building democracy? Or will women once again accept the rules of the game foisted on them from above – either the theory of women's 'natural mission' (to be wives and mothers) or a combination of roles – worker and mother? Or shall we try to enable each member of society to have a real choice in how he or she earns a living, how to coordinate our working and personal lives (both women's and men's) with family life as well as developing as individuals? We need democracy for this to take place.

Concepts of democracy, solidarity, liberation, freedom of choice, sex equality and human rights are discredited in our society, but they have steadily gained credibility during the last eight years. People in the former socialist countries are experiencing a revolution in their consciousness, they are shaking off the militaristic, imperialistic and chauvinistic ethos. The old totalitarian state and social structures are being dismantled or modernized. The empire has collapsed, the Berlin Wall has fallen and the Iron Curtain has at last been lifted. Our language has begun to free itself of newspeak, national democratic movements are growing and a new-found inner freedom is finding ways of expressing itself. But still only the first inroads are being made on patriarchy, supported for so long by religion, sexist language and the totalitarian system itself. So in these tentative early stages, what are the chances of women being able to organize their public and private lives in the way they would like?

The reforms begun in 1986 have resulted in a situation full of paradoxes: women have suffered sackings, they have stood in queues, put up with poor services, etc. But freedom has meant we have been able to say what we think, to go to meetings and to form associations. We can also use our initiative to set up our own businesses, which gives us a feeling of self-fulfilment. None of this was possible before: most women have not yet fully grasped or begun to appreciate this freedom. And as yet most women are not making use of their new opportunities. The process of liberation is painful. We seem to have inherited fear in our very genes, fear bred in us by total dependence on 'the bosses' and our own internal bondage.

We break out of the thick shell of our prejudices and fears, only to find ourselves defenceless and vulnerable in the face of all that we have to tackle. A civil society is only just taking shape, there are still too few organizations, pressure groups and lobbies that can express and defend the interests of individual citizens or groups and defend them socially and psychologically. Some already blame our new democracy and the democrats for all our problems, and put forward the idea of an enlightened dictatorship. This approach is simply taking advantage of people's discontent during the difficulties of the transition period.

For the time being we still have to admit that in Russia the public sphere belongs to men, and the private sphere to women. Sociological data may show that 'men are potentially eager to integrate into the sphere of family relationships',[2] but to what extent are women prepared to get involved in social and political affairs? And to what extent are men prepared to make room for women and particularly to give up leadership posts to women? How can gender asymmetry in social and political affairs be neutralized? We cannot wait for the involvement of women in every aspect of society to develop 'naturally': it is a political problem. Active involvement of women is both a prerequisite and a consequence of the democratic ideals which are beginning to take root in these post-totalitarian societies. Real sex equality will only be incorporated into government policy if the political will is there; and if there is an efficient decision-making process and an effective means of putting these decisions into operation at the grassroots level.[3] We are only just beginning to glimpse the emergence of such conditions amid the social, economic, political and cultural upheavals of our time.

Much needs to be done if we are to develop that political will. We need a civil society; we need new democratic media dealing with gender issues and relationships; we need more responsive politics and politicians; we need to reform the process by which leading personnel are selected. We need special programmes to support women: we must encourage campaigns by women's organizations to back progressive women candidates; government bodies should be set up to act as watchdogs for the process of providing equal opportunities. Only then will we see a significant number of women occupying key positions of power.

A Civil Society: Not Yet Democracy

'Life has become not so much better as more fun!'
From a radio broadcast, November 1991[4]

Society is moving from a state of dismal uniformity, conformism, monopoly and orthodoxy – in ideology, in the economy, culture and politics – in which human rights were totally ignored, to the rudiments of pluralism, social tolerance and recognition of human rights and freedoms. It is an extremely painful process, more so in the former Soviet Union than in the countries of eastern and central Europe. Three generations of Soviet people lived under the conditions of a repressive regime, the 'big brother' described by George Orwell. With perestroika came the legalizing of political parties which had been operating underground. And new protest groups began to emerge: ecological, anti-nuclear, women's, workers' and civil rights movements, as well as various religious groups and organizations.

An American expert on US social movements, Bill Moyer, defines these as 'collective actions':

> Social movements are collective actions in which the population is alerted, educated and mobilized over years and decades, to challenge the power-holders and the whole society, to redress social problems or grievances and restore critical social values. By involving the populace directly in the political process, social movements also foster the concept of government of, by and for the people. The power of movements is directly proportional to the forcefulness with which the grassroots exert their discontent and demand change.[5]

Moyer describes social movements passing through eight 'stages of development': (1) the normal condition – i.e. a critical social problem exists; (2) a stage of proving the failure of official institutions; (3) ripening conditions; (4) the social movement's take-off; (5) perception of failure; (6) majority public opinion; (7) success; (8) continuation of the struggle.[6]

We can assume that in Russia most movements are going through the second of Moyer's 'stages', but with new groupings emerging all the time. However, I feel it is impossible to compare the situation in the United States – a stable democratic society – with what is happening here. Geoffrey Hosking describes the 1989 miners' strikes in Russia and the Ukraine as an expression of the 'primitive solidarity' of earlier periods.[7] This seems to over-simplify the miners' strike of 1989, since they were putting forward political demands despite the fear of repression, and without much hope that their demands would find support in Moscow. I think it is true to say that the miners' conscious political position – showing a new level of political culture – contributed to the fact that Yeltsin's democratic government has remained in power. But there was no central, coordinated democratic movement at that time, so in 1989 it was unrealistic to expect links to be forged between the various movements. These do exist now, but it is still too early to speak of any serious coordinated action.

The new social movements share several interesting characteristics. Many of them, like the civil rights movements, are based on small dissident groups that emerged in the late 1960s. Most have no coherent ideology as they have arisen spontaneously, and problems are as yet seen mainly at an emotional level. The groups' demands are not based on any research or statistics, nor do they suggest solutions to problems. No information network has been established between the various groups or their equivalents in other parts of the world. There is a lack of experience in organizational work and big problems are experienced in cooperating with official public and state organizations of the former USSR (the Soviet Women's Committee, departments of the Russian Ministry of Foreign Affairs, the Friendship Society, the Peace Committee, etc.). There has been much criticism of these public organizations over recent years, and they continue to be widely distrusted. They strive to maintain a monopoly, which makes working with them difficult, but they need contact with new organizations and new ideas to improve their image.

The new groups desperately need better material and technical resources. There is no legislation enabling businesses to support these new groups financially. Society's attitude to political groups depends largely on the popularity of their leaders (for example, Yelena Bonner and Larissa Bogoraz in the civil rights movement), rather than their ideology or practical work (the general public knows little of them, again due to lack of information).

So how and why do these groups manage to prosper? In part because people have become politicized, and are searching for new ideas and theories to fill the ideological vacuum. Most importantly, we believe we can actually at last take part in changing things. The women's movement is now an important part of our newly emerging civil society.

The Women's Movement: A Ghost Is Stalking Russia

It is obvious that the problem of the struggle for equal rights is not on the agenda for us at present – it is a problem at a different level of life, a different economy and a different level of civilization.
Yevgeniya Albats, '*According to Sex*'[8]

An independent women's movement is a new phenomenon in our society,[9] and one which is being greeted with some hostility. But even in its present form, it is a prototype for a future broad democratic protest movement.

Patriarchalism in Russia has yet to be studied. Theoretical and practical research is needed, as is comparative analysis of the various kinds of patriarchy. Post-totalitarian patriarchalism is not just on the defensive, it is baring its teeth at the changed conditions and the timid challenge thrown down by the few feminists in this country and in the West.

The present state of our women's movement is the result of the interruption in tradition of the women's movement in Russia soon after the 1917 Revolution. Monolithic Party and government control suppressed any differing ideas or initiative from below. The Party had sole power and imposed a strict hierarchical system on the women's movement. During the rise of the women's movement from the late 1960s onwards feminist ideas, whether of national origin or from the West, were dismissed out of hand.

Stereotypes and myths about the women's movement are still powerful factors that influence public opinion. I will mention just a few.

'The women's movement is a "social monster".' There is enough tension in society already, without the women's movement making things worse by setting women against men. This could lead to social unrest.

'Women are bent on power.' Women are trying to gain even more power over men. Haven't they got enough power as it is? In the family they are the bosses, they bring up the children as they see fit and are increasingly earning more than men. What more do they need?

'The women's movement is an impermissible luxury.' Feminist movements and ideologies are suitable for a 'well-fed' society, but we have other problems on our plate. Let's first solve our social and economic problems, and 'women's' problems will automatically be resolved.

'The division of society by sex is a dead end.' It is silly to divide society according to sex. Why should women have privileges? Separate quotas for women simply belittle women. Leading posts should be filled by competent responsible people; women should not be given preferential treatment.

'Blue stockings on a red banner.' Only former *apparat* women who did not manage to excel in other fields find fulfilment in women's organizations.

'Emancipation is to blame for everything.' The goal of the women's movement is women's liberation. But in Russia they have already achieved liberation. And what is the result? Women are overburdened; children are left to fend for themselves; juvenile delinquency and drugs are on the increase; more and more children are abandoned by their mothers (our mothers did not give us up!); prostitution and pornography are flourishing. All because the traditional roles of men and women have been forgotten.

'Feminists are CIA agents.' The feminist movement in Russia is inspired and financed by special Western agencies. Their aim is to destabilize society by destroying the stability of the family. Feminism is alien to the Russian soul and was imported from amoral Western society.

'Women are always looking for special advantages.' Feminists are always trying to improve things for themselves and promote women. Whether it's white-collar positions (be it president, cosmonaut or politician), or blue-collar work involving heavy, unskilled labour, they are always demanding 'women's liberation'.

'All feminists are lesbians'. Women politicians are discredited if they take part in the feminist movement.

'Feminism is like Bolshevism.' Feminists try to force their ideology on people as the Bolsheviks did with Communism, while hypocritically promising universal happiness and equality.

'The women's movement is a "demographic monster".' The women's movement has caused demographic changes all over the world: a reduction in the birthrate, an increase in the number of divorces and the number of children born outside wedlock.

Is there any truth in all of this? Let me examine these myths one by one.

The 'social monster' myth. There might be 'saucepan' uprisings during the difficult transition period. Data from the All-Union Institute of Public Opinion (VTsIOM) for mid December 1991 show that 'the most disillusioned and least inclined to wait [for the success of the reforms] are unskilled women workers, who have the lowest incomes and least chance of buying food and goods, because they live in the small towns of Russia'.[10] Only women's or workers' movements are likely to be able to politicize women and give their protest a more civilized edge. Job cuts affecting women must be monitored and new jobs created, which will contribute to the growth of women's businesses. Training and retraining programmes are vital, as are psychological support and assertiveness courses.

The 'women are bent on power' myth. Men ignore the issues that concern women: the burden of their everyday lives, poor nurseries and crêches, having to fit their work around the needs of their families, and so on. The women's movement ought to put this on the agenda – a fairer shouldering of responsibility for decisions that are of importance not just to women, but to society as a whole.

'The women's movement is a luxury we cannot afford.' The women's movement is part of the new civil society we are trying to build and it is a normal social phenomenon. As incredible as it may seem today, the hoary old idea that women's demands must wait is now an important topic of private discussions among our new 'democratic' politicians. And this is before equal opportunities are even on the political agenda!

'The division of society by sex will lead us nowhere.' Studies have shown that society is already divided according to sex and social status. Women suffer discrimination in pay, in career promotion and in access to decision-making. We have to overcome these social and sexual obstacles and create conditions so that the individual can best fulfil him- or herself as befits his or her abilities and goals.

'Blue stockings on a red banner.' The so-called 'leaders' of the old women's movement in the former Soviet Union were representatives of the nomenklatura and did not represent the interests of different groups of women. The independent women's movement has attracted idealistic women, who identify with the democratic movement.

'Emancipation is to blame for everything.' Not only women in our society require liberation. Society as a whole is not free. Proclaimed human rights and freedoms and equal rights between men and women were never put into practice. Women were drawn into production more for economic reasons than from any concern to implement their rights and freedoms. The problems of discrimination against women and their lack of political freedom were never raised.

'Feminists are CIA agents.' Today's cheering patriots have now embraced the class approach, preserving a false understanding of ideological purity and social intolerance. The first wave of feminism existed in Russia before the 1917 Revolution; who was behind it then? Perhaps it is an objective phenomenon after all?

'Women are always seeking special advantages.' It would appear that until now it is men who have sought special advantages: most men took it for granted that they should play an active role in managing society. Neither men nor women should work in jobs which are dangerous and injurious to their health. Yet it turns out that it is women who want these jobs to be retained, because these few jobs offer higher wages and allow workers to retire earlier. It is doubtful whether this can be considered a 'special advantage', when it comes at the expense of their health.

'All feminists are lesbians.' Issues of female sexuality have not yet been raised by the new women's movement. One of the reasons is the absence of feminist research into this subject. The habit of labelling dies hard and has often contributed to discrediting normal behaviour.

'Feminism is like Bolshevism.' There are profound differences between feminism and Bolshevism. Bolshevism is an ideology of violence and suppression that has hidden behind proclamations of equality and justice. Feminists want to build a non-violent world; they propose cooperation instead of competition, joint forces in place of 'I won, you lost', and 'enough is fine' instead of 'the more the better'. Bolshevism is blinkered by its monolithic class approach. The ideology of feminism is pluralistic and varied: socialist feminism, reformist (liberal) feminism and radical feminism.

The 'demographic monster' myth. The demographic changes that have taken place in the developed industrialized countries of the West over the last decades (the fall in birthrate and increase in divorces and in the numbers of children born outside wedlock) are also happening in Russia. These changes cannot be blamed entirely on the women's movement, since until a few years ago there was in fact no such thing in this country. Clearly there must be other factors behind these changes.

These, then, are my comments on the myths surrounding the women's movement: a detailed scientific analysis has yet to be made. Such myths have not yet achieved wide currency, but they exist. Stereotypes about women's liberation that were widely accepted in the former USSR still persist. Yet at the same time you hear more and more people say that at this turning-point only women can save society.

Who does the newly emerging women's movement in fact represent? Women's groups at present are both organizationally and ideologically separate and are not yet a credible political force. But it is their potential that counts. It is impossible to say how many movements there are at present. The social base tends to be professional and intellectual women, but women workers are also becoming active. There are practically no information networks, papers or magazines that reflect the new, unconventional approach. At present there is a definite ideological vacuum (the class approach has been discredited, but feminist ideas are little known as yet), which is being filled mainly by spontaneous reactions to pressing problems. The movement's aim is to improve the lot of women, mainly in the economic and political sense.

The politicization of our society has led to women's active participation in women's organizations. But the level of feminist consciousness among women as a whole is low. Women's groups have become accustomed to expressing their opinions, whether the subject be democracy, national sovereignty, pluralism, the market economy, reform in the armed forces or feminism. But not one of these groups has come to grips with the problem of sex discrimination. Five distinct trends can now be observed in the women's movement: democratic, feminist, traditionalist reform, undemocratic and radical.[11]

The most developed of these groups is the 'democratic' trend, which encompasses women's organizations supporting a variety of democratic reforms. For example, committees of soldiers' mothers want changes in the army. Changes in local government are demanded by groups such as the political club in the town of Zhukovsky. Women active in the Social Democratic Party of Russia set up a women's wing in December 1991. An association called the Independent Women's Democratic Initiative in Kemerovo is part of the Union of Kuzbass Workers, thus setting a precedent for the trade unions; in the civil rights movement the Independent Organization of Women's Initiatives (NOZhI) in the city of Kaluga defends women's legal and civil rights; and now a political party called Women of Sovereign Russia has been founded in Tomsk.

The 'feminist' trend is represented by such groups as the League for Liberation from Stereotypes (Lotos),[12] which was founded some six years ago; the Independent Women's Democratic Initiative (Moscow),[13] founded in 1990; the Free Association of Feminist Organizations (SAFO), which provides support and psychological counselling for women; research departments such as the Centre for Gender Studies at the Russian Academy of Sciences' Institute for Socio-Economic Population Studies; an independent organization called Ariadna, which supports gender research.[14] Ariadna is a new type of organization, which aims to change the old structures from within while at the same time developing new groupings. This strategy is fraught with but probably has a greater chance of success than many of the others.

The 'radical' trend is small in numbers, but active: organizations of lesbians – and homosexuals – have held several demonstrations, blocking the traffic in the centre of Moscow.

The 'undemocratic' trend, in my view, includes a wide range of both government and public women's organizations; some set up prior to 1985 and others since then. These include the Soviet Women's Committee and the Russian Union of Women, *zhensoviety* at all levels, for example in factories, residential areas or at district, town and republican levels; two parliamentary committees on women, the family and demographic policy; and Russian and Soviet government departments. During perestroika not one of these organizations proved able to declare openly and unequivocally the need to campaign for equal rights, nor did they argue that discrimination against women should be made illegal. They were unable to react appropriately to political events (in April 1990 in Tbilisi,[15] in January 1991 in Lithuania,[16] or in August 1991 in Moscow[17]). The apparat of most of these organizations is, it seems, incapable of a new mentality. Unofficial women's organizations such as the 'pro-life' groups in Lithuania and Moldova, or the nationalist-chauvinistic organizations in Russia will probably grow as religion gains in influence.

The 'traditionalist reform' trend is attempting to revive women's clubs, like sewing and knitting circles, literary groups, etc.; and to draw women into business and encourage them to create jobs for women. Various associations of businesswomen are being set up.

We have only begun to lay the foundations of an independent women's movement. Future developments are not altogether clear. Two stages in the movement's formation may be discerned. The first is the emergence of new women's groups along professional, political and feminist lines (1989–90); and the second is the merging of several old (e.g. *zhensoviety*) and new democratically minded or feminist groups of women, although these are still on a rather small scale. Women's solidarity is not yet on the agenda. An optimistic forecast would be that the present attacks on the rights of women might serve as a stimulus for the women's movement to expand, as long as feminist work continues to raise women's consciousness.

Revolution without Feminists?

Our people were deprived of one of the great passions, male passions – the opportunity to engage in politics. . . . This greatly impoverished our lives.

Yuri Shcherbak[18]

Society is at last hearing the truth about the past and the present and this offers us great moral strength. The opportunity to take a real, not merely formal, part in the 'revolution'[19] attracted new people, both women and men, into politics. The first democratic elections, or rather, the pre-electoral campaign, gave women candidates the chance to have their say and show their worth. They became prominent, not only in their own cities and villages, but some even at national level. But so far very few of these women are concerned about the question of achieving sexual equality.

At the time of the 1917 Revolution, there were women leaders who could put women's problems on the agenda;[20] whereas during perestroika women only emerged as political leaders about five years ago. Unfortunately, however, even popular, democratically minded women politicians still deny in public the existence of discrimination against women. They do not see the value of special measures for women or understand the importance of the women's movement. They follow the traditional male pattern of political behaviour: self-assertiveness, competitiveness, strict rationality, absence of emotion, insistence on their own point of view. Their refusal to acknowledge that the 'woman question' exists can partly be explained by the fact that the woman question had not really been settled. At first it was seen as part of the overall democratic struggle, then later it was considered 'solved', and no one seemed to know of any other way to deal with the problem. In addition, women deputies of the Soviet parliament, who were in the main loyal Party apparatchiks, always put the stress on simply extending entitlements for working mothers.[21] The traditional stereotype 'politics is men's dirty business' has always held sway,[22] and helped to maintain the situation where the corridors of power were only open to women loyal to the regime and by quota. The new women politicians, by contrast, have been elected to parliament without quotas of any kind and are proud of the fact.

One might expect that the emerging independent women's movement would embrace democratic and humanistic ideals and values – against violence, for cooperation, sensitivity, solidarity, freedom and sex equality. However, we must admit that old concepts and ideas die hard. In March 1991 some 180 women attended the First Independent Women's Forum in Dubna. A survey conducted there showed that delegates represented forty-eight women's organizations and twenty-five cities.[23] In answer to a question about future tasks for the women's movement, 68 per cent stressed the importance of achieving real sex equality, consolidation of the rights they had won and the need to fight against existing stereotypes; 62 per cent of the respondents thought it 'very important' that the number of women in the highest echelons of power should be increased; while only 2.4 per cent thought this unimportant. In response to a question as to why women's representation was important, nearly half of those questioned thought that women politicians would be more likely to 'pay attention to other areas of politics and social problems'; 36 per cent thought that women should be represented at decision-making levels, since they constitute more than half the population. A large majority of the women questioned (83 per cent) expressed the conviction that a woman could 'cope with the responsibilities of president, chair of the Supreme Soviet, or general secretary'.[24] However, when it came to the question of whom they would propose for these posts, 34 per cent answered that they could not think of any suitable woman candidate, 35 per cent left the question unanswered and 7 per cent could not say. Galina Starovoitova received the highest number of votes (17 per cent). On the subject of existing leaders, 36 per cent of the respondents could not say which leaders' policies they supported; 25 per cent supported Yeltsin, with significant numbers (3.8 per cent) showing support for Sobchak,[25] 3 per cent supported Bush, and 2.3 per cent Thatcher.

So, have women made any significant inroads in the new political parties and social movements? In Russia there are now over twenty-five political parties, whereas in October 1991 there were only four. In Moscow alone there are some ten civil rights groups. Their unofficial, informal nature has to do with the crisis in our political system: people have lost confidence in any kind of authority – a reflection of the alienation and apathy they experience. The facts indicate that there is a growing awakening of political activity among women – especially from 1989–90 onwards – but that this is still at a very low level, compared with men.[26]

Women are poorly represented at decision-making levels, in both state and political affairs. As a result of the partial lifting of quotas for women in parliament, the proportion of women deputies in the former USSR Supreme Soviet dropped from 33 per cent to 15.7 per cent; in the RSFSR Supreme Soviet from 35 per cent to 5 per cent; and in the Supreme Soviets of Ukraine, Belarus and Kazakhstan, it dropped to 7 per cent. This decrease was recorded even during the period when quotas were still partially in force – those allotted to the so-called public organizations (the Soviet Women's Committee, Soviet Peace Committee, Council of Veterans, the CPSU, etc.). Women's representation in local councils fell: in Estonia, it dropped to 23 per cent; in Latvia, 34 per cent; in Russia, 35 per cent. The electorate in the main showed a preference for male candidates. There were no women on two of the USSR Supreme Soviet committees (Committee on Defence and Security and the Committee on Science and Technology) nor on eight of the committees of the RSFSR Supreme Soviet.[27]

Most of the new political parties, independent trade unions and civil rights groups have not put equal rights for women on their agendas. Only 'pro-socialist' parties or chauvinistic nationalist groups such as the Russian Popular Front mention women's problems, but then only in terms of their importance for strengthening the family – and men are not mentioned at all in this context. Others, like the Socialist Party, aim to increase social benefits for mothers. In general, it may be said that the more politicized the movement or group, the fewer women are active in it. There are few women in pro-socialist parties or in parties modelling themselves on Western 'bourgeois' democracies, as the following statistics show: Democratic Party, less than 1 per cent; Socialist Party, 2–3 per cent; Social-Democratic Party of Russia, 1–2 per cent; Party of Urban Proprietors and Landowners, 10 per cent.

This is an indication not so much of women's conservatism as of their more unconventional understanding of the term 'politics'. Women understand the priority of global problems, like the environment, human rights and peace. One-third of the Green Party's members are women; about 30 per cent of the Transnational Radical Party are women; women make up half of the Blue ('for human ecology') Movement; half the Christian Democratic Union's members are women; and 40–50 per cent of the members of the Andrei Sakharov Union of Democratic Forces are women.

But women tend not to be in the leaderships of these new organizations. In the Committee for Social Protection, for example, only one of the four leaders is a woman, though half the membership is female; out of sixteen leaders of the Russian People's Front, only three are women; however, 40 per cent of the Blue Movement's leadership are women.

Women have played a very active role in the many demonstrations and mass meetings organized by the democratic forces in Moscow, St Petersburg, Yekaterinburg and other large cities. Women are joining new independent trades unions of miners, air-traffic controllers, and cooperative members. Women make up twenty of the sixty members of the independent trades union called Justice in St Petersburg. The fear of losing their jobs is one motivation for women to join such trades unions. Strikes by nursery-school staff and doctors were threatened in early 1991 and Moscow teachers (87 per cent of whom are women) actually went on strike in February 1991, closing down one-third of all the capital's schools. It was the first time women had taken part in a strike in this country. Women made up two-thirds of all the strike committee members, but only 40 per cent of the leadership.

In 1991, out of 160 postings abroad in international non-governmental organizations and in the diplomatic service, only 13–18 per cent of posts were held by women at junior and middle levels and there were only three women ambassadors.[28] Of 1,962 leading officials in the former USSR – top leaders, first deputy posts and other officials – there were 55 women. In the Russian Federation 16 women out of 5,111 held such posts, according to data from 1990.[29] The day when significant numbers of women occupy key positions of power is, it seems, still a long way off.

Some Conclusions

'Young democracy is like a young girl who is seduced. Immature democracy is like pornography. Mature democracy is like a mature man.'
From the speech of Kazakh poet Olzhas Suleimenov at the
First Congress of People's Deputies in Moscow, 1989

Gender relations in politics were at the heart of the patriarchal system that existed in the USSR and was reinforced by the totalitarian regime. Democratization has given rise to complex and contradictory processes affecting the system of gender relations. Gender relations of the patriarchal type are not stable in this transitional period; they are subject to change, and may even be somewhat influenced by new ideas and practices. The democracy that is coming into being during this transitional period offers women new opportunities in theoretical and practical work. We must admit that women have so far not made use of this historic opportunity to change their status. We must take into consideration that gender relations in politics are tied to gender relations in other fields. Unfortunately, no studies have been conducted on these links.

One serious failing of the new democracy of the post-totalitarian period is that it is taking shape without the active participation of women. Patriarchal gender relations are becoming stronger – or perhaps they are simply becoming more evident – in official bodies and institutions. The representation of women in parliament (of both the former Soviet Union and the Russian Federation) and in executive bodies has decreased. But this decrease in the number of women deputies merely reflects the real situation – the low status of women in society. The new women that have appeared in the upper echelons of power, in diplomatic circles and in non-governmental organizations represent women only formally.

Nevertheless, politics is no longer depersonalized and anonymous. Women are becoming visible in the political arena (among both left and right, both democrats and conservatives). As yet few of them have voiced concern about the existence of discrimination against women. But we can hope that, as experience elsewhere in the world has shown, they will turn to these issues as they go through the school of the women's movement and introduce a feminist consciousness into politics. My research, based on available data, indicates that gender relations in the new political parties and democratic protest movements (anti-nuclear, women's, ecological, etc.) and in civil rights organizations and independent trades unions have undergone changes. The activity and enthusiasm of women is evident in the new political groups, especially in the social movements, although women are not adequately represented in their leaderships.

Much research needs to be undertaken to study power relations as a whole and power relations between men and women. We need to analyse in particular masculinity and the type of patriarchal system in place, the role of the family and the effect of role models on the political choices of women. We need to look into the relationship between 'public' and 'private' life, the nature of political elites, the importance of informal communications networks in promoting women, so that we can do away with what we have so often seen in the past – the purely formal participation by women in politics.

What is needed to neutralize patriarchal gender relations in politics are measures aimed at improving the political system itself. We need to teach children about democracy in schools and to change our electoral system to ensure sufficient political freedom. Steps should be taken to encourage women to assume a more active role in politics. We need mechanisms to promote women at the national level, to increase the number of women at decision-making levels. We need special programmes to train women leaders at all levels. We need women who will undertake research into gender roles.

The model of our future democracy is hardly discussed in Russia among social scientists, much less among the population as a whole. But we all hope for a democratic society – non-violent, neutral from the gender point of view, both national and international, moral and humanistic. We are happy that we have bid farewell to Communism, but . . . is it not time that we launched an attack on patriarchalism?

Notes

1. Rutthy Taubb, in *Rise Up Singing*, ed. Peter Blood-Patterson (Bethlehem, PA 1988), p. 249.
2. A. Posadskaya, *Gender Aspects of the Way of Life of Inhabitants of Taganrog before Economic and Political Reforms* (Moscow 1991). For instance, roughly equal numbers of men and women were in favour of giving fathers paternity leave (the right to take leave to look after children, the right to shorter working hours, etc.); 44.1% of men wanted to distribute their working time equally between work and their families; 31.8% of women wanted to do the same.

3. E.C. Seminar, 'Institutional Conditions for Equality Between Men and Women in the Member States of the European Community', Bielefeld, 1989.

4. In the 1930s the Stalinist dictum: 'Life is better now, life is now more fun!' became a popular saying.

5. Bill Moyer, *The Movement Action Plan: A Strategic Framework Describing the Eight Stages of Successful Social Movements*, Spring, 1987, p. 1.

6. Moyer, p. 16.

7. Cited by Peter Reddaway in 'The End of the Empire' *New York Review of Books*, 7 November 1991, p. 56; Geoffrey Hosking, *The Awakening of the Soviet Union*, Cambridge 1990. This had developed at one time in tsarist Russia owing to the *mir* (the traditional peasant communities) and the *artel* (cooperatives): 'The workers' movement illustrates the traditionally strong and weak sides to popular movements in Russia.'

8. *Ogonyok*, no. 10, 1990, p. 9.

9. See Valentina Konstantinova, 'The Women's Movement in the USSR: A Myth or a Real Challenge?', in *Women in the Face of Change: The Soviet Union, Eastern Europe and China*, ed. A. Phizacklea, S. Rai and H. Pilkington (London 1992), pp. 200–17.

10. A. Levinson 'The Patience of Russians: How Much Is There?' *Izvestiya*, no. 296, 13 December 1991, p. 2.

11. More detailed descriptions of these trends can be found in Konstantinova, 'The Women's Movement in the USSR'.

12. More details about Lotos can be found in the book by Swedish journalist Kerstin Gustafsson, *Perestrojkans kvinnor*, Prisma 1991, pp. 41–5.

13. More details on this organization (NeZhDI) can be found in 'Women in Action, Country by Country: The Soviet Union', *Feminist Review*, no. 39, 1991, pp. 127–32.

14. 'Ariadna' aims to support research on women's and gender issues and the independent women's movement in Russia, to examine and adapt various schemes for women (both Russian and foreign) and introduce various programmes to help women (in business, political leadership, etc.).

15. *Translator's note*: A peaceful demonstration in the centre of Tbilisi was forcibly broken up by the use of chemical gases and by soldiers wielding shovels, resulting in several deaths.

16. *Translator's note*: Tanks and troops were sent in to occupy key government buildings in Vilnius, and fourteen people were killed as paratroopers seized the TV station.

17. *Translator's note*: The attempted hardline coup which resulted in the downfall of Gorbachev, the dissolution of the Communist Party and collapse of the Soviet Union.

18. Yuri Shcherbak, 'How I Became a People's Deputy', *Yunost*, no. 6, 1989, p. 74.

19. Ralf Dahrendorf, in his book *Reflections on the Revolution in Europe*, uses the term coined by historian T.G. Ash in characterizing the events of 1989 in Poland and Budapest as 'refolution', and those of Prague, Berlin and Bucharest as 'revolution'. Ralf Dahrendorf, *Reflections on the Revolution in Europe*, London 1990, p. 5.

20. American researcher N. Noonan thinks the female revolutionaries of 1917 can be divided into three groups: (1) those who gave no importance at all to the woman question (these included V. Zasulich and Stasova); (2) revolutionaries who thought it important, but as part of the overall revolutionary struggle; and (3) those who can be called feminists in the modern sense of the word (Alexandra Kollontai and Inessa Armand), who wanted to treat the woman question as a separate issue.

21. Many women deputies were Soviet Women's Committee apparatchiks. This committee has shown that it is incapable of reexamining its strategy and tactics from radical positions. See interview with the Committee's chairwoman, V. Fedulova: 'The Market, Yes, But Without Loss of Our Entitlements', *Izvestiya*, 6 August 1991, p. 2.

22. According to British academic Mary Buckley, the subject of women and politics were given less importance under Stalin and Brezhnev. The problem of women's political role was raised in the 1920s and 1950s more than in the 1930s or 1970s. Mary Buckley, *Women and Ideology in the Soviet Union* (Hemel Hempstead 1989), pp. 224–5.

23. For this research the author used a questionnaire compiled by the organizers of the First Independent Women's Forum.

24. *Translator's note*: The survey was conducted in March 1991, before the collapse of the old Soviet Union parliament and the Communist Party following the August 1991 putsch.

25. *Translator's note*: Anatoli Sobchak was a prominent radical parliamentary deputy, now Mayor of St Petersburg.

26. More details about women's participation in the new political parties and social movements in Russia (up to March 1991) can be found in Konstantinova, 'The Women's Movement in the USSR'.

27. Data obtained from the Committee for Women, the Family and Demographic Policy of the USSR Supreme Soviet, in March 1991.

28. Taken from a speech by V.F. Piotrovski, USSR Deputy Minister of Foreign Affairs, at parliamentary hearings to celebrate the tenth anniversary of the signing by the USSR of the Convention on the Elimination of All Forms of Discrimination against Women (26 October 1990).

29. Data from the Committee on Women, the Family and Demographic Policy of the USSR Supreme Soviet, March 1991.

5

What Does The Future Hold? (Some Thoughts on the Prospects for Women's Employment)

Yelena Mezentseva

What will become of us tomorrow? Shall we be able to survive? How can we adapt to the new market situation? How are we to find our place in the labour market and hold out in a situation where there is competition for jobs? Today everybody is worried about these questions. But they are particularly worrying for women, who are the first to experience directly the difficulties of this transitional period. In fact, today women are the first to be dismissed and, in comparison with men, it is much more difficult for women to find a new job. And we are constantly being reminded that our main workplace is the home: at the kitchen stove, in the shops and with our children.

Taking the country as a whole, a greater proportion of the new unemployed are women than men.The situation is particularly bad in Moscow and other major cities, where women constitute 80 per cent of the unemployed. Those who inevitably fall into the highest risk category are young mothers with small children and women professionals approaching retirement age – engineers, economists, accountants, lecturers and research staff.

Many people today, both men and women, are frightened by the prospect of losing their jobs. This is understandable, since the overwhelming majority of workers in our country have no source of income other than their wages, nor do they have much hope of receiving the paltry unemployment benefit. For example, in the first six months of 1991, out of one million people who registered at labour exchanges as looking for work, only a tenth were granted unemployed status, which entitled them to unemployment benefit.

Moreover, unemployed women suffer double discrimination: on the one hand, the amount of unemployment benefit they receive is almost always lower than that of men, since the benefit depends on wages earned in the last month of work. On the other hand, it is much harder for women to find a new job; many firms refuse to hire them simply because they are women, completely disregarding their professional experience and skills.

As we look into the future to try to forecast female employment prospects, we are forced to ask ourselves a number of questions:

- What factors will most affect the pattern of female employment?
- What demands will a market economy place on working women?
- Which of women's professional and business qualities will be of most value in a market economy?
- What must women do to learn how to compete for jobs on equal terms with men?
- What are the main trends in promoting women's employment in the near and distant future?

In the final analysis, we have to know what the strengths and weaknesses of the female labour-force are in order to learn to make use of our advantages and neutralize our shortcomings.

Our best-known economists and politicians are fond of repeating the assertion that 'the market has no sex', since in the conditions of competition it is the strongest person who wins, regardless of whether it is a man or a woman. In my opinion, this point of view bears little relation to reality. If we analyse what is happening in the labour market at present, for example, the specific gender dimension in employment can easily be seen, since men and women compete for jobs on quite different terms. The fact is that the position of women today as regards jobs is much less favourable than that of men. Moreover, not only is the gap between men and women not narrowing, but a number of developments indicate that it is actually widening, despite the propaganda about 'no discrimination against women', 'equal opportunities', 'equal pay for equal work' and so on. The high employment rate of women in jobs where working conditions are hazardous to employees' health, the fact that women's wage levels lag considerably behind those of men, and the existence of a great many obstacles in the path of women gaining further qualifications and career promotion, all testify to the unfavourable position of women in the workplace.

If we take all these circumstances into account, we can conclude that women are in a much worse position than men when it comes to competing on the labour market. An additional factor that exacerbates

the position of working women is the increasingly patriarchal consciousness and direct appeals to reduce female employment and 'return women
to the home'. Supporters of such views base their argument on their
desire to reduce working women's overall burden, to enable mothers to
give more time and attention to bringing up their children – which, they
say, would strengthen family relationships and contribute to reducing the
number of divorces.

In my opinion, the sharp upsurge in this ideology when a labour market
is only just taking shape can be interpreted as a preventive measure aimed
at artificially lowering the level of potential unemployment by first taking
women off the list of contenders for jobs. I believe that this method of
regulating employment not only fails to satisfy the majority of working
women, but also will have negative consequences for the future.

When we consider employment prospects for women, we must first
determine the most important factors that will have the greatest influence
on the position of women in the labour market. Undoubtedly the main
trends will be determined by the nature of the social and economic
transformation implemented to extricate the economy from crisis and to
institute new market relations, as well as how rapidly these changes are
effected. In the process of transition to a market economy various
scenarios of development can be envisaged, differing both in objectives
and in the means used to achieve them. Nevertheless, today we can
already identify certain stages in the transition process that will most
likely have to be traversed whatever our future development.

As far as the economy is concerned, the first stage involves completing
the process of initial accumulation of capital, which should then be
followed by a gradual transition from primarily speculative activity
(which is what we are seeing at present) to the manufacture of actual
goods and the provision of services that consumers need. The second
stage may be characterized as a period of active expansion of
manufacturing, accompanied by the radical transformation of its
economic and technological base. The most important feature of this
period is that structural changes in the economy will begin 'from below',
that is, under the influence of market production regulators. Those
sectors guaranteeing the fastest turnover of capital will develop most
quickly. At the same time the economy will be transformed structurally
'from above' – either by capital investments or by encouraging private
investment in priority areas. Structural policy will probably be oriented
towards modernizing those factories with more complex technologies
requiring large initial investments. The third and final stage is the period
after the process of structural change has in the main been completed. We
can expect that by this time we shall see further normal development of a
market-type economy equipped with a new technological base and within

the framework of a new system of production in all sectors of the economy.

I am dwelling in such detail on these economic questions because it is important for us to have at least a general understanding of how our economic system will develop. We need to estimate which sectors will develop more rapidly and which will decline. Changes in the demand for labour and in the demands of the workplace on its personnel will depend on this. We also need to know what will happen in those sectors that at present mainly employ women. If we are guided by the forecast for the economy as a whole, we can predict changes in the extent and structure of women's employment and give an approximate estimate of the level of potential unemployment. With these considerations in mind, we shall be able to analyse the most important employment trends for women in the context of the economic problems that are emerging as we move towards a market system.

So, what can working women expect from the first stage of the market economy? During this period, as a result of a drop in production and the closure of a whole range of technically obsolete and uncompetitive sectors, the trend towards shifting women from paid labour to unpaid domestic labour is likely to intensify. The theory about women's 'natural mission' and appeals to their role as mothers and homemakers serve as ideological grounds for this displacement of women. At the level of state policy, this ideology translates into a system of 'social protection' measures for women, 'assistance to mothers' and the aspiration to 'liberate' women from their double burden at work and in the home. These measures complicate the situation even further, since they make the female labour-force an extremely unattractive proposition for employers. This stage has already begun, as the unemployment statistics graphically demonstrate: the majority of unemployed persons registering at Moscow labour exchanges are women. Moreover, their chances of finding work are very small, since many firms openly refuse to hire them despite recommendations from the labour exchange. Researchers have observed these same tendencies in most former socialist countries. In Poland, for instance, cuts in certain sectors of heavy industry and closure of the coal mines resulted in mass unemployment for women, but few new jobs were created for them. The situation was worsened by the deceleration of production at textile factories and in light industry. In some provinces, there were 37.3 unemployed women for every available job, compared with 9.5 unemployed men and in six provinces there were over 100 women applicants for every newly created job: in places the number of women applying for each new vacancy reached incredible figures. Young women just out of school, who often have young children, have the worst chances of finding work. A similar picture is also seen in the former GDR, the former Czechoslovakia and, to a lesser extent, in Hungary (where the process of economic reform started earlier).[1]

Data about levels of skills and education of unemployed women show that most have either completed secondary school or have entered higher education. Secondary school graduates are not likely to have specific vocational training or trade skills. Graduates from higher education establishments usually have good educational qualifications. A similar tendency can be observed in practically all the former socialist countries: women shop-floor workers (both skilled and unskilled) who become unemployed find it much easier to get another job than women with a higher level of education.

As in our country, most politicians and public figures in the countries of Central and Eastern Europe clearly underestimate the social perils of excluding women from employment. The notion has become widespread that women who face unemployment experience far fewer problems than men, since they can always stay at home and devote themselves to their family responsibilities. This is why society passively accepts the fact that unemployment among women is growing much faster than among men in all the former socialist countries of Europe.

It is revealing that not all women in the countries of Central and Eastern Europe are opposed to the prospect of staying at home with their children for a period of time. However, we must bear in mind that 'socialist' women are only now learning the reality of unemployment; they have been schooled in a regime of social protection that allows people not to be too concerned about earning a living. These women have not previously experienced the economic and psychological pressures of unemployment and therefore do not fully understand that 'staying at home with the children for a couple of years' might mean that they never manage to find work again throughout the rest of their lives. By the same token, women unwittingly find themselves in the position of hostages of their own husbands: many are forced to remain in unhappy marriages because they cannot support themselves.

Obviously, during this stage of development fundamental changes are likely to occur in the demand and type of work performed by women. One can easily predict a further reduction in demand for women's vocational skills on the part of employers; their education and job experience is likely to be devalued. We shall hear demands that the nation should look after the health of its women by enabling them to stay at home and calls for women to care about those 'female qualities' dearest to the patriarchal consciousness: attractive appearance, ability to run the home, submissiveness, efficiency, etc. This stage will witness the painful process whereby one 'social norm' is replaced by another. For example, instead of women realizing their potential in the family, at work and in public life being the social norm, we shall see women setting themselves the goal of realizing their potential not in society or as individuals but only as wives and mothers. In this sense we can say that society's demands on women will appeal to their qualities as a *social sex*, not to their qualities as individual personalities.

A development strategy of this kind, although it may offer certain superficial, short-term advantages, will have serious social costs. The ideology of social protectionism towards women, if there are no resources to support these measures financially, may result in the majority of women becoming disillusioned with their new situation, which could lead to serious gender conflicts. The skills and experience of the female labour-force will remain untapped by society, the labour market will split along gender lines and the low-prestige jobs and jobs that do not appeal to men will remain female: replacing the norm of the 'working woman' with the patriarchal social norm of the 'housewife' will greatly reduce the opportunities women have of fulfilling themselves as people. All the various types of self-realization will be reduced to one alone: fulfilment as a social sex. Not only will this signify a personal tragedy for many women, it will also result in a further lowering of cultural and moral standards throughout society.

During the second stage of transition, new growth factors will come into play while the basic employment trends of the previous stage remain in place. The flow of capital out of speculative and into productive circulation will most likely take place in those sectors which can guarantee the fastest turnover of capital. In these conditions, we can expect accelerated growth in those sectors which employ mainly women at present: the service sector, food and light industries. It will be these branches of the economy that will start to show increased demand for various categories of labour, and women will begin to see a real opportunity to improve their position in the labour market. At this stage the trend towards lower female employment might be reversed, showing a gradual increase.

We can predict a comparatively new trend in women's employment: employers might attract women into the sort of jobs where female labour is more profitable because they can pay lower wages. This will mainly be various kinds of monotonous assembly-line work in which female productivity is likely to be as high as male. Faced with the lack of other job possibilities, this form of employment might become quite an attractive proposition for women. It will also be a good bargain for the employer, enabling him to increase his profit margins by paying lower wages for female labour.

In this situation, we can expect changes in the way the female labour problem is viewed ideologically. The rigidly patriarchal model may be replaced by a 'softer' version of the same rhetoric, similar to the ideological line of stagnation times: the social norm of 'housewife' will be replaced by that of 'the woman who not only looks after her family and raises her children but also sees to her family's material welfare'. The pattern of society's requirements for the qualitative features of female labour will be shaped according to this model. In particular, when it comes to women's job skills, the accent will be on the abilities acquired in the process of working at home. In this sense, public opinion about women going to work will be based on the theory that women's work outside the home is a continuation of their domestic duties and as such does not require new skills or vocational training. During the stage we are describing we expect to see women looking for new means of creating jobs for themselves and to see a big expansion in independent employment. This will take the form of a wide range of enterprises, from one-woman businesses to the formation of all-women firms: all-women by choice, not by compulsion (as in the textile and garment-making industries, for instance).

A widespread increase in various kinds of women's self-employment may become a relatively gentle and painless way of incorporating one section of working women into the market economy. But it is likely that the demands of competition will force women who have chosen this path to work harder without commensurate remuneration.

The various forms of self-employment should become a safety net which will enable women to survive if they lose their jobs. Quite apart from this, self-employment for many women may become an effective means of personal development, a way of realizing those qualities and skills that women acquire in the course of running the home: personal responsibility, good management, punctiliousness, ability to plan their work and time, and so on. The expansion of self-employment will demand more of women in terms of job commitment, better qualifications and a broader education. The traditional pattern of women's working lives will change as self-employment becomes more common. Until now women have had relatively uninterrupted working lives in the trades or professions, usually interrupted only when they have children. In the future, however, women's working lives may consist of several parts: working until the birth of the first child, then a gap while looking after children, then a job in the former position or a new job or trade, then perhaps redundancy, a period of self-employment, then another new job and so on. In this sense, self-employment can serve as an effective means of enabling women to survive if they are forced out of a job. For many in developed countries self-employment is gradually becoming a 'job for life' chosen voluntarily and in preference to working for an employer.

During the third stage of market transformation we can expect a further increase and improvement in the pattern of female employment described above. The situation will be similar to that in developed capitalist countries, in which it is becoming the norm for most women to work during their entire working lives. Fewer women are choosing the role of housewife: in Denmark, Finland and Sweden, for example, only 10 per cent of women between the ages of 25 and 54 are housewives; in Iceland and Norway, the figure is slightly higher at 15 per cent, but decreasing steadily. Despite the general impression formed in Russia, the role of housewife was never very popular in Western countries: in Finland, for example, in the period from 1940 to the beginning of the 1960s only 25 per cent of women aged 15 and older were housewives. About one-third of Swedish women were housewives during the same period.

Since working outside the home is becoming part of the lifestyle of the majority of Western women, the working lives of women are becoming more and more like men's. Until the mid seventies (mid sixties in Finland) women's employment outside the home could be represented by a zig-zag line: women worked outside the home before marriage, when their children were born they became housewives, and they returned to work in middle age once the children no longer needed looking after. The situation is different now: with state support for families with small children and widespread provision of childcare, women are able to go back to work much sooner, and the vast majority of them do so. In Sweden, for example, 86 per cent of women with children under 7 and 93 per cent with children aged between 11 and 16 worked outside the home in 1986; in Finland the figures were 70 per cent and 85 per cent respectively.

These statistics indicate that the actual pattern of women's employment in many developed countries differs significantly from the model that our mass media are propagating at present. This is true both for the levels of women's employment (including among women with small children) and the numbers of women opting for a shorter working day. In Russia the impression has been created that the vast majority of women in Western countries work for only two or three hours a day, and that they work not so much for financial reasons, but to have contact with people outside the home and earn some 'pin-money' of their own. The real picture, however, is quite different. In 1986, for example, 78 per cent of American women aged between 25 and 54 worked full-time – that is, not less than thirty-five hours per week. Of those working less than thirty-five hours, 5 per cent would have preferred to work full-time. Only 17 per cent of American women worked a shorter working week by choice. A similar situation was observed in Finland, where in 1986 only 16 per cent of employed women worked less than thirty-five hours a week.

An analysis of the real problems of female employment in the developed countries of the West allows us to draw some conclusions that relate directly to our forecast for women's employment at the final stage of market transformation:

- The overwhelming majority of women in countries with a highly developed market economy work outside the home, and over half of them work full-time.
- The 1970s and 1980s saw a big increase in the number of women returning to work soon after childbirth (in Finland the majority of women go back to work a year after the birth of a child; in the USA over 50 per cent of women resume work even before the infant is one year old).
- Practically all developed countries show a gradual decrease in the number of women choosing to be housewives exclusively.
- Women are actively mastering new kinds of work that until recently were almost exclusively the domain of men.
- In most developed countries sex discrimination in employment is illegal, and in many countries special government agencies have been set up to supervise the enforcement of such legislation.
- In a number of countries equal pay for men and women doing work of equal value is legally required, as a result of which the gap between wages for men and women for similar work has narrowed.

Obviously these Western employment trends for women cannot be automatically transplanted to Russian soil. This would be just as unnatural and pointless as the campaign conducted at present to revive patriarchal values. It is important to note that not one of the above-mentioned countries has been able to do without women's labour or the part played by women in public and political life and in decision-making processes. This is very important since it is precisely the countries of northern Europe, Sweden in particular, which enjoy the most popularity as models for us to emulate. It is difficult to imagine how calls to build the 'Swedish model of capitalism' fit in with persistent calls for women 'to go back to the home', 'to devote themselves to the home' and so on.

When making forecasts today about our social and economic life once we have a real market economy in this country, we should make it clear what type of capitalism we intend to build. Obviously the West European model is only one of the possible variants of development. But at the same time there are no serious grounds for believing that economic efficiency or social and political stability can be achieved in our country by creating a society of the Japanese type, with marked gender opposition according to the principle: 'the world of men is society, the world of women is the family'. Most likely, our experience of transition to the market will lead us to take a middle option, combining features from different models. There is no point in saying now what quantitative indices will characterize the pattern of employment in this period, but we can try to outline its most important features and future trends.

After the stage of denationalization and privatization has been completed, it is likely that the proportion of working women will stop falling and this index will stabilize somewhat, probably at the level of 60–70 per cent; employment levels will probably fluctuate considerably in future due to structural economic reforms.

There is likely to be far greater regional variation in statistics for women's employment. This goes both for the former USSR and for the Russian Federation whose regions differ sharply from one another in socioeconomic, national and cultural respects.

There will be fundamental changes in the pattern of women's employment as far as education and qualifications are concerned, as well as the sectors in which women work. There will most probably be a shift in employment patterns towards typically 'female' jobs, mainly owing to growth of the service sector. This process should be accompanied by a well-planned system of vocational retraining for women coming from other sectors. At the same time, we can expect a gradual increase in the number of women employed in various kinds of assembly-line work, and an increase in the number of women engaged in manual work in industry. Changes in the educational level of working women will be expressed in the parallel development of two trends: on the one hand, a certain fall in the proportion of women obtaining higher education; and on the other hand, an increase in the proportion of women receiving secondary vocational education and training in those trades where there is a demand for female labour.

There will be an increase in the number of women working part-time. Different estimates put the figure at between 20 per cent and 40 per cent of the overall number of working women. There will also be an increase in the number of women working on temporary contracts and as self-employed individuals.

To sum up, we can say that the changes we forecast in the volume and pattern of female employment will not signify an improvement in the social and economic position of women. According to this scenario, women will have to content themselves with jobs offering few career prospects or chances for job promotion. As a result of these changes, women's part in decision-making and management will be reduced to a minimum: women will work outside the home for economic reasons only.

Note

1. The statistics are for October 1990.

6

Women in the Labour Market:
Yesterday, Today and Tomorrow

Zoya Khotkina

Today we are witnessing profound social and economic upheavals in our country: the collapse of the Union; economic crisis and the breakdown in economic and political links; the transition towards a market economy entailing new forms of ownership; unprecedented inflation and cuts in social programmes. Most people see their standards of living fall as prices rise astronomically for food and consumer goods in short supply. We are witnessing unemployment and the marginalization of a large part of the population unprotected by society, as well as an increase in social tension and national conflicts.

All these political, social and economic changes affect the system of gender relations, but they affect men and women very differently. Experience throughout the world has shown that in periods of structural reforms, women are always more negatively affected than men, because of men's position in power structures and the division of labour. But it would not be correct to see women merely as passive, long-suffering victims of this transition period. Women are playing an important role in the transition, by giving a certain flexibility to the reform processes at this most critical time. By adapting their role in society to the new economic conditions, women are making what Unicef has called 'an invisible adjustment'.

We must also remember that women are not a single group who all have the same problems. Even the job discrimination that all women experience varies according to social group: women in the state sector experience job segregation; unemployed women face employers' reluctance to hire qualified professional women; women entrepreneurs find it difficult to obtain market information, finance and credit, and so on. Apart from these problems, there are many other social and professional groups of women whose problems are no less serious. Their job situations are different and they experience varying degrees of success in adapting to the transition to a market economy.

In this article I have attempted to use two main approaches: historical and structural. The historical approach traces the ways in which women's employment developed in the past and outlines the current situation and prospects for changing the position of women in the labour market. The structural approach examines the employment problems of several groups of women who occupy different positions in the labour market: women who are still employed at state enterprises; unemployed women who have lost their jobs as a result of the present economic crisis or structural changes; and finally, women entrepreneurs who have become self-employed or who have set up small enterprises and have adapted very well to market economy conditions. The structural approach to investigating the position of women in the labour market is now assuming particular importance, since plurality of forms of ownership is replacing the former situation of state ownership. Instead of labour uniformity we are now seeing labour differentiation.

The Historical Context: Formation of the Female Labour Market

In the early 1990s, women in Russia are being increasingly pushed out of remunerated employment (especially highly skilled and intellectual work) into unpaid domestic labour and/or occasional unskilled employment. In order to assess accurately women's position in the labour market today, we need to take at least a brief look at how women's employment began and the changes it has undergone at different stages of the country's social and economic development.

The history of women's employment in any country has seen both periods of labour mobilization, in which women have played a crucial role in industry, and periods of 'demobilization', in which women have been excluded from traditionally male skilled jobs and limited to low-paid traditionally female jobs.

The manipulation of the role of women in our country at different historical periods bears a striking resemblance to similar Western mobilization campaigns. Of course there is a huge difference between the period of Stalinism, when women were mobilized to work, and the present stage in our country, when we are building a 'democratic' society and women's labour is tending to be 'demobilized'. There are examples of the mobilization of female labour in democratic capitalist countries – for example, Britain and the USA – and these parallels are significant.

Comparing the experiences of women in different countries might improve our understanding of women's labour problems and patterns of women's inequality.

History is full of examples in this country and elsewhere of how women have responded to the calls of society whenever the need arose. At times of economic boom and during wartime, when there was a labour shortage, women have played an active part in their countries' economic development. But at times of crisis and unemployment, women have been the first to be ousted from the workplace and into unpaid domestic labour. The role and function of women, as well as their position and their image, have undergone changes at different stages of economic, social and political development in accordance with society's demands.

We all know that the USSR was the first country in the world in which equal rights between the sexes was enshrined in the constitution, in all walks of life: in politics, labour and in domestic life. But though it did away with women's inequality before the law, socialism did not create real equality. It drew women into active public and political life but it did not liberate them from domestic burdens – in fact it actually perpetuated their enslavement in the home. This continues as a result of widespread stereotypes which even now ensure an unequal attitude towards men and women as regards their contribution to the economy. Women's domestic bondage is also due to the poor infrastructure of our social services, which have been severely underfunded for years.

Thus from the early years of the Soviet regime, two ideologies emerged with regard to the status of women in society. An ideology of equality existed in laws and statutes, while a patriarchal ideology operated in real life. The labour market took shape within the framework of these two ideologies. At certain periods women were drawn into employment, at others they were ousted. As a result of male losses sustained during the First World War and the Civil War, by the late 1920s the country had a population imbalance – there were five million more women than men. At that time the state was putting all its efforts into industrialization. Yet the republics of the USSR were primarily agrarian and many areas were affected by famine, forcing huge numbers of peasant women to flood into the towns in search of work and food.

By the mid 1930s the goal of bringing as many women as possible into the state sector had been achieved: the number of women working in industry had increased fourfold as compared with pre-war times – at a rate twice as fast as the overall increase in numbers of workers. In the seven years of the first five-year plan (1929–36) the number of women workers and office staff in all branches of the national economy increased by over five million, of whom only 1.4 million were urban women.[1]

Female labour was introduced in large numbers into what were considered 'male' sectors. In the construction industry, the proportion of women practically tripled during that time (from 7 per cent in 1929 to 19 per cent in 1936); in transportation, it doubled (from 8 per cent to 17.5 per cent); there was a substantial rise in the number of women office-workers (from 19 per cent to 30 per cent); and in retail trade the percentage also rose (from 15.5 per cent to 31.8 per cent). Meanwhile, the proportion of women employed in day-labour or seasonal work and in domestic service fell (from 16.5 per cent to 2.4 per cent). Thus, profound changes were brought about in the structure of women's employment in each industrial sector.

In pre-revolutionary Russia, two-thirds of all women workers were employed in the textile industry, whereas by 1936, only 30.9 per cent of the total of women employed were female textile workers. In 23 of the 26 largest sectors of industry, women made up more than 20 per cent of the workforce. The policy of actively involving women in production enabled them to enter into sectors that paid higher wages. Society was so interested in women's labour-power in those years that it allowed women to receive wages close to men's pay levels and even to exceed those levels in certain jobs. In October 1934, for instance, wages of unskilled female turners, capstan lathe operators, welders and grinders were 1–10 per cent higher than the male wage. At this time women played an increasingly important role within the intelligentsia, as teachers, doctors and scientists. In 1935, about 22 per cent of higher education lecturers were women, and 11 per cent of academics with higher degrees were women. The number of women doctors grew particularly rapidly. In 1936, there were 42,000 women doctors in the USSR, compared with less than 2,000 in pre-revolutionary Russia; more than a twenty-fold increase.

But as large numbers of women entered education and healthcare, the work of these vital sectors became devalued. Priority was given to heavy industry, and sectors of the social infrastructure were declared secondary and of lesser importance, which was reflected in the wage levels of workers in these sectors. This disproportion in different sectors' pay levels is maintained to the present day.

The large-scale entry of women into both higher and secondary vocational education – in 1936 women comprised 39.5 per cent and 43 per cent of students respectively – contributed to a rapid increase of professional women. However, according to data for 1936, the rate of illiteracy among working women under 25 was twice as high as among young working men. Among older female workers illiteracy was practically universal, since, as has already been said, the majority of women brought into socialized labour were formerly peasants. The labour of illiterate women was mainly used in heavy, unskilled work. This particular use of female labour became 'traditional' for our economy.

Thus a female labour market was rapidly formed during the early years of the USSR. But the female labour-force was low-grade, which resulted in the segregation of women into low-status unskilled jobs. Elimination of illiteracy and the higher educational standards women attained in subsequent years still could not break down this structural discrimination against women in the workplace. Even today, when the educational level of working women is higher than that of men, their labour continues to be used mainly in less skilled work at lower pay levels.

If the state's policy towards working women was not discriminatory, such a discrepancy between women's educational level and their status in the labour market would be impossible. We have attempted to give a brief description of the history of the female labour market and to note both the positive and negative aspects of the process. We saw how women actively supported state policy aimed at bringing them into paid work at a time when there was an urgent need for their labour, how they built an industrial society with their own hands (in the literal sense of the word, since then as now, their labour has been primarily manual and unmechanized). But the situation in the labour market started to change in the early 1930s. The new wave of famine and enforced collectivization in the countryside drove considerable numbers of peasants, men and women, from their homes. Industry, which was then developing, though still inefficiently, was not in a position to cope with large numbers of unskilled workers unsuited to industrial labour. There was less need for female labour-power.

As a result, state policy on the employment of women gradually began to change. The policy of mobilization of women to work changed to one of the 'demobilization' of women from the workplace. The first step towards implementing this policy was the decision to disband the women's sections (*zhensektory*) and women's councils (*zhensoviety*), which conducted ideological work among women during the period when women were being encouraged to enter the workforce. In 1934 the *zhensoviety* were closed down by order of the Party. A new attempt to revive the *zhensoviety* was only made fifty years later – in 1986, at the beginning of the perestroika period, when the Communist Party, which had already begun to lose its grip on power, tried to attract women to its side.

The 1936 law banning abortions must be seen as one of the state measures aimed at curtailing female employment in the mid thirties, and a veiled attempt later to oust women from remunerated work. This law has an illustrious history. 1936 was the year mass repression started against the urban population, in particular the intelligentsia. A number of draconian laws were passed to break the will of the people during this period, including what is known as the 'Stalin Constitution'. All these laws were introduced amid a barrage of propaganda intended to make them seem as if they expressed the will of the people. But only the bill on abortion was submitted to nationwide discussion, two months before it became law. How should we interpret such a show of democracy in the midst of raging totalitarianism? Why was it precisely this law affecting women that was granted such a privilege? The reason is probably that women in the 1930s represented a force in society that would have been dangerous to ignore. The authorities were afraid that women might openly protest against the abortion law that limited not only their reproductive rights but also their human rights in the wider sense of the term.

Therefore the mass media launched a propaganda campaign in support of the new anti-abortion policy. The campaign started with an article by Semashko, the Minister of Health (People's Commissar for Health, as it was then called) in *Pravda* entitled 'What a Magnificent Law!' After that all the newspapers were filled with letters from women expressing their joy at the new abortion law. The mass media supported the position that 'abortions cripple the lives and health of thousands and tens of thousands of women' and started singing the virtues of big families. It was at this time that women who had given birth to several children began to be awarded the order of 'Heroine Mother' and the medal 'Maternal Glory'. The increase in nursery schools was inadequate to meet the demand. Many mothers with four, five or more young children were forced to stop working and return to unpaid housework. It was at this time that Stalin declared the 'woman question' completely and definitively resolved in our country. The publication of statistics on the position of women ceased until 1957. Information on women's issues was replaced by propaganda about the advantages of socialism in settling the 'woman question'.

All these measures aimed at reducing female employment and forcing women out of the labour market produced the desired result. Thus, statistics from the last pre-war year, 1940, show that female employment in industry actually fell from 38.8 per cent to 37 per cent. During the war years, the situation in the labour market changed once again. Once more women had to take the places of the men who had left for the front. Once again the ideology of motherhood was replaced by that of civic duty, which called women to the factories and mines.

This rotation of ideologies continues to the present day: first patriarchal calls to women to go back to the home, then calls for 'selfless labour for the sake of the Motherland'. By manipulating this reserve army, the female labour-force, the state can regulate strains in the labour market by conducting a discriminatory policy towards women.

During our country's history, as everyone knows, the 'Mother country' has called women to the tractor and the communist building projects, all of which gave rise to the myth about strong Russian women. The other periods when the home and motherhood took pride of place are perhaps less well known. Therefore, nobody should be deluded when in the current economic crisis of slump and unemployment, we again hear calls for women to go back to the home, in accordance with their 'natural mission'. We must understand that as always when our society finds itself in an impasse, it tries to solve the crisis at women's expense, taking advantage of their ability to adapt to new situations. But who takes their traumas and losses into account? Thus, the state ensures that both old and new social and economic structures operate flexibly during the transition to a market economy.

But the educated women of the 1990s are not at all like their illiterate sisters at the turn of the century. Today's situation also differs from earlier periods in that we know that the roles today's women play in society are irreversible: it is impossible to turn back the tide of history. Women have become active members of society; they form part of work collectives; they enjoy public recognition and economic independence – all this has become a means of self-expression and self-fulfilment for the majority of women. Therefore attempts to return women to the home and remove them from the economic plane are unrealistic.

We should also recognize that if women have responded to society's need, society should in turn respond to the needs of women. Women prove at work and at home that their place is not restricted to the family; that the family is not their sole responsibility. Men should play a more active role in family matters and rearing children. If these facts were recognized in a new conception of the position of women in society, this would significantly help to correct mistaken policies on women.

Problems of Female Job Segregation

We have already shown that in the 1920s and 1930s the female labour market formed rapidly under pressure from a number of specific social, economic and political measures. Moreover, women's employment did not form an independent structure but merely supplemented the already existing jobs structure, which was oriented towards men. Although women had been allowed to fill the vacuum caused by wartime losses, they ended up being given only those jobs which men avoided – the low-prestige, low-status and low-paid, mostly unskilled, manual jobs. The structure of female employment retains this inherent distortion to the present day.

No other developed country in the world has as many women employed in physical labour as this country. According to the 1989 census, 38.3 million women, or 56.3 per cent of the overall number of working women, were employed in physical labour. In comparison, the proportion of women employed in similar work in 1987–88 was 13.1 per cent in Germany; 14.8 per cent in Spain; 11.3 per cent in the U.S.; and 26.8 per cent in Japan.[2]

A high proportion of women are working on obsolete machinery and equipment and in factories with poor social provision and services. The majority of working women are concentrated in industry, construction, transport and communications, agriculture and forestry – a total of 34.1 million women, of whom over half do physical jobs. The labour of millions of women entails lifting and moving heavy objects without any kind of mechanization. There are more women than men among manual workers. The legally prescribed norm (!) for manual lifting and moving of heavy weights by women is 7 tonnes per working day. But tens of thousands of women have to move 20–25 tonnes per shift – all by hand! Over two hundred thousand women are engaged in heavy physical work. Over 4 million women work in conditions that do not meet health and safety regulations – i.e., conditions injurious to health. Some 44.5 per cent of women in industry are employed in workshops with heavy, injurious or very injurious working conditions. In construction, the proportion is 17 per cent. But it is women in agriculture who have the worst working conditions. It is impossible to think of loving such work, nor can there be any question of 'the individual's development and self-fulfilment in labour'! There are very great differences in job specialization between men and women doing physical work. Driver, tractor-driver, and lathe-operator are the main mechanized jobs for men. Women's mechanized jobs include garment-maker and operator of looms, spinning machines and other machines.

The differences between 'female' and 'male' trades are even greater among those engaged in manual labour. Men employed in manual work on the whole do highly skilled and highly paid work such as repair and adjustment of machines and equipment, whereas the majority of women's manual work has long since been replaced by mechanization in the rest of the civilized world. Women clean workshop floors, plant and weed vegetables or milk cows by hand, haul goods from place to place at warehouses and in shops (what is more, goods which are not wrapped, but packed in barrels, boxes and sacks). As we can see from this list, these 'female' jobs do not in the main require qualifications: they are heavy, dirty, monotonous and low-status jobs. And they are paid at the lowest rates.

'Occupational censuses' are held periodically in industry and other sectors. From these censuses, we picked five of the most common 'female' jobs, in which women comprise 75 per cent of the workforce. In the censuses of five and ten years ago, the 'trade' of cleaner took pride of place. There are 1,860,900 women cleaners and auxiliary workers employed in the economy, i.e. 8.2 per cent of the total number of all women workers employed. 'Technical progress' has done nothing to eradicate or reduce numbers in this most female of jobs. Even the number of machine operatives falls short of the number of cleaners in this country. In 1989 there were 1,574,200 female machine operatives – this is the second biggest category of women workers. Then come shop assistants, at 1,370,000; quality controllers, at 961,300; and garment-makers, at 821,600.

As we can see, out of the five most common female jobs, only two – machine operatives and garment-makers – involve mechanized and automated labour, while cleaners, shop assistants and quality-controllers in the main carry out their work manually (the proportion of manual labour in these jobs being 96 per cent, 93 per cent and 87 per cent respectively). Of the five most common female jobs, only one – that of operative – can be considered at all advanced; all the others involve heavy, boring and monotonous work.

If we analyse the prospects within the employment structure for women, we can conclude that women are at present mainly employed in jobs which are likely to change (controllers, cleaners, office-workers and so on) or become obsolete as a result of automation and the introduction of new technologies (storekeepers, washerwomen, cleaners, cooks, etc.). The women's employment problems discussed here reveal marked job segregation, both horizontal (in terms of sector and trade), and vertical (in terms of qualifications, status and pay levels). When consideration is given to the fact that the educational level of women employed in the economy is higher than that of men, it becomes clear that this gender structure in employment is not only irrational, but discriminatory. It proves the inefficient use of women's educational and intellectual potential at work. In addition, many types of work are injurious to women's health.

There are both objective and subjective reasons why this discriminatory female employment structure remains. Segregated jobs give women little opportunity for professional advancement, which leads to a fall-off in motivation. This, in turn, reinforces stereotypes that the female labour-force is inferior. A 'vicious circle' is created; women cannot break out of it by themselves, and there have been no government programmes in this country aimed at creating equal conditions. Society is simply not interested in creating equal opportunities for men and women at work. Moreover, keeping women in low-status jobs makes it easier to manipulate the female labour-force. This is very clear now that mass unemployment, which affects more women than men, has started.

'Objective' reasons are given for sacking women first of all, in that they are employed in less skilled jobs than men.

The discrepancy between women's level of general and vocational education and the fact that women's job skills lag behind men's has always been one of the greatest problems as far as women's employment is concerned. But this has become all the more important today in the transition to a market economy, when there is competition for jobs on the labour market. We therefore need to take a closer look at this problem to try to understand whether the reasons for this relate to the specific nature of the female labour-force or whether they go deeper and have to do with society's attitude towards women.

Women's job skills have lagged behind men's for a long time and there is a tendency for the gap to widen. The number of unskilled women workers is twice as high as that of unskilled men. The main reason for the level of women's skills being lower than men's is usually given as women's 'double burden' of work and domestic duties, which limits the amount of time they can spend on improving skills. Not only in everyday life, but even in academic studies one frequently comes across opinions like: 'women's possibilities in choosing a career are restricted by their family and domestic circumstances'.

Without denying the negative effect of women's double occupation on their level of qualifications, I should like to emphasize that this is not as simple as it is usually made out to be, and relates not to women's inherent weaknesses but to the specific deficiencies in our social structure. First, the 'double burden' could be lessened if the country had an adequate domestic infrastructure (services, household appliances, pre-packed foodstuffs, convenience foods, etc.) and if food and other goods were easily available. This would cut the time spent on laborious and essentially routine domestic work and on queuing, which consumes so much of women's free time in Russia. In addition, simply to assign all domestic concerns to women alone is nothing more than the typical patriarchal understanding of their role in society and in the family. Second, although there are certainly a number of careers and jobs that women are not so eager to choose because they do not easily fit in with their family responsibilities, to a far greater extent it is society that limits their range of job choices. This happens primarily through the system of job training, that is, upon women entering the workforce.

According to the official *Handbook of Wage Rates and Qualifications*, only about six hundred, or 20 per cent, of the more than three thousand jobs listed are prohibited for women. Yet the number of jobs for which women are trained within the job training system is five times less than the number of jobs for which men are trained. There is no justification for this sharp delimiting of job and career choice. For the 'double burden' is more likely to affect the possibilities for married women who are already working to improve their skills than to affect the range of initial job training options that young women can choose.

How do women regard the issue of improving skills? Data obtained from research into the conditions of women both at home and at work, conducted by the USSR State Statistics Committee in 1989, may help to answer this question. The survey of 85,000 working women revealed that over half of them (54 per cent) would like to improve their job skills. Moreover, women consider that both workers and managers of enterprises should be mutually interested in improving workers' qualifications. But the research showed that there was little management interest in women improving their skills. Most managers (78 per cent) were not interested in the career development of their women workers. This attitude results in a situation where the majority of women who go on training courses actually fail to get promotion. Thus, 90.7 per cent of women after training continued to work in the same job at the same skills grade, and 81.5 per cent of women did not even get a wage rise after their training courses. The State Statistics Committee research confirmed the results I obtained in an earlier investigation. But one very important circumstance must be noted here. In my 1985 survey I interviewed both women and men. It revealed that after completing training courses, men's careers invariably improve – their jobs, grades and wages – whereas for the majority of women they do not.

We can see, therefore, that when entering the workforce and during employment, both within society as a whole and in individual enterprises, discriminatory barriers exist that block the promotion of women and bar them from improving their job status. The following chain of interrelated events may thus be observed: when women enter the workforce, the range of jobs open to them is restricted, then they meet barriers to improving their skills and job status, and then, when the question of job cuts arises, they are the first to be dismissed on the grounds that their skills level is lower than that of men. Yet there can be no doubt that positive changes in the position of women in employment will not be achieved without an improvement in their job training and qualifications. The solution to most other problems relating to female labour depends largely on the successful resolution of this question. These problems include: how to improve their competitiveness in the labour market (since highly skilled workers are practically always in demand); raising wage levels (since skilled work is more highly paid); improving working conditions (because skilled work usually entails more pleasant working conditions); raising the level of labour mechanization (since low skills are a feature only of those employed in manual labour); and finally and most importantly, making work more creative and satisfying, thus enabling women to develop their personalities.

Trends in the employment of women workers do not arouse much optimism. However, the situation is no better when it comes to the employment of professional women. Women are tolerated just as unwillingly in business and economic decision-making as in top political circles. This is shown by data on the proportion and number of top women managers of enterprises and organizations. On 1 January 1991 the proportion of women managers in the former USSR stood at 5.6 per cent. The percentage of women managers broken down into sectors was as follows: industry, 9.5 per cent; communications, 7.9 per cent; agriculture, 6.3 per cent; construction, 0.9 per cent; and transport, 0.6 per cent. There are fewer women managers in the Transcaucasian republics and Central Asia: in Armenia, 0.9 per cent; Azerbaijan, 1.4 per cent; Georgia, 1.7 per cent; Uzbekistan, 2.4 per cent; Turkmenia, 2.5 per cent. Moreover, a negative trend can be observed whereby the proportion of women managers has actually decreased in eight out of the fifteen former Union republics. In 1991 the proportion of women managers fell from the 1990 level in Ukraine, Uzbekistan, Georgia, Azerbaijan, Lithuania, Latvia, Kirgizia and Turkmenia. Only Estonia saw a slight increase in women managers – from 2.9 per cent to 3.2 per cent. The proportion of female managers in Russia (6.5 per cent) was somewhat higher than the average for the former USSR as a whole. However there was considerable regional variation: 15.3 per cent in Novgorod region; 11.1–11.4 per cent in Kostroma, Ivanovo and Vologod regions; down to 3.2 per cent in Ulyanovsk region, and 3.7 per cent in Belgorod region. Such differences between regions suggest considerable unused potential among women at this level of employment.

There is an even lower proportion of women managers in the largest social, economic and cultural centres of the country – Moscow and St Petersburg. It cannot be that in these cities there are not enough skilled women to occupy managerial posts, since the greatest number of professional women in all sectors of the economy are concentrated in these cities. We must therefore conclude that it is due to flagrant discrimination against women, who are refused entry in every way possible to the highest echelons of the economy. The result is that in St Petersburg, the proportion of women managers is only 3.5 per cent, and in Moscow 4.2 per cent – much lower than the average for the former USSR and Russia as a whole.

The educational system provides another blatant example of discrimination against professional women. Statistics show that teaching is traditionally a woman's profession, whereas the post of secondary school head is a male profession: although 83 per cent of schoolteachers are women, only 39 per cent of headteachers are women. When we consider that more professional women possess university degrees than men, the fact that they are barred from managerial posts indicates vertical discrimination and segregation of women. It is also wasteful in the sense that it is an inefficient use of human resources.

The present economic situation, in which the former state-owned, integrated system is being transformed into a much more varied economic structure, brings forth new employment problems. In place of a single employer – the state – we now have various non-state 'bosses' of leased, cooperative, joint-stock, privately owned and joint enterprises. At the end of 1991 one in four workers was working in the non-state sector. Wage levels at such enterprises are, as a rule, considerably higher than in the state sector. And this is hardly surprising, since the new forms of ownership are based on the profit-motive, which is only possible where new technology, new ways of organizing labour or other innovations have been introduced. Women lose out everywhere in the competition for highly paid jobs in the non-state sector of the economy. There is practically no information about such jobs at labour exchanges. The new private firms select their staff carefully and in private. The system for privatization of former state enterprises allows managements to get rid of all 'unwelcome' staff. More often than not, these turn out to be women near retirement and young women with small children.

Men are eagerly transferring to enterprises outside the state sector, leaving their less well-paid and less prestigious jobs at state enterprises to women. In 1991 an increase was observed, after a five-year gap, in the proportion of women employed at state industrial and construction enterprises. Today we can already say that two labour markets have emerged in this country. The first belongs to the private sector, with highly profitable firms equipped with new technology in all areas of the economy. Here there is a demand for highly qualified, enterprising personnel who can show initiative, and the demand tends to be principally for men. The second is the traditional labour market, where there is a great demand for unskilled workers to perform mainly physical work. The struggle for survival forces workers to accept such jobs, under any conditions, on obsolete equipment or without any mechanization. These are the job vacancies that the state employment service is offering the unemployed.

These processes are taking place not only in manufacturing, but also among professionals and intellectuals. For instance, if we look at the country as a whole, education and health care are feminized sectors, yet the private schools, gymnasia and lycées now opening up attract mainly male teachers. It is male doctors who have been the first to take up private practice. But it is higher education that is suffering the worst effects, as the most highly qualified professors and lecturers are leaving in droves for various private associations, business schools and so on. In 1992, a lecturer in these new educational institutions was paid ten times more than in the state sector. This 'brain drain' from the state educational system will very soon begin to tell on the quality of training of specialists, especially women. At the prestigious private institutes and business schools, both teachers and students are mainly male. In the elite Higher Commercial School in Moscow, for example, the proportion of women students does not exceed 10 per cent. Enterprises and organizations sending their staff on courses at the HCS do not want to put money into the training of women.

To prevent further job segregation of women, we need good programmes to integrate women into the market economy. These should encompass women workers in manufacturing, professional women, and women who want to go into business. The interests of all groups of women should be taken into account in legislation and in any state-run programmes for market transition. None of this as yet exists. Moreover, due to the lack of any organized women's movement, women are not demanding that their specific interests, including their economic interests, be taken into account, and their problems remain 'invisible' to the rest of society.

The Female Face of Unemployment

Unemployment figures, which began to be recorded in the USSR on 1 July 1991, show that unemployment is a female problem. Some 70–80 per cent of registered unemployed are women. The problem is so severe that it has taken precedence over all other female labour problems. During the six years of perestroika, employment problems were seen as an issue separate from the social and economic transformations taking place. Only in mid 1991, when the prospect of mass unemployment became a reality, did the Soviet and Russian parliaments enact laws on employment.

Despite the obvious inadequacies of the RSFSR Law on Employment of the Population and its clear failure to regulate the labour market, the very fact that the law was passed is of great importance: it is an acknowledgement in law of the fact that the system of 'state employment' – an essential part of the command-administrative economic system – is incompatible with the social and economic changes that were taking place.

This law contains a fundamentally new interpretation of the concept of employment, which reflects the transition from totalitarian to democratic principles. Whereas under previous legislation labour was universally compulsory, now it is voluntary and people are free to choose what job they want to do, the hours they work, and whether they want to work in a state-owned, joint-stock or private enterprise. Instead of employment for everybody at low wages, we now have voluntary and better-paid employment – but it is not guaranteed for everybody and for all time. Unemployment, which had long since been forgotten in this country, has once again become a reality. The Law on Employment recognizes this, and guarantees assistance to those who have lost their jobs but still want to work. The Law commits the state to help people find work, to grant unemployment benefits and other financial assistance to the temporarily unemployed and members of their families, and to organize job training and re-training programmes out of the Employment Fund.

Society was in a state of social and economic crisis when the Law on Employment came into effect. The economy was experiencing a slump in output, links between enterprises had broken down and former economic structures had collapsed. New structures were slow in taking their place, and new forms of ownership were emerging with difficulty. Many jobs have been lost as a result of cuts in production and economic restructuring.

Some enterprises and organizations are being abolished altogether, others are changing hands after liquidation, which is invariably accompanied by job cuts or replacement of some personnel. Workers thus made redundant find themselves on the labour market. Those who want to continue working but who cannot find work by themselves turn for help to the labour exchange: if the labour exchange cannot find suitable work for them, they are registered as unemployed. The Law on Employment of the Population regulates dismissal and hiring of workers, registration of the unemployed and conditions under which benefits can be paid.

The Law 'guarantees equal opportunities for all citizens living on the territory of the Russian Federation, irrespective of nationality, sex, age or social status . . . in implementing the right to work and to free choice of employment' (Article 5). But there is nothing in the Law to show how these equal opportunities can be put into effect. Article 13 of the Law contains 'additional employment safeguards for particular categories of the population'. The Law puts 'young people, single parents with children under the age of 18 and women with pre-school-age children' into the category of those 'experiencing difficulties in looking for work and requiring special social protection'. Article 13 seems to contradict Article 5. The Law categorizes women with pre-school-age children, single parents and parents of several children as 'social invalids', but rather than 'guaranteeing equal opportunities in implementing the right to work and to free choice of employment', the state instead pledges to 'set up specialized enterprises and create additional jobs'. Local Soviets, using their own finances (but will local Soviets find money for women?) can establish quotas of 'special jobs for certain categories of citizens'. Thus the Law ensures, as it were, that 'female ghettos' are created in state enterprises, rather than enabling women to integrate into normal economic structures, for example, by means of 'guaranteeing part-time employment, flexible schedules for work and holidays', as recommended by the United Nations Commission on the Position of Women (34th Session, 1990). This UN document emphasizes that 'women should be included in the main strategies for development, not singled out as a separate object of specific projects intended for women, which might turn out to be totally ineffective for them and, in the long-term, for the economy as a whole.'

The new law is infused with the spirit of the paternalistic ideology so prevalent in our country. It expresses specific concern for unemployed women who have children, but fails to mention rights or social protection for other categories of women with children. The logic of this legislation is that people who work, those who do not work and the unemployed all have the same rights (Article 1). The Law even states that people have a responsibility to work (Article 45). But the Law says nothing about the social protection of citizens who do not work, or of their children. This means that the entire system of social assistance to families, as in the past, applies only to working mothers. The pernicious effect of this unjustifiable policy towards women was quite clear in the compensatory payments issued after the April 1991 price rises. On this occasion all categories of women in practice became victims of the state's concern about women. Working women, because of all their social entitlements (which are actually meant for the family, not for the women themselves), ended up being an unprofitable proposition for enterprises. Enterprises began to get rid of their female workers, using any kind of specious pretext to sack them. Women who did not work simply had to go without the payments made to compensate for the price increases.

Neither does the Law on Employment envisage any social protection for pregnant women or workers who happen to be on parental leave when an enterprise goes into liquidation. They do not come under the category of paid redundancies: when an enterprise goes into liquidation (this is the means used to turn a state enterprise into a joint-stock company or some other form of ownership) pregnant women and all those on parental leave are instead dismissed, as the management is usually reluctant to include them on the payroll of the newly formed enterprise. The question of who should then pay maternity grants or compensation has not been legally resolved. These women can only receive unemployment benefit if they register for work, which they are hardly in a position to do.

The new Law on Employment, therefore, has adopted all the old approaches and principles in policy towards women. Not simply old, but long since obsolete and condemned by all international declarations on women's rights. The result is that 'social protection' is interpreted as 'assistance' that the state offers women; 'equal opportunities' and 'freedom of choice' are something imposed by the state forcing women to choose between economic or domestic responsibilities.

The current social and economic crisis is making it clear what the position and role of women is in society. Experience in the rest of the world shows that economic crisis has a more negative effect on both women as a whole and particular groups of women. The reasons for women's special vulnerability relate to the fact that the crisis and measures taken to overcome it are passed on to enterprises and institutions where equality between men and women did not exist. So when there is a crisis, this inequality becomes more marked.

The current state of the labour market offers a striking example of the asymmetrical effect of the economic crisis on men and women, and of the need for a new employment law. During times of full employment and manpower shortages discrimination against women was partially camouflaged, but the worsening of the employment problem, as a result of redundancies and unemployment, has made the inequality between men and women in the workplace more glaring than ever. The fact that there are as many as four times more women unemployed than men can be explained principally by the discrimination that exists against women in the workplace. In comparison, in 1988, 8.3 per cent of men and 13.4 per cent of women were unemployed in EEC countries.

It is true that the higher level of unemployment among women is determined by a number of reasons, but in my opinion the main reason remains discrimination. The proof of this is that if cuts in the workforce were non-discriminatory, then all categories of men and women would become unemployed in roughly equal measure, both in prestigious jobs with good working conditions, and those working in poorer conditions. In practice, however, women cannot stand up against the competition from men and are ousted precisely and only from specialized jobs. Men are not interested in competing with women for manual or heavy jobs or work which is injurious to health.

As many as 90 per cent of the unemployed who register at labour exchanges are professionals with higher and secondary vocational education, and the majority of these are women. Only 10 per cent are manual workers (here the numbers of men and women are about equal). Yet in the kind of vacancies on offer, we see an inverse proportion: about 90 per cent of vacancies are for manual labour. Female engineers and office-workers, accountants and book-keeping staff (except the most experienced and highly qualified), scientists, lecturers, goods managers and secretaries – all have become 'unwanted' on the labour market. Nearly all these professional groups are feminized, though this may change in the future. Our research conducted at Moscow's labour exchange shows that enterprises are only interested in recruiting men to fill the post of engineer. This is surely documentary proof of the discrimination that faces women. As far as vacancies are concerned, the greatest demand in the labour market is for lathe-operators of all kinds, metalworkers, adjusters – and all these are skilled, primarily male, jobs. The only 'female' jobs in demand by employers are sewing-machinists and cleaners (women make up 93–98 per cent of these job categories). It is practically impossible to find work for unemployed women specialists under the present conditions and they are therefore given unemployment benefit. However, receipt of benefits is not a solution to the problem. For in a year's time the need to find jobs for these women will still be there, but it will be that much worse. Then it is going to be a question of survival and the need for some minimal means of subsistence. Our research shows that the families of 69 per cent of women registered as unemployed at the Moscow labour exchange are living below the poverty line. One in four unemployed women are either widows or divorced – i.e., they are the sole breadwinners in the family and have no means of support apart from their wages.

The reasons for women's lack of competitiveness in the labour market are both objective, or socioeconomic, and subjective, or socio-psychological. They also have to do with prevailing patriarchal stereotypes about the role of women in society and in the family. Among objective factors we can list the following: lower level of vocational qualifications and training, compared with men; a high level of formal education, but one which is not kept up through their working lives, since there is no system in Russia for continuing education; and the fact that their many social entitlements and preferential terms make them an unattractive proposition for employers. Among subjective factors it should be noted that women are not psychologically prepared for job competition: they are accustomed to labour security, even if their abilities are under-utilized. This has made them (and many men too) lethargic, incapable of asserting themselves independently in their work and in life generally. Three generations of Soviet people have become used to the state being 'obliged' to solve many of the problems that in a competitive market system every person has to solve for him- or herself.

In a poll carried out by the Institute of Public Opinion, over three thousand people were asked the question: 'Should the government take responsibility for guaranteeing work for all who want it?', and 85 per cent of those questioned answered 'Yes.' A survey we conducted found that, in answer to the question, 'Did you try to look for work independently after you received notice of redundancy?', only a quarter of the unemployed women we questioned answered 'Yes.' About 13 per cent of unemployed women envision a hopeless situation when their unemployment benefit ends, and do not expect to be able to work in their field. Only about 8 per cent intend to set up their own business or become self-employed. Half of the respondents were willing to pay for retraining, if this would help them to find work. The rest were categorically opposed to, or were not in a position to finance, their own retraining.

The Employment Law's interpretation of 'suitable and unsuitable work' lends a particular edge to the problem of unemployed women finding work. Article 4 says that criteria for deciding whether a job is unsuitable are: 'if it entails changing residence against a citizen's wishes; if working conditions do not meet health and safety regulations and standards; if wages offered are below those of the person's last place of work.' As we can see, in the criteria for what is unsuitable, important aspects such as education, trade skills or profession are not even mentioned. And in the instructions – we do so love supplementary legal documentation, despite our many fine words about a 'law-based state'! – which the Moscow labour exchange follows in its work, it is even emphasized that: 'Work may be considered suitable if it requires a *lower* educational or training level than that possessed and if there are no other counter-indications.' According to this instruction, it is perfectly lawful to offer a person with higher or secondary vocational education work requiring only minimal skills. Finance clerks and engineers were being offered work as consumer services inspectors, or as wardens, caretakers etc.

One might get the impression that our labour-force is too highly educated. This is not the case, however, as there is a shortage of highly-trained specialists. We can see this quite clearly in the case of accountants: among the vacancies there were nearly twenty requests for experienced chief accountants, whereas these employers turned down newly-qualified accountants and cashiers.

The survey shows, therefore, that if social tension is to be reduced and the psychological climate in families is to improve, women must have the chance to work and contribute to the family's income. Without their income, families cannot survive or enjoy a decent standard of living, especially in today's conditions of inflation and price rises. For most women, work is a vital necessity and they can only 'save' their families and children if they have work, not if they are forced back into the home. An employment policy that is not for women, but at their expense (because they are being ousted from the workplace) cannot satisfy the majority of working women. Apart from that, it may lead to a number of negative consequences in the future, for example: ineffective utilization of the female labour-force's potential; devaluation of the education they have received and loss of professional qualities; a decline in their financial independence; and the feminization of poverty. This sad list could of course easily be added to, but every effort must be made to force the situation to develop along different lines.

Conditions of this sort heighten the importance of state policy regulating the labour position of women. The paternalistic policy aimed at funding various kinds of entitlements, grants and compensatory payments should be replaced by a policy for a large increase in investments to improve the quality of the female labour-force, with the aim of improving women's ability to compete on the labour market and creating equal conditions for such competition. The way out of crisis in this country is a transition to a market economy. But market forces and increased demand for labour cannot by themselves ensure that women are included in economic progress unless the state acts to remove certain barriers, including the evident need to improve employment legislation and the work of the employment service and labour exchanges. Measures must be taken to ensure that women are conversant with legislation so that they can make practical use of their equal labour rights. Over half those registering with Moscow's labour exchange do not know what the Law on Employment of the Population actually entails. This is fertile ground for the Law to be used in ways unfavourable to women. Measures are needed to help set up suitable childcare arrangements in nurseries and crêches and to guarantee women the necessary training and retraining.

There is an urgent need for new strategies to raise women's role in the economy; we need to work out ways of fostering women's businesses and assisting women to take advantage of the opportunities offered by privatization of small and medium-sized enterprises, especially in the service sector. To this end it is necessary first to expand the network of business courses and schools for women and create a market infrastructure oriented towards, not against, businesswomen (funds, banks etc.). Secondly, we need to elaborate a wide range of programmes to provide psychological support and training for unemployed women to help them understand the new social and economic realities which will help them adapt to new conditions and relieve some of the tension in society.

Reducing strains on the labour market will also create flexibility, so that, apart from traditional full-time jobs, more part-time jobs and home-based work, which is especially important for the unemployed women of today (not only the monotonous kind, as now, but intellectual work too), will become available. It is not only a question of preserving or increasing the number of jobs for women, but also of raising the level of these jobs, so that women can actually influence decision-making. We need, therefore, to protect and improve the professionalism of the female labour-force and retain their work skills. Nor should this process mean the retraining of well-educated women to do the kind of unskilled jobs presently offered (an idea the labour exchanges are now busy popularizing). Changes are also needed in the orientation of vocational training programmes. These should be effective and geared towards the future, not the past, and should prepare people who are not only well-qualified in their jobs, but experienced and capable of working as managers in various sectors of the economy.

An Opportunity Not To Be Missed: New Strategies for Women in the Transition to a Market Economy

The social and historical essence of the changes now taking place is the transition from a bureaucratic command economy to a market economy, from the monopolism of state ownership to the pluralism of different forms of ownership. This restructuring gives rise to the need to raise output and leads to new strategies aimed at enabling people to make a living by adapting to the new conditions.

I would like to focus here on women's businesses in Russia, as one of the new models that can be adopted by women who want to work during this transition period. It is better to think more in terms of the social effect than the economic effect of female entrepreneurship. In my opinion, women's businesses provide a vivid example of the fracturing of dogmatic, patriarchal stereotypes about the role of women in our society. The economic effect has yet to be seen, since there are no statistics on this as yet, and the process of women setting up small enterprises, firms, foundations and associations, which began so recently, is so dynamic that even information a month old is out of date. Studies of women's businesses in our country are only just beginning. No results have yet been published and no official statistics are available. I shall therefore use here the results of small polls and observations I have made from many meetings with women entrepreneurs in Moscow and other cities. These data do not, of course, claim to represent the overall picture.

Over the years a negative attitude has formed towards so-called 'career women' in our society. The small number of nomenklatura 'iron ladies' in administrative posts and praesidiums – not elected by anyone but appointed by the Party and state apparatus, obedient to the will of the top bosses, always ready to vote 'in favour' and carry out directives 'from above' – have created a negative stereotype of career women. Even today this stereotype is very much alive. When millions of viewers watched the unseemly campaign by Svetlana Goryacheva[3] (Deputy Chair of RSFSR Supreme Soviet) against Boris Yeltsin, the following could often be heard: 'Typical woman, you can't let them get into power!' But when Galina Starovoitova[4] speaks, they say: 'She's an exception – there are not many women like her.' Thus we see that the negative features of a particular person are extended to all women, whereas positive qualities are recognized only in a particular woman leader.

Of course women entrepreneurs have not yet made themselves heard as political leaders have done, so they are only known in narrow business circles, yet even here negative stereotypes are an obstacle to their work. One partner in the recently formed independent firm Dini said: 'Men had to accept me as a professional designer, but no way do they want to accept me as a businesswomen.'

I have talked to women entrepreneurs at a variety of seminars and conferences; at the First Independent Women's Forum; at businesswomen's clubs and schools. They vary widely, of course, in age, education, profession and social status. I would put them into three groups, although this is only an approximate classification.

The first group comprises women directors of state enterprises, usually in food and light industries, trade or the service sector. Acting in the spirit of the times, they are involved in the lease or privatization of their enterprises, or have set up small enterprises at their factories. Most of them are quite progressive professionals in their own fields. Many of them are young, but many are already experienced women managers.

The second group of female entrepreneurs could be called managers. They are mainly young, well-educated women who are second in command at various types of joint enterprise with foreign firms; they tend to be commercial directors, assistant directors, heads of departments, vice-presidents, experts, researchers, or in charge of some particular programme. These young women are competent, sociable, purposeful and businesslike.

Finally, the third category is women entrepreneurs. Some are in charge of associations, societies, leagues and foundations. Others sit on the boards of directors of these associations and foundations or are in charge of small enterprises. The most striking feature in these women is their enthusiasm, their creative approach, optimism and independence. In response to our question: 'What attracts you to small businesses?' they answered, 'The opportunity to realize my creative potential'; 'independence and freedom'; 'the opportunity to show what I can do'; 'it enables me stand up for my own interests'; 'the chance to do my own thing and see the results of my work', etc. But at the same time many businesswomen are cautious: yes, they view business as something that allows them the opportunity to show what they are worth, to test their powers and to earn additional income, but more often than not they continue to work at their primary jobs, if only on a part-time basis. This dual attitude towards entrepreneurship can be explained by the fact that many of them have taken up commercial activity in unfamiliar fields. I know a woman engineer, for example, who has gone into the leisure business. Or an architect, who teaches economics; a scientist who is in charge of a commercial partnership involved in a variety of businesses; and a school headmistress who manages a small enterprise manufacturing consumer goods. Only doctors, lawyers and financiers tend to keep to their own professions when they go into business.

For many Soviet women the transition to a market system is associated with unemployment, a drop in living standards and shortages of goods; which, in turn, gives rise to pessimism and repeated demands for social protection. This attitude contrasts with that of the modern businesswomen, who tend to be self-reliant and optimistic, and ready to help others. These businesswomen have banded together in all sorts of associations, clubs and societies, with the aim of support, exchange of experience and information and creation of new jobs for women in small enterprises.

The new businesswomen understand that the parasitic attitude of the past is a losing proposition. They find it humiliating to be the object of social assistance and protection from the state. Their goal is to take charge of their own lives. It is interesting that they do not want to fit into conventional male structures: their aim is to change these not only in their own businesses, but in society as a whole. They do not want their businesses to be the pragmatic, technocratic structures that men have set up. They tend to be aware that they owe something to society, and strive to give their businesses a humanistic face. Thus many of the associations and clubs which have sprung up have started funds to go towards creating new jobs for unemployed women and for charitable purposes.

Another feature of new Russian businesswomen is their active participation in the social life of the country. Their commercial activity is tied to the new forms of ownership the market economy has introduced, and their political views, too, tend to be progressive. Now that they have shown themselves capable of standing on their own feet, these women have no intention of going back to the old totalitarian structures that treated them as second-class citizens who received pathetic hand-outs instead of salaries commensurate with their work.

Many problems exist, however, as in any new endeavour. The lack of knowledge, experience and information; the impossibility of obtaining loans, when most of these businesses start from scratch; difficulties in getting premises and equipment, endless bureaucratic obstacles and checks, having to account for every step they take to prove that what they are doing is within the law. This is a real problem at present because of the 'war of laws' and confusion that exists in current legislation. Another equally important factor is that of male chauvinism, when men claim to want to help women's business, but are not at all keen to have enterprising and talented women as rivals and competitors. Finding it hard to counter these difficulties on their own, businesswomen have banded together in associations and societies so that they have their own network for informal communication and exchange of information. Male managers have always had this sort of network, since most top managerial personnel were always men, and they had the opportunity to meet at a wide range of conferences and symposia. Now women have also come together in order to discuss their mutual business problems and interests, to formulate demands, to express themselves and to be heard.

Russian businesswomen are not only interested in the commercial aspect. They are taking an active part in the emerging unofficial women's movement, which is evidenced in part by their active participation at the two Independent Women's Forums in 1991 and 1992 and in setting up an independent women's information network (ZhISET). In the first forum, sixteen out of forty-eight (that is, one in three) unofficial women's organizations were represented by businesswomen. Businesswomen want to maintain contacts not only among themselves but also with the Centre for Gender Studies and feminist organizations. In my opinion, the emergence of public-minded businesswomen now forms one of the most important trends in the independent women's movement of Russia today.

Notes

1. All factual data are taken from the volume of statistics *Women in the USSR* (*Zhenshchina v SSSR*), published in the USSR in 1937.
2. *Mirovoi obzor*, 1989 (*World Survey on the Role of Women in Development*, 1989). United Nations, New York, 1990, p. 243.
3. *Translator's note*: Goryacheva, a conservative parliamentary deputy from Siberia, was the first openly to accuse Yeltsin of authoritarianism, early in 1991.
4. *Translator's note*: A radical deputy from the Democratic Russia bloc.

7

Equal Opportunities or Protectionist Measures? The Choice Facing Women

Yelena Mezentseva

The Soviet regime declared right from the start that one of its main goals was to achieve full equality between men and women. For almost seventy years different Soviet leaderships repeated the claim that the USSR had achieved full sexual equality in the workplace.

The USSR Constitution and labour legislation were usually cited as evidence of this. It is true that these do formally enshrine equal rights of both sexes to secondary and professional education, job placement in their chosen fields, and so on. They also laid down special provision for the labour rights of women during pregnancy and breastfeeding – women were supposed to be transferred to lighter types of work and could not be sacked because of pregnancy, and so on. This 'protectionist' tendency in labour legislation extended to all policies on women's employment. This was the Soviet authorities' way of implementing the principle of equal opportunities.

In the present economic, political and social crisis, we are finding that we face a number of longstanding employment problems. Many of these problems were at one time pronounced to be 'fully resolved' since a new, more 'advanced' social system had taken over. And it is true that we had all become accustomed to there being no unemployment and no threat of redundancy in the USSR. In the unlikely event that people lost their jobs, the state always looked after them by offering a choice of other suitable jobs. We were also accustomed to having just one employer in the country – the state. Moreover, only the state – i.e., state officials – could determine pay levels. We all accepted the myth that in the USSR there was no discrimination against women at work, and that women's rights were reliably safeguarded by the state.

But the real situation was quite different. In practice, women's labour rights were openly being violated. This is still the situation today, aggravated by the fact that now their employment prospects are increasingly poor.

Is the Principle of Equal Employment Opportunities for Women Being Observed?

The principles laid down in the United Nations Convention on the Elimination of All Forms of Discrimination against Women are only partially observed in our country. While it is true that women are equal before the law and have the legal right to education and employment, it is unfortunately only the letter of the Convention's guidelines that is being implemented, not the spirit. The practical implementation of equal rights, on which the UN Convention lays particular emphasis, is often ignored altogether. Soviet reports to the United Nations on how the Convention was being observed usually stated that its legal statutes were being carried out. Thus they avoided both the problem of having to reveal actual discrimination against women and that of differentiating between direct and indirect discrimination. The logic behind this was quite simple: if sex discrimination is forbidden by law, then it does not exist.

The second way in which the authorities have claimed to observe international anti-discrimination obligations is by laying the emphasis on the state's social protection of women. Women are being given an increasing number of social benefits and entitlements, they say. Yet real, as opposed to proclaimed, equality of opportunity in employment is practically lost from sight. Recent practice confirms that public opinion prefers social protectionism to equal opportunities. The highest state authorities are convinced of the value of substantial social protection for working women. The republics, regions, enterprises and the public at large think likewise: we only have to recall recent elections, when candidates offering significant improvements in social benefits and entitlements for women stood the best chance of getting elected.

Failure to implement many of the provisions of the UN Convention and the International Labour Organization tends not to be considered as constituting discrimination. In fact discriminatory practices even tend to be justified from an ideological point of view. This is mainly due to a significant increase in patriarchal views on women's place in society, and the widespread ideology of social protectionism towards women. In politicians' speeches and official documents, not to mention views expressed by the mass media or by the public, women are increasingly shown simply as the object of social policy – as a single passive mass without a stance or interests of their own. Moreover, public opinion tends to view the 'renaissance' of patriarchalism as an inevitable consequence of the transition to a market economy, the onset of mass unemployment and tougher competition for jobs.

In such circumstances, infringement of many provisions of both the UN Convention and ILO conventions and recommendations goes practically unnoticed. It even tends to be excused by citing the need to ease women's heavy domestic burden. Women have considerable difficulties, the argument goes, in combining their roles as wives, mothers and workers, and exhibit poor motivation towards their work.

Clearly neither political declarations (and the reports this country presents to the United Nations and ILO concerning observation of ratified conventions can be seen in this light), nor public opinion proves the existence or absence of discrimination. To answer the question posed in the title of this essay, we must deal with the real situation of women at work.

Data analysis reveals significant differences in the employment situation of men and women. These concern levels of educational and vocational qualifications, the kinds of jobs and industrial sectors in which men and women are employed, pay levels, working conditions, opportunities for improving skills, career promotion and participation in industrial management.

Women are very unevenly represented in certain sectors of the economy. Over half of all working women are employed in manufacturing and industry. From 1985 to 1990, the proportion of people employed in this sector fell from 55.2 per cent to 54.1 per cent; this drop was mainly due to cuts in the numbers of women employed in agriculture and, to a lesser extent, in industry. Over the same period there was a gradual increase in the numbers and proportion of women employed in non-manufacturing sectors.

The sectors outside manufacturing are highly feminized. For instance, in finance and state insurance women comprise 67 per cent of the total employed, they constitute 82 per cent of all shop and food service workers, 81 per cent of the health and fitness sectors and social security; 75 per cent in education and 72 per cent in the arts. A number of industrial sectors also come close to these figures: the textile industry, for instance, where women comprise 70 per cent of workers, 89 per cent of garment-makers, 71 per cent of bakery-workers, 72 per cent of confectionary workers, and 69 per cent in the leather, fur and shoe industries. These data show that despite this country's proclaimed sexual equality at work, and in particular, in the choice of job, women in fact work in a limited number of sectors, while other sectors and jobs remain virtually closed to them. As a result, nearly 80 per cent of working women are employed in so-called 'female' sectors and jobs, in predominantly 'female' work collectives. We find precisely the same situation in terms of what manufacturing trades women are employed in: women are concentrated in a limited number of trades and in comparatively junior positions.

The low technological level of present-day production corresponds to the large-scale employment of women in unskilled jobs. The number of unskilled women workers is more than twice the corresponding figure for men. Women's skills are 2 to 3 grades lower than those of men in a number of sectors. In machine-building and metalworking, 70 per cent of women workers possess skill grades 1 to 3, and only 1.3 per cent of women workers possess the 6th grade. In light industry, which is considered a traditional area of women's work, the average overall grade is 4.17, whereas for women it is only 2.91 (37 per cent possess the 1st and 2nd grades); in the food industry – another typically 'female' sector – the average figure is 3.89, but for women it is 3.0 (and 33 per cent of women possess the lower 1st and 2nd grades). Only 10 to 16 per cent of men employed in these sectors have grades as low as 1 and 2.

Female office-workers are in a similar position: many have never had a chance throughout their working lives to improve their job status or be promoted. This is especially true of sectors or enterprises with a mixed workforce: here, even in enterprises where more women are employed than men, women are to be found in the least important jobs. In the main, they service the work of others and carry out orders. Women in jobs of this kind have practically no opportunity to show initiative or imagination, or obtain job satisfaction.

Nevertheless, despite such modest employment prospects, most women and young girls attempt to choose interesting, stimulating kinds of work and try to achieve high educational standards. The proportion of professional women with higher or vocational secondary education is steadily increasing (it rose from 59 per cent in 1980 to 61 per cent in 1989). Most of these women work in the most common professions – engineers, teachers and doctors. However, various surveys have shown that a considerable proportion of professional women remain at the bottom of the career structure throughout their working lives, despite their level of education and professional experience.

Frequent calls have been heard in recent years to free women from their double burden, to return them to the home, to return mothers to their children, and so on. People holding these views usually claim to express women's 'real' interests by alleviating the situation of working women. However, in practice, it turns out that first in line to be 'returned to the hearth' are not women engaged in hard, monotonous, unskilled jobs. On the contrary – the first to be made redundant are women office-workers and professional women. The majority of those registering at labour exchanges are from this category. The reasons are obvious: few men would agree to fill those jobs at present done by women in industry, since the work is low-paid and arduous. Statistics show that in the sort of jobs where mainly women are employed, labour is less mechanized and consists mainly of heavy, physical operations carried out manually.

Pay levels show massive discrimination. In 1990 only 25 per cent of women received wages of more than 200 roubles per month. In the 30–39 and 40–49 age groups, over 12 per cent of women did not earn more than 100 roubles, whereas for men the figure was just over 3 per cent. Only 9 per cent of women were highly paid (over 300 roubles per month), compared to 25 per cent of men. It is important to note that this situation exists at an age when most women have raised their families and are thus in a position to spend far more time and energy on their work.

Of course the fact that inequality exists in practice does not in itself prove that there is inequality of opportunity. In fact, studies on female employment problems often attribute such inequality to a number of factors – for example, that women are less work-motivated and less career-oriented than men; or that they have little aptitude for complex technical work, that they are no good at making decisions and do not want to bear responsibility for them. In short, 'women's functions' at work are simply to perform assigned tasks, which as a rule serve the main activity. Moreover, we are treated to the theory that the present employment situation for women is 'natural' or 'normal', fits in with 'women's nature' and corresponds to their own interests.

Unfortunately, such views are very widespread. They are usually not based on scientific conclusions, but on the commonplace patriarchal ideas about women's place in the family and at work. However widespread such ideas, they do not help to solve the question: Is inequality in employment due to the lack of opportunity, or the result of concealed – or overt – discrimination against women? Again the reply must be sought by taking a look at the real situation. The main questions are: Is the present employment situation for women the result of their 'free choice'? Does the sex of a worker provide grounds for direct or indirect discrimination in our country? Does a worker's sex affect wages?

Factors affecting achievement of real equality of opportunity for men and women in employment are of two types:

(1) Factors found in education and employment (displays of direct or indirect discrimination against women applies particularly to this group).

(2) Limiting factors (or conditioning factors) which are not directly connected to the work women do, but which determine the extent to which they are really free to choose what they want to do in life, and what

trade or profession they choose to pursue. This group contains several sub-groups:

- the social and economic conditions of women's lives;
- the domestic conditions of women's lives;
- women's value orientations;
- the social environment (value systems, cultural stereotypes etc.)

It is obvious that the two types overlap. Let us take a closer look at the first set of factors – i.e., those that have a direct bearing on women's opportunities in education and employment.

Freedom of Opportunity

Let us begin with education. There are a number of jobs that are prohibited for women. If we analyse the list of jobs in the Skill Grades Handbook, we will find that the percentage of jobs prohibited for women does not exceed 20 per cent of the overall number listed. One would expect corresponding percentages in technical and vocational education. That is, the number of trades which only girls can go in for should be 20 per cent less than the number open both to boys and girls. But in fact we see something quite different: 'female' trades form only 20 per cent of all trades taught at PTU[1].

So, for girls choosing to go on to PTU or tekhnikum the range of possibilities is much narrower than for boys. Therefore the principle of equal opportunity in employment is violated right at the start of their working lives, at a time when the vast majority of girls have no family commitments and can devote as much time and effort to their education and training as boys can. The Skill Grades Handbook also reveals that 'male' trades normally have a wider range of skill grades than 'female' trades. The highest grade of the most common industrial trades, for example, fitter or turner is no. 6; whereas for many 'female' trades, the highest skill grade is only no. 4.

This gap between starting positions does not diminish with time; on the contrary, it widens. Goskomstat[2] figures for 1988 show that only 7.9 per cent of women attended training courses to upgrade their skills. Most obtained no real improvements in job status or pay as a result. The following statistics illustrate this very clearly: 65.5 per cent of all women who had attended skills-upgrading courses reported that afterwards nothing had changed at work; 90.7 per cent had received no promotion; 88.9 per cent had not been placed on a new skills grade; and 81.5 per cent had received no pay increase!

Despite the fact that over 40 per cent of women think the work they do does not correspond to their qualifications, the overwhelming majority continue in those jobs. Their mobility in terms of jobs, skills and place of work is considerably less than the corresponding indices for men. What prevents women from changing their jobs and choosing something more suited to their trade and level of skills? What do women themselves think? Women gave the following as the main reasons for staying in the same job: difficulties in finding work in their own trade, 28 per cent of women questioned; proximity of workplace to home, 25 per cent; higher wages, 18 per cent; having young children, 15 per cent. The reasons women themselves give to explain why they stay in the same jobs are mostly to do with their family responsibilities, not job interest. It was particularly hard for women in Armenia and Georgia (42–51 per cent) and in Lithuania, Latvia, Kazakhstan, Azerbaijan, Belarus and Kyrghyzstan (32–37 per cent) to find work in their own fields. Women in the 18–23 age group (42 per cent) and 24–29 (34 per cent) had most difficulties in finding work in their own fields.

Women factory-workers, office-workers and professionals all experience great difficulty in realizing their potential at work. At present, professional women's higher level of education not only fails to ensure better prospects for them in finding work or in getting promotion, but even acts as a kind of additional 'risk factor' at practically all stages of their working lives.

At the very start of their working lives – immediately following graduation – women come up against considerably greater difficulties than men. When graduates are competing for work placement, gender is an extremely important factor in deciding who gets the most coveted placements. In job vacancy descriptions, organizations often directly specify the preferred sex of the young professional they wish to recruit. With the exception of so-called 'typically female' trades, practically all organizations prefer young professionals to be men. Women professionals with higher or vocational secondary specialized education who lose their jobs have considerably worse prospects of finding work in their profession than men. These difficulties are becoming worse as the situation on the labour market gets tougher: in the present economic crisis redundancies are occurring at a faster rate among professionals than among industrial workers.

Nor does a high level of education guarantee promotion for professional women. Whereas 50 per cent of all men with higher or vocational secondary education are somewhere on the management scale, only 7 per cent of women graduates are in managerial posts. These figures seem to indicate a lack of equality of opportunity for professional women. In fact, recent years have seen a marked decrease in the already small numbers of women in high managerial positions. This decrease should certainly not be seen as the result of women's 'free choice'. It is the natural consequence of a policy aimed at excluding women from decision-making and management.

These trends are extremely dangerous, because during the transition to a market economy there has been a marked tendency towards increasing masculinization of highly skilled work requiring extensive specialized training. This trend is particularly evident in professional posts and in management. It can be observed in the form of concealed – although recently it has become much more overt – sex discrimination in hiring and dismissing staff. The problem of equal opportunity and treatment of women in the workplace is not confined to accessibility of education and job training or promotion prospects.

No less important is the problem of women's pay. The principle of equal pay for equal work is laid down both in the preamble to and Article 36 of the Fundamentals of Labour Legislation. The USSR had also in 1956 ratified ILO Convention no. 100 concerning equal pay for equal work. One would think that this principle ought to have been strictly observed – since it is guaranteed both by our internal labour laws and by international obligations. How does women's pay compare with men's? Data from many surveys carried out by Goskomstat[3] and Goskomtrud,[4] labour research institutes, and other organizations indicate that women's wages are in fact one-third lower than men's wages. This apparent gap in earnings is usually justified by arguments about women having lower qualifications, lower labour productivity and output, doing less overtime, and so on. We shall look at the problem from a different angle – by analysing pay differences between the different sectors.

Our data show that the higher the proportion of women employed in a particular sector of the economy, the lower the average pay in that sector. If we compare pay levels between sectors in the republics, we find the same relation for each republic. It is particularly revealing in this sense to compare 'female' sectors of the economy with predominantly 'male' sectors or sectors with a mixed workforce.

Over the four years 1985–89, all the feminized sectors of the economy (with the exception of banking and state insurance) dropped further below average pay levels, despite declared measures to raise the salaries of doctors, teachers etc. The most unfavourable situation as regards pay is in education, culture and the arts. In industry during the period 1986 (when pay rises started) to 1989, pay increased by 22 per cent, and by 30 per cent in the construction industry; whereas in the education sector pay rose by only 13 per cent, in culture 15 per cent and in the arts 12 per cent, there was a somewhat bigger pay increase – 21 per cent – in health, housing and communal services and trade sectors. Obviously, these trends in workers' wages in the predominantly female sectors of the economy cannot be explained by variations in vocational skills or labour productivity. There can be no serious grounds for arguing that the level of education and qualifications required for work in the health service or education sector is less than that required in industry or in construction. It seems to me that the fact that almost all the 'female' sectors of the economy correspond to the most low-paid is a clear example of discrimination in pay between male and female labour. The data indicate that the gap in earnings between 'male' and 'female' sectors has not only failed to close; it has in fact widened even further.

This marked discrepancy in earnings in favour of the production sectors is a result of the way our economy was structured in the past. From the 1920s onwards, it was declared that our country's main task was to build the material and technological basis first for socialism and then for Communism. This plan was put into effect during the period of industrialization and collectivization. The whole pay system was subordinated to the solution of these technological and production problems: wage rates were set so as to ensure the necessary influx of workers into the priority sectors – industry (primarily heavy industry), construction, transport, and so on. Sectors servicing the needs of the individual (education, healthcare, the arts, services) were never considered a priority – after all, the state never cared particularly about the 'quality' of its population. What was important was merely the quantitative aspect – the state needed a constant influx of new workers into manufacturing, new soldiers into the army, and so on. Moreover, production technology was (and still is) at an extremely low level, requiring neither a good education, nor professional skills.

The main function of the non-manufacturing sectors was therefore to show the whole world the 'outstanding achievements' of the socialist state's social policy. The job of preparing educated, cultured people and keeping present and future generations healthy had to take second place. These sectors were considered 'ballast', which did not actually produce anything useful, apart from propagating a positive image of socialism. But the state could not do without them entirely, since it proclaimed itself a state *of* the workers and *for* the workers.

The factors of the first type described above are evidence of direct or indirect discrimination against women in education and employment. Factors of the second type do not lead to employment discrimination. They do, however, foster the conditions that prevent women from enjoying equal employment opportunities.

Freedom of Choice

Of overwhelming importance is the double burden working women bear
– combining the roles of wife, mother and housewife, as well as that of
worker. It has been estimated that the average work-load for working
women is 76.3 hours per week. Under such circumstances, how can
women recuperate their strength for the next working day or realize their
potential as individuals at work, in social and political affairs, or in the
family?

The economic pattern that has emerged from the influx of women into
the economy is that the Soviet family came to depend on two incomes.
The results of a survey carried out by the State Statistics Committee in
1990 showed that over 80 per cent of the women respondents gave the
need to support their families as the main reason for going out to work.
Only about 15 per cent said that their work enabled them to feel
independent. Office-workers experienced the highest level of financial
dependence – 48 per cent of them emphasized this fact; the most
financially dependent women were those with children under 7 (53 per
cent) and those with children between the ages of 7 and 16 (50 per cent),
and the least financially dependent were women between the ages of 51
and 55. Since this survey was conducted, women have become even more
financially dependent, both as a result of lower pay in the feminized
sectors and a sharp increase in the numbers of women losing their jobs. In
this situation, of course, women are virtually deprived of the chance of
choosing between work and home. Redundancies have deprived women
of any choice between low-paid professional work or higher-paid manual
work.

But there is one 'escape route' of sorts: jobs entailing arduous or
dangerous working conditions offer an 'attractive' alternative to women.
Over 25 per cent of working women, and an even higher percentage (39
per cent) of women manual workers, say their working conditions are
unsatisfactory. Of these, 44 per cent class their working conditions as
hard or very hard, 20 per cent as injurious or highly injurious to health,
and 36 per cent as monotonous and tiring. The figures for women in
agriculture were 12 per cent, 17 per cent and 72 per cent respectively.
Only 12 per cent of women working in unsatisfactory conditions were
satisfied with their earnings.

Although critical of their poor working conditions, these women resist
any attempt to make the transfer from such jobs to lighter work. One
reason is obviously loss of earnings, since other jobs would not include
compensatory pay for poor working conditions. And many women
unable to make a decent wage by upgrading their skills have compensated
for this by moving to heavy but better-paid jobs. But an even more

important reason why women are reluctant to leave heavy jobs or work which is injurious to their health is that this work allows them to retire earlier. In a system where all able-bodied people were obliged to work, this right and the guarantee of a higher pension always formed a very attractive proposition. All governmental resolutions and instructions notwithstanding, the prospect of a higher pension still keeps women in unhealthy jobs.

Women's behaviour at work and the opportunities they have for self-advancement in their chosen trade depend to a great extent on their actual family and financial situation. The vast majority of women today and in the foreseeable future simply cannot manage without paid employment outside the home – their wages are an essential component of the family income. Moreover, women have to put financial considerations first when changing jobs or choosing working conditions. In any case, the opportunity to choose where to work and in what conditions is very limited, since our labour market is not sufficiently flexible to enable women to combine to best effect the demands of work and home.

Most women are weighed down with domestic responsibilities, which explains why they are interested in jobs with shorter hours. We do not have the kind of services that can relieve women of exhausting and time-consuming housework and shopping, so the shorter working day tends to be a compromise that reconciles the interests of women and the workplace. Surveys have shown that 81 per cent would prefer to work a shorter day, yet only one per cent of the women surveyed actually had the opportunity. Women in Moldova, Russia, Belarus, Latvia, Kyrghyzstan, Turkmenistan and Tajikistan were particularly interested in working shorter hours: 78–91 per cent of women in these republics wanted a shorter working day. The breakdown of women wanting to work a shorter day but for various reasons unable to make use of this right is as follows: 50.2 per cent of women wanting to work shorter hours cannot do so for financial reasons – the woman is the sole breadwinner in the family; 17.3 per cent of women indicated that conditions at work did not permit them to work shorter hours; 16.4 per cent said that working shorter hours would cause problems for the rest of the work collective; 11.5 per cent said management did not agree to it; 18.8 per cent said it was difficult to find work of this kind; 3.8 per cent gave other reasons. The majority of women, therefore, are unable to make use of their right to work shorter hours because they lack the financial means; 45 per cent of women would have worked shorter hours if the nature of their employment or their managements allowed them to do so. This example confirms the theory that the present structure of women's employment is to a large extent forced on them and corresponds neither to women's own interests nor to the interests of the nation's economic development.

In addition to the limitations imposed by family and domestic commitments, women's own value orientations play an important role in influencing their attitude to work. If it is true that society does not ensure equal opportunity in employment, we should also ask whether women are psychologically ready to take advantage of equal opportunities. Analysis of the statistical data does not draw a very comforting picture. Only 13 per cent of women, according to the results of our survey, wanted to take up a higher post, whereas over 85 per cent of working women expressed no such desire. Women under 30 are the most career-minded: 36 per cent of the women who want promotion are in this age group. Career motivation is also relatively strong in the 30–40 age group: 75 per cent of women wanting promotion are thus under 40. Least career-inclined are women in the Baltics (8–9 per cent of respondents), Belarus, Russia and Moldova (11–13 per cent). This seems rather surprising, since these republics are among the most highly developed. Clearly, the overwhelming majority of women go to work for financial reasons alone: only a very small number of women see their work as a means of personal fulfilment.

Only a very small number of women cite reasons for changing jobs as having to do with the nature of the work or as a career move: 18 per cent of industrial workers; 14.7 per cent of agricultural workers; and 25.5 per cent of office-workers. Economic factors are by far the predominant motive: over 45 per cent of women questioned in all social groups gave dissatisfaction with pay levels as their reason for changing jobs.

Data on the reasons for changing jobs reveal a striking similarity with results obtained during a survey in the city of Naberezhnye Chelny (1989–90). We discovered that women's main concerns when changing jobs were, in order of preference: (1) to find a job with more flexible working hours (32.8 per cent); (2) to earn higher wages (32.4 per cent); (3) to work nearer to home (27.4 per cent); (4) to get a job with better working conditions (23.7 per cent). Other reasons for changing jobs were rarely given: 10.5 per cent of women questioned said they wanted to find more interesting work where they could use their initiative; 8.5 per cent said they wanted to improve their qualifications and get a better job. Only 1.4 per cent expressed the desire for a managerial post and only 0.34 per cent said they wanted to make a career for themselves.

The question: 'If your husband were to get a significant wage rise, would you continue working?' was also asked. About 20 per cent of engineers and technical staff, and 26 per cent of shop-floor workers, said they would stay in their present jobs; 64 per cent of engineers and technical staff, and 32 per cent of shop-floor workers, said they would switch to shorter working hours; 12 per cent of engineers and technical staff, and 30 per cent of shop-floor workers, said they would seek more pleasant work; 4 per cent of engineers and technical staff, and 3 per cent of shop-floor workers, said they would stop working altogether. From these responses we can see that the majority of women expect to combine the two roles, but for most women the interests of the family come first.

This is further illustrated by answers to the question: 'What do you consider most important in life?' First in the hierarchy of values in life was health (84.1 per cent); followed by financial prosperity (34.8 per cent); family happiness (30.7 per cent); their children's development (29.0 per cent); career (25.3 per cent); public service (23.9 per cent); interesting work (21.6 per cent); friendships (21.6 per cent); love, sex, intimate life (11.2 per cent). We can see that here, too, a significant proportion of the women surveyed are guided by material living standards, while only a fifth named their career or interesting work as important.

We can conclude from these data that women are not at present showing great interest in job satisfaction, nor are they particularly concerned about achieving equality of opportunity at work. They view their various labour entitlements and social benefits as being more important. While not denying the need for a system that offers social protection to everyone, it must be said that the policy of social protectionism towards women goes somewhat against the practical implementation of equal job opportunities. Protectionism causes employers to adopt a negative attitude towards women workers, who are seen as a burden because of their many benefits and entitlements. Women are viewed primarily as recipients of benefits rather than as potential workers with their own merits in terms of skills and experience. This tendency can already be observed: enterprises quite often refuse to hire women without even looking at their professional qualifications or experience.

To return to the question in our title: has the principle of equal job opportunities been fully implemented? Or is it just a political declaration? And are women ready to take advantage of equal opportunities? Are women striving for freedom of choice as regards trade or profession and equal opportunities alongside men?

The majority of women have not yet internalized the need for equality of opportunity in employment. Many women, overburdened with their many social roles and functions, regard their jobs as something forced on them by purely financial considerations. As we indicated earlier (in the example of shorter hours), their choice of employment is extremely limited, since today's labour market cannot offer these women the type of employment that is most suitable for them.

It is also true that women who are psychologically and professionally ready to take advantage of equal opportunities come up against a number of obstacles both in employment and education: official and unofficial barriers to prestigious professions and to top career and social status, and in their social environment. These women often experience social pressure not only from prevailing views about the place and role of women, but also from their family environments. We can suppose that these women will find the adaptation to a market economy more difficult, since society is not ready to offer them real employment opportunities on a par with men, yet they are not likely to want to reconcile themselves to the social role men have assigned them.

Notes

1. *Translator's note*: 'PTU' – *Professional'no-tekhnicheskiye uchilishcha*, or Vocational-technical schools.
2. *Translator's note*: 'Goskomstat' – State Statistics Committee.
3. *Translator's note*: 'Goskomstat' – State Statistics Committee.
4. *Translator's note*: 'Goskomtrud' – State Committee for Employment.

8

The Mythology of Womanhood in Contemporary 'Soviet' Culture[1]

Olga Lipovskaya

What does a person need? –
A woman at his side . . .
From a Soviet poem

A young woman with long legs wearing a mini-skirt and high heels represents an advertising agency; an attractive young woman wearing sexy black underwear advertises computers – the barely covered curves are supposed to remind us of the smooth design of IBM equipment. The new, seductive image of the Soviet woman floods the cinema and TV screens, commercials, newspapers, magazines and cartoons. Where is the old familiar woman-comrade, dressed in the buttoned-up uniform, modest business suit or sexless gown of the milkmaid, house-painter or collective-farm girl? No, she hasn't disappeared, she has merely changed her representation from positive to negative, from plus to minus.

Social, political and economic changes in Soviet society have brought about a reassessment of values, a reconsideration of historical events – to put it metaphorically, the exchange of pluses for minuses. The right has become the left, previously positive historical achievements are now considered to be negative, the good has turned into bad in societal and cultural values. The image of woman as a meaningful cultural concept has also changed radically.

Sofia Vlasievna, or, From Plus to Minus

A charming young woman looks out from the cover of the magazine *Stolitsa* (Capital).[2] Her hair is intricately braided to imitate a hammer and

sickle, her body is draped in the red Soviet flag. Her hand holds a real
sickle to her throat; the viewer can perceive that the girl's head plays the
role of the hammer. Like everything avant-garde, this photographic
portrait leaves plenty of room for the ironic imagination.

This young lady could be called 'Sofia Vlasievna' – the nickname given
to the Power of the Soviets (*Vlast' Sovietov*) by the dissidents of the past.
Every era has its own names. The angry, often childish and passionate
rejection of the 'Communist' totalitarian past is inherent in the
contemporary Soviet consciousness. A trendy new expression has
appeared in Russian slang: *sovok*, which is applied to people with the
Soviet mentality. Almost all examples and subjects of Soviet culture may
be labelled by this word. Both men and women can be called *sovok*. The
female *sovok* is principally characterized by her asexuality. Typical
attributes are severity in dress, a certain mannishness or, even if she is
quite feminine, a strict professional orientation outweighing family
responsibilities. In a word, she is the *emancipée*, and the tradition of her
negative portrayal can be traced to Tolstoy and Turgenev. (Of the many
contemporary portrayals of emancipated women, only one has been
positive: that of the four women in the film *Adam's Rib*, directed by
Krishtofovich.)

This image has a dramatic history, because it never reflected existing
reality. The socialist realist tradition was intended to create an ideal
reality and utilized this model to portray the exemplary woman of the
radiant Communist future. Every Soviet woman was supposed to acquire
those traits and become like her. But in real life we were also supposed to
take care of our children and husbands and dedicate ourselves to
exhausting domestic chores. In fact, it was impossible to combine these
tasks and women were always torn between the two, never truly content
because they could not be their real selves.

This metaphorical image, taken further, culminates in a real-life
person – Nina Andreyeva. An arch conservative, rigid fanatical
Communist and Stalinist, she passionately attacks all forms of liberalism,
from economic reforms to sexual freedom. Nina Andreyeva achieved
fame in 1988 with her angry article 'I Cannot Forgo My Principles',
published in the conservative newspaper *Soviet Russia*. Since then she has
been widely interviewed and quoted by the media in Russia and the West,
and gradually came to epitomize the hateful Soviet system. A real, living
woman has become the personification of a system. To some extent, this
in itself reflects the tradition of cultural misogyny in Russian and Soviet
culture. This personification has taken place in a country where political
and economic power belongs almost exclusively to men. Detached from
its owner, the name 'Nina Andreyeva' has become a label for
conservatism and totalitarianism and has replaced the former term 'Sofia

Vlasievna'. It is true that certain conservative male politicians, for example Yegor Ligachev, former Prime Minister Valentin Pavlov or his fellow accomplices in the August 1991 *coup d'état* have also acquired iconic status and are often used symbolically in the mass media to characterize the ideology of conservatism. However, their masculine gender saves them from being used to personify a 'system' (*sistema*) which takes the feminine gender in Russian, as do the words 'power' (*vlast'*) and 'authority' (*avtoritetnost'*). After all, in many cultures men have often been considered more human, and women more often objectified and regarded as secondary to men, exemplifying the tradition of *cultural misogyny*, where all that is negative (bearing the minus sign) is ascribed to the female gender.

Cultural hostility towards women – misogyny – requires only one real Nina Andreyeva for the myth to become reality. The dreadful image of the 'Communist emancipée' frightens most women away, although previously it had been extolled as a role model. Women are now afraid to display independence and self-confidence in any way, for fear of being linked to this stereotype, and so it is increasingly risky to be 'emancipated' or to call oneself a feminist.

The reaction of rejection and hatred towards our totalitarian past is finding its expression in our culture: in the cinema, theatre, literature and the mass media. The sharp increase in violence in society and in everyday life is reflected by a new type of film on television and in the cinema that contains scenes of violence against women – either rape or the aggressive erotica now in fashion, in which women are portrayed as mere sexual objects. Film critics have been quick to interpret this image as a metaphor for the evil past: the raped woman, they say, is the reviled totalitarian system, against which the slave, who has now risen in revolt, is discharging his anger. Sex, almost completely identified with freedom from the fetters of totalitarianism, is thus converted into an instrument, a weapon of liberation in overthrowing the system. Through this transformation, violence changes its sign from minus to plus.

The liberation of sexuality from ideological dictates is undoubtedly a positive factor if we compare it with the earlier ideological rigidity towards sexuality. Thirty years after the Western sexual revolution, it is time for Russia to experience one as well. But this version of free love does not guarantee sexual freedom for all – because its form and content are overtly phallocentric, it is 'sex according to male rules'. Woman is assigned the role of a passive object in this new cultural niche. Only by this passive role, and in this context, can she achieve her own 'positive' self-realization in contemporary Soviet reality, and thus acquire a *plus sign*.

Madonna and Whore, or, From Minus to Plus

Today's positive heroine is more complex than before. Like Janus, she is double-faced. As in the ancient male definition of woman as two opposing, mutually contradictory personae which is relentlessly imposed upon us, she is both Madonna and whore; the Virgin Mary and Mary Magdalene.

The first persona is as old as the earth itself and possesses enormous power over men due to its ideal purity. If this has always been a model for all women (a model that male power has foisted on them) then the second model, the seductive whore, is a phenomenon new to Soviet culture in the perestroika era.

The image of woman as whore, or lascivious seductress, is, however, proceeding with difficulty. The period of sexual liberation in Russia has been too short for it to be fully accepted into Soviet culture. Puritanism – whether it be Christianity, Judaism, Islam or the totalitarian Communist faith – always tends to suppress natural sexual desires. When the forces of suppression are removed, the unleashed energy can cause an explosion.

In the last three or four years the doors of censorship have opened and released an incredible amount of erotica and pornography on to the Soviet market, only a fraction of which can be classed as useful educational material. Needless to say, almost all of this literature, video and cinema is primarily male-centred and sexist. It is made by men for men, and it is men who reap its huge profits. Women are merely exploited and utilized as objects.

Many sexual cartoons, which are published not only in pornographic collections of sexual jokes but also in established media like the newspaper *Moskovski Komsomolets*, are overtly misogynistic in content. This is perfectly understandable, since a repressed, enslaved mentality is incapable of light-hearted, non-aggressive humour. But the choice of subject for this sort of woman-hating humour is certainly not accidental.

Nevertheless, the overall tendency and goal of this new socio-sexual phenomenon undoubtedly bears the plus sign. Women are now no longer forbidden to be sexy – on the contrary, their sexuality is much encouraged. If in the very recent past the image of a pretty, but brainless, young woman was ridiculed and criticized, it has now become the desired model, her external appearance more and more fitting the image of a Barbie doll or pin-up beauty. Together with the image of good wife and mother, this model is now being promoted as the real, feminine woman so dear to Russian male culture.

Encouraging women to emulate this model is not only ideological but quite commercial. The numerous beauty contests, which have already become a tradition, broadcast to millions of TV viewers their award ceremonies. Often the prizes look most impressive, especially against the backdrop of our general poverty and scrambling for food: fur coats and watches, make-up, tape-recorders and VCRs are an enticement to young women dreaming of a better life, who know the worth (in material terms) of their own bodies.

The new trend is to reward not the whole woman, but a particular part of her. *Moskovski Komsomolets* organized two contests called 'Miss Bust' and 'Miss Legs'. The value difference in the prizes ('Bust' received a VCR; whereas 'Legs' merely a dual cassette tape-recorder) sends women a clear message that one part of their body is more important than another. The beauty market is developing rapidly; plastic surgery is available to those who want to 'correct' their inadequacies (and statistics show that breast enhancements are the most popular). Not only beauty but other traits of 'real feminine' women are now tested. New competitions have appeared on TV in which mothers and their adult daughters demonstrate their dancing abilities, answer simple questions, recognize French perfumes, and show how well they can cook. Again, prizes are awarded by the show's male host.

Socially and ideologically, the image of women as sex objects is fostered by numerous articles in the press about the successful careers of Soviet models (the most fortunate being, of course, those working in the West). You can now see personal ads in newspapers placed by foreigners wanting to marry a Soviet woman. This new version of the Cinderella story has become the dream of many Russian women.

Articles about prostitution, once indignant, angry, and puritanical in tone, now exhibit a more 'objective' and sympathetic attitude. The profession is increasingly seen as a successful means of making a living. And in a way it is, considering the rapid increase in female unemployment, especially in large cities and among educated women. Trading one's body becomes not only economically necessary but also socially justified. Conceptually prostitution is rationalized by the identification of sexual freedom with freedom as such.

Having stripped women of the military uniform and modest suits of the totalitarian past, our culture is now creating a conventional image of compliant, sexualized femininity so dear to men's hearts – submissive, tender or passionate, as the client orders.

Going against the current of the Western women's liberation movement, we are returning to the past, to the old formula of the popular tag: 'A woman should be a whore in the bedroom, a cook in the kitchen, a governess in the nursery and a lady in the drawing-room.' Despite the variety of functions, this formula narrows the sphere of a woman's existence, limiting it to the walls of her home. This model does not allow women to move out into full social activity and hence it deprives them of creative social self-realization.

Unburdened by an acquaintance with Western feminist writing, particularly in the area of sexuality, Soviet women do not understand that the celebrated sexual freedom sung by the heralds of perestroika's sexual liberation does not affect them personally; there is no place here for female sexuality as such.

In 1991 the *Leningradsky Universitet* published a series of articles by a professor of child psychology, A. Shchogolyev, under the title 'False Woman'. He describes a number of 'false' types of contemporary Soviet women, whom he calls, for example, 'falsely social', 'falsely religious', 'falsely political' (i.e., too involved in social, religious or political affairs). Similarly, the section titled 'falsely sexual woman' describes women who are sexually too active. By describing her opposite, the author constructs an image of the 'real', 'natural', 'standard' woman, who is quite simply the one who satisfies his masculine requirements and sexual appetite. The very appearance of such a tendentious and unscientific publication in an academic newspaper is shameful enough in itself, but worse is the popularity of such ideas, especially among the 'educated' circles of our society.

Also in 1991, the well-known Petersburg sexologist Lev Shcheglov published a book on sex education entitled *Sex is a Normal Thing*. The author, who specializes in male sexual disorders, carefully restricts women's sexuality to men's sexual arousal, maintaining, for example, that 'contraception should be entirely the woman's concern', and that 'if a woman takes the initiative in sex, this causes sexual disorders in the male because of her aggressive and too active attitudes'. His assessment of how women should behave sexually is determined by how easily men's needs can be satisfied. The author's reputation as an acknowledged specialist enables him to make a serious impact in creating and sustaining patriarchal mythology in Soviet society.

The other 'good' sacral part of the positive image of women does not require further establishing in our culture. The cult of motherhood has always played an important role in our society. A childless or infertile woman was always considered 'less of a woman'; someone who had not fulfilled the most important task of her life. A childless woman is perceived by our society more negatively than a woman who has children but has not managed to find herself a husband. Throughout her life the childless woman bears the stigma of being defective, and it is no coincidence that there are so many single mothers in our country. In this sense, in our social and cultural development we are close to the primates, where the pack is divided into two groups: females with their young and, separately, the males.

Motherhood has become more accentuated in the mass media, cinema, theatre and literature. It has become popular to publish pictures of actresses, women writers and professional women with their children, as if the man behind the camera – the social portrait artist – is prompting the woman, reminding her of her paramount role in this life. Thus, wholesale 'domestication' of the once supposedly emancipated Soviet woman proceeds apace. Her social and professional functions recede into the background and to the fore come qualities befitting the traditional Russian model of 'womanliness'. Since birth rates have fallen significantly in the last four years owing to economic and political instability, and nationalist tendencies in the former republics of the USSR have strengthened, the role of Mother of the Nation is becoming not just an ideal, but a political reality – a call to women to accept their social responsibility.

In the media this tendency is evidenced by articles on the domestic abilities of professional women, by the appearance of new women's and 'ladies' magazines – all those 'Leningradki' and 'Moskvichki', 'Madams' and 'Natalias' dazzle the reader with useful housekeeping advice, beauty tips and dress patterns, all washed down with second-rate sentimental fiction. Simplistic prose and poetry preach love for one's man, submissiveness and self-sacrifice; they glorify an image of men as knights, breadwinners and handsome princes, the likes of which are not to be found on this earth. To entertain their readers, these magazines repeat old sexist jokes, depicting the 'weaker sex' as petty, unintelligent, and second-rate human beings.

There is a growing tendency towards bolstering and reinforcing sex stereotypes: women lament the lost manliness and unchivalrous ways of modern Soviet men – who, in turn, reproach women for their lack of femininity. It simply never occurred to any of us in Russia that a battle would erupt around the invented myth about femininity and manliness. I think it was Jung who said that the range of differences between individuals is wider than that of differences between the sexes. That is, there can be more significant differences between any two women or any two men than may exist between the two sexes.

Even the traditionally respectable function of women – motherhood, always praised and sanctified – no longer helps women to improve their status. The motherhood of the Holy Virgin is just a myth, whereas the reality for Soviet mothers means hard daily labour. In Russian and Soviet culture, most of the parental responsibility is shouldered by the mother. Yet the poor economic and cultural state of Russian society today, and its reluctance to recognize women's right to equality, means that it is incapable of providing decent conditions or a high status for motherhood.

So the living space of real women is being limited by contemporary ideology to the confines of the home. Gradually being driven out of political, social and professional areas, woman as a real, living, creative and thinking individual is approaching zero level.

Zero Position or Starting Point?

The French philosopher Jacques Lacan once made the statement that 'woman does not exist'. The whole of contemporary civilization is constructed in the male image and likeness; man is the standard. In many languages the word 'man' is a synonym for 'human being'. Woman, as Simone de Beauvoir shrewdly observed, occupies the position of 'the other', the one that is different from the human being. The abstract, philosophical meaning of Lacan's dictum is almost becoming a physical reality in present-day Soviet culture.

Look at what the popular author V. Pyetsukh writes in his story 'Central Yermolayevsk War':

> Let's suppose that out of boredom a *person* has just taken a much-needed shed to pieces, . . . he has beaten *his wife* with a kitchen towel, and now here he is, sitting on his porch, smiling contentedly at the beautiful evening, when suddenly he says : 'Shall I think up a new religion or what?' [my emphasis]

A precise and well-written attitude towards human relationships. The 'person' is the creator, invested with almost divine strength; endowed, as it were, with the right to create religions, the freedom to take delight in the fine day, and to disassemble sheds. The 'wife' is an objectified creature, inserted into the enunciation between shed and kitchen towel. Any attempt to perceive her as a person in possession of her own 'I' is doomed to failure: as far as the concept of person is concerned, she is equivalent to zero, she does not exist.

At the Museum of Ethnography of the Peoples of the USSR I once viewed an exhibit showing the hierarchical distribution of power among one of the Central Asian peoples. The diagram included the usual symbolic little figures of men, sitting cross-legged against a background drawing of tents. The figures were arranged in a hierarchical pyramid, with a lone patriarch at the top. Missing from the picture were those 'other' beings who ensured the very existence of that clan, those who give birth to all the clans and tribes that exist on earth.

Reproduction, however, is a function that connects us with the whole of the living, animal kingdom – nothing more. One of the most important criteria for distinguishing the rational human being from the irrational animal is the human's ability to create, to construct and produce material and spiritual values. It is in this area that women of the perestroika era are gradually losing ground. Today's cultural environment leaves less and less room for women to fulfil themselves creatively.

Over the last five years the space for creativity has expanded considerably due to glasnost. Many new authors have appeared, both young writers and previously unpublished authors. But in this loud chorus of male voices, women can hardly be heard. Even fewer of them have been noticed: Tatiana Tolstaya, Lyudmila Petrushevskaya, Valeria Narbikova and perhaps half a dozen women poets.

The masculinization of contemporary Russian literature is evident not only in quality and content, but also in its quantity. Most perestroika publications concentrated on particularly male values: the army and war, politics and the gulag prison camps (described in memoirs and articles by men). Writing about love, feelings and emotions was replaced by primitive, barbaric and explicit depictions of sex – something quite new in the Russian literary tradition.

The gradual exclusion of women from the spheres of public life narrows the framework of their literary image as well. They are left in the main with the image of objectified sexuality or the metaphorical personification of the hateful totalitarian system – in characters like teachers or the Party officials of the Stalinist era. Sometimes we also find a model of 'positive', 'natural' femininity – an idyllic image of the ideal wife and mother, usually lacking in flesh and blood.

Who else, if not women themselves, can express their own feelings and experiences? But many Soviet male writers subscribe to the notion that women are not fit for the writing profession. Women's writing is considered second-rate. No wonder some women writers prefer to conform to the traditional masculine model of writing. The female view of the world, their feelings and heartfelt emotions, has become un-fashionable.

Male writers' egoism cannot accept that a woman can write just as well as a man. Are we supposed to feel touched when the only attention shown to a woman writer is when her age is omitted in the blurb accompanying her published work? This looks all the more silly in collections by writers of both sexes, where only the male authors' dates of birth are indicated. Surely women are not being complimented in having their age taken away from them, but are in fact being deprived of part of their personality?

Women writers, however, since they are part of the given culture, usually conform to the male model. With the exception of Lyudmila Petrushevskaya, Larissa Vaneyeva, and Marina Palei, who certainly have their own inimitable and distinctly feminine style, nearly all other women writers (in literature and journalism, on television and in the cinema), deprived of their own 'I', sing along with this male chorus. Practically all the new papers and magazines with 'feminine' names and topics follow the masculinist cultural imperative, shaping a traditional, conformist type of woman.

Some authors go further, for example, Tatiana Tolstaya. Annoyed at Western feminists, Tolstaya has published several irate anti-feminist articles in the Soviet press and abroad. Her articles in *Moscow News* entitled 'Let's Not Teach Grandad How to Cough' is surprising, since the writer's fury is directed at a feminist movement that scarcely exists in Russia. The lady authors in tabloids such as *Natalya* or *Womanly Happiness* have a much milder, more 'feminine' approach. Their publications often feature banal 'ladies'' jokes tinged with misogyny, which paint the stereotypical one-sided image of women as silly, naïve and helpless consumers.

In the popular new erotic magazine for men, *Andrei*, artist Svetlana Borisova has a cartoon series depicting sexy little kittens under the heading 'Svetlana Borisova in Search of a Heroine'. The text accompanying these saucy little sketches continually stresses the theme of female devotion to lord and master.

The nullified personality and objectified function of images of women can be seen particularly clearly in contemporary Soviet advertisements and commercials. The most striking of these, patriarchal in the extreme, shows a woman who, with her back to the viewer, portrays the submissive secretary of a young businessman – a boy of nursery-school age playing with a model steamship. Deprived of her face (her personality), the various parts of her body dismembered in order to sell anything, the image of women in advertisements is utterly deprived of all individuality and reduced to nothing.

The rapid development in Soviet journalism that took place with the advent of glasnost brought many talented journalists to the fore, including some outstanding women. It is paradoxical that not one of these has so far actually made a statement on her own behalf or on behalf of women as a group, despite the vanguard position occupied by the mass media in today's cultural scene. Moreover, in the majority of 'progressive', 'democratic' publications like the Moscow magazine *Stolitsa* (Capital), or papers like *Kuranty* (Chimes) and *Moskovskiye Novosti* (Moscow News), articles on women's issues make up less than one-hundredth of all material published.

Journalists' attitude to the mystical concept of 'feminism' deserves special attention. It was only three or four years ago that the word began appearing in the papers. The context is invariably negative or, at best, ironic in character and provides no useful information. Slowly but surely the mythology of antifeminism is being created. Thus, for example, an article in the youth magazine *Pulse*[3] dedicates an entire ode to the anniversary of the ladies' bra. The word 'feminism' can be found in the text, in the following connection: 'Burnt in public during the aggressively feminist years, the brassière last year celebrated its one hundredth anniversary in an atmosphere of total rehabilitation.' The two are clearly polarized: *aggressive* feminism vs blessed brassière, the symbol of femininity. In one of its issues the paper *Moskovsky Komsomolets* published a sexy photograph of a heavy-metal rock singer, headlined 'She Calls Herself a Feminist.' The text accompanying the photograph was full of sexual innuendo and had nothing to do with feminism.

The aggressive rejection of feminism in Russia is on the rise, especially in 'democratic' and 'progressive' circles. The notion that the concept of democracy unquestionably entails a movement towards equality has not yet penetrated the consciousness of our progressives. This is emphasized by the present discord among nationalities. There can surely be no radiant future unless we learn to be tolerant, unless we truly understand the meaning of the word 'pluralism'.

And yet new feminist thinking is gradually filtering into Russian culture. Words and expressions such as 'feminist', 'emancipation', 'women's liberation', 'equality of the sexes', etc., can now be encountered and are beginning to be debated in Russian society. There is still a very strong reaction to them and reluctance to accept such ideas, but the first step has been taken.

Myths have always played an important role in our irrational, ritualistic Russian culture. The image of the Holy Virgin or the fairy tale of Cinderella seem more real than real life – which, especially nowadays, has become a daily struggle for survival, with the problems of unemployment, inflation, and childcare (the last too expensive for many women). So it becomes preferable for reality not to exist, for real women to escape this harsh reality and become reduced to nothing – a zero. Yet our history teaches us that reality is inexorable and unavoidable. The real, living Soviet woman cannot exist in the narrow confines of two-dimensional images. Every one of us contains pluses and minuses, but also our own authentic self – our hopes and desires, ambitions and talents.

And in many ways Russian women have already begun their journey back to reality. Many new independent women's organizations – professional, political, humanitarian – have appeared during the last four or five years. Between 1990 and 1992 women writers published four collections of female writing. There are many talented women among them and each has her own voice and style. These publications are an indication of how women have been brought together by the sheer necessity of creative survival in a world of male competition.

New kinds of women's magazines have appeared that show an interest in issues of gender equality – for example, *IEVA*, published in two languages in Lithuania, *The Women's Club*, a quarterly, and newspapers like *New Woman* and *Businesswomen*, published in Moscow. Also in the forefront are the talented film director Kira Muratova and a women's rock-group, Kolibri, whose style is unmistakable. A young generation of poets and prose writers is also demonstrating great potential for independent creative development.

The influx of information from the West gives us knowledge and experience of the women's liberation movement, and I am sure that these influences will bear fruit in the near future. With the revival of our historical memory we can find many examples from the past of great, intelligent and brave women who fought for our equality, and this will also help us to acquire dignity and self-respect. We have already moved from our zero starting-point. The rest is simply a matter of time.

Notes

1. The word 'Soviet' signifies the cultural reality and mentality of society in the former USSR.
2. *Stolitsa*, no. 23, 1991.
3. *Pulse*, no. 11, 1991.

9

Virgin Mary or Mary Magdalene? The Construction and Reconstruction of Sex during the Perestroika Period

Olga Voronina

At the very beginning of that process we call perestroika, the Soviet mass media began to change public awareness by opening up new topics for public discussion and interpreting old topics – such as the Revolution or Stalinism – anew, and by publishing previously unknown historical materials and testimonies in mass-circulation newspapers and magazines. In doing so, the press contributed in no small measure to freeing people's consciousness. However, none of these innovative publications ever found the space to discuss the problem of discrimination against women in Soviet society. The women's issue actually disappeared altogether from the pages of the press and from our TV screens at the very beginning of perestroika.

But after journalists had had their fill of sensational topics and facts too hot to handle, they discovered the need for something new, and did in fact get around to discussing the position of children, women and the elderly. After a number of articles on the plight of women in the workplace, on their gynaecological and obstetric problems, on the strain of women's everyday lives and on children left to fend for themselves, it became obvious that the position of women in Soviet society was far from desirable. But from the very beginning, media discussion of this issue took a strange turn. Not only were women's issues viewed quite openly as being a matter for women alone and not for society as a whole, but discussion of these topics gradually turned into a debate on the nature of the Soviet woman and what she should be in order to be a 'real' woman, not a 'Soviet' woman.

The well-known Russian writer Valentin Rasputin, with the dignity his position affords, reminds us that women's responsibilities are to 'feed her family, surround her husband with loving care, raise her children, be a good neighbour'.[1] Poetess Larissa Vasilyeva suggests we concern ourselves with raising 'womanly, not sexless beings', with the aid of more space in the press devoted to 'Housekeeping', 'How To Be Beautiful', 'The Kitchen and Culinary Problems' and so forth.[2] This identification of women with the kitchen is to be found practically everywhere. In an article intended as a teaching aid, one author stresses that emancipation should not be understood as 'freedom from every-thing that makes women womanly, such as freedom from bothering about a shirt for her husband or getting his dinner ready'.[3] (Following this logic, we should no doubt regard as 'non-women' all those who for one reason or another are not burdened with worrying about their husbands' shirts – that is, widows, unmarried and divorced women, women who send their husbands' shirts to the laundry or those whose husbands wash their own!)

In a short piece entitled 'Professional Dedication', *Pravda* reports that in contests for best nurse and best female doctor, not only professional qualities were taken into account, but also . . . the contes-tants' culinary abilities! 'And this is understandable,' the paper writes, 'after all, most medical staff are women.'[4] This is a typical example of covert sexism, one of the ways in which our patriarchal Soviet society exercises control over women, who are never allowed to forget what it means to be a 'real' woman.

The notion that a woman's culinary abilities are an integral part of her existence and the best proof of her 'real nature' is so deeply embedded in our national consciousness that it is virtually impossible to find anything in the media about women that does not mention the kitchen or the family.

An *Izvestiya* feature about Academician Tatiana Zaslavskaya, for instance, showed her holding a samovar; a television report about Professor Natalya Rimashevskaya showed her alongside a spinning wheel. In a feature about a female police lieutenant-colonel, one journalist (a woman) not only described in great detail how her heroine could knit and what a good cook she was, but even let readers into a special 'secret of feminine wisdom' by relating that when her lieutenant-colonel policewoman is at home, 'she doesn't begin the washing, cooking and cleaning until she has dressed and put her make-up on'.[5]

Even organizations one would have expected to take a different view of women follow the popular notion of 'women's mission' and 'woman's nature'. Tass information bulletins and those of the Soviet Women's Committee, for instance, alongside stories about outstanding women of the world, invariably carry recipes, tips on make-up and advice by psychologists and sexologists on how to achieve harmony in the family and success in personal relationships.

Incidentally, innumerable items of advice in the mass media from professional psychologists contribute towards disseminating and keeping alive the patriarchal ideology about 'women's mission'. The main point of all this advice is to remind women that it is they who are the guardians of the home fires, that their place is in the home, but that at the same time they should not forget that the head of the family is of course the man. Thus, in one issue of the popular women's magazine *Rabotnitsa* (Working Woman), a Doctor of Medical Sciences authoritatively asserts: 'In addition to their traditional *biological* functions – childbirth, feeding, rearing, *culinary concerns* – women now have a new role: active participation in public life. Not all women can manage to combine both functions' [my emphasis]. He goes on to propose a simple solution to this situation: 'Let women have a shorter working day . . . and give their husbands a wage rise. This will raise the man's role and authority in the family and make him into the real leader.' He is echoed by another writer – incidentally a woman Ph.D. candidate in Psychology – who gives this arrogant instruction to 'irrational' women, ostensibly with all the authority of her discipline: 'Male psychology is such that the man has to feel that he is the head of the family, whatever the conditions. Even if it is the woman who shoulders all the problems, the husband should not be made aware of this.' She shows no interest at all, as a professional psychologist or as a woman, in the psychology of women – what they want, what they feel, or what husbands ought to do to make their wives feel good within the family!

I could go on for a long time listing views of this kind, but I think I have given enough examples to show the general trend. It is not even a question of whether women's social destiny is determined by certain characteristics 'of nature'.[6] I look on the mass media's homilies that women should be selfless and self-sacrificing (as if these were essential features of their nature) simply as a demagogic cover for the prevailing utilitarian, consumerist and disdainful attitude towards women.

Men's predetermination of the role and place of women in society according to sex ('a woman's place is in the home') is as old as the world itself. Nowadays public opinion in civilized countries looks on such ideas as discriminatory against women – and therefore anti-democratic and anti-humanistic. But in our country the campaign to revive patriarchal ideology unfolds against a backdrop of proclaimed principles of democratization and humanization of society and the formation of a rule of law[7] and under the slogans of a critical reappraisal of the past and alleviating the lot of women.

What is paradoxical and ambiguous in this situation is, first, that it is

intended to 'return women to the home' without taking any account of
our opinion (for nobody is seriously interested in finding this out) and,
second, that the ideology of women's mission is now actually being used
in this country to justify and intensify discrimination against women both
at work and in the family. The ideology which says that 'the family is the
woman's business' fulfils an extremely important function in patriarchal
Soviet society: it allows responsibility for the results of many years of
shortcomings and errors in the state's social policy with regard to the
family to be put on to the shoulders of 'emancipated women', 'carried
away' by their careers and forgetting their mission in life. The founder of
a special school for young people, K. Rash, accuses working women of
'not considering it a disgrace to put their children in a nursery'. Writing in
Pravda, Rash goes on: 'It does not break their hearts to leave their
children there, nor does it cause them to stop gratifying their vanity by
working and stay at home with their children instead'. 'Women working
outside the home means disintegration of the family and a low birth-rate',
Rash warns.[8]

A newspaper with a different political orientation, *Kuranty*, is,
however, at one with its ideological opponent *Pravda* on this issue:
'Women who work outside the home cannot really be called mothers or
wives', lectures one cabaret artiste, who for the last thirty years has
carefully avoided following that stereotype of the woman's mission which
she considers *de rigueur* for all other women.[9] Or to take another
example: 'There's always a woman behind each and every kind of
trouble', claims Valentin Rasputin.[10]

On the other hand, despite all the media calls for women to return to
the home, it is doubtful whether the state is preparing the real conditions
to enable those women who want to do so to be reasonably well provided
for. In a country whose backward economy literally rests on the
large-scale cheap manual labour of women in the fields, in factories, on
the railways, in warehouses, in shops and hospitals (where 81 per cent of
health service personnel, 75 per cent of education staff and 61 per cent of
specialists are women), turning the huge numbers of working women into
housewives will spell social and economic disaster. Clearly, in this
situation reviving the stereotype about 'women's mission' has a quite
definite ideological function: it enables women to be kept in secondary
and subsidiary roles, in low-prestige and low-paid jobs and, more
importantly, it justifies the isolation of women from politics and
management.[11] And during the present economic crisis the return to
patriarchal stereotypes legalizes mass sackings of women and preservation of jobs for men – 'the family breadwinners' (and quite often it is
through female job losses that the conditions are created for raising the
wages of the remaining men).[12]

Good to point out the contradiction of female unemployment, but the stereotype of woman's mission is not purely ideological. It has a material base – reproduction.

The resurgence of patriarchal ideology paves the way for another trend – to regard women who are keen on their jobs, who are 'career-minded' or who want to be socially and politically active, as unfeminine and anti-family. It is especially interesting that this is the view within certain 'intellectual' circles which actively support and sustain this trend in the public consciousness – the Russophile writers and, in particular, psychologists. The poet Larissa Vasilyeva argues: 'A woman wants to be a person among people, an active member of society. Is this a natural aspiration? Yes, if it does not negate her desire to be a wife and mother.'[13] Thus, a woman's right to be called a person is made dependent on her willingness to follow her 'innate mission'. The writer Valentin Rasputin is convinced that 'emancipation is the degeneration of the weaker sex, a moral mutation'.[14] Similar ideas about women can be found in Vasily Belov's celebrated novel *Everything Lies Ahead*; in Anatoly Kurchatkin's novel *Evening Light*; and in V. Gusev's short story 'Alien Woman'.

But I would like to look particularly at the negative role our professional psychologists play in implanting the patriarchal outlook in the public consciousness. Not only do they possess a sacred belief in the absolute truth that the different sociological (gender) roles of people are determined by nature (biologically), but they even propagate these ideas in the mass media. For many years professional psychologists have been playing up the negative consequences of the 'masculinization' of women and the 'feminization' of men as a consequence of women's emancipation. They appeal to women in a variety of ways to be (or at least to appear) weak, tender and passive, since, according to them, men can only be made strong through interaction with weak women. Thus over-emancipated women are to blame, psychologists often conclude, for the weakness of today's men.

Other arguments along the same lines are that 'career orientation and independence of thought in girls' entails the 'inculcation of male characteristics, marking a considerable deviation from normal development',[15] to quote a scientific journal.

But I was struck most of all by the article by a psychotherapist, A. Shchogolyev, published in three issues of the newspaper *Leningradsky Universitet* under the sensational title 'False Woman'. Not troubling himself with reflections or an acquaintance with world experience in analysing women's issues, the author asserts, as if it stands to reason: 'A woman's aspirations towards primordial male creativity – and it is in this that the "intellectual woman" wants to succeed – is direct proof that she has closed herself to what is genuinely feminine in herself.' 'Hypertrophic intellectualism in a woman is clearly a neurotic phenomenon', he writes, and later continues:

At moments of profound spiritual crisis the 'intellectual woman' feels as if her intellect were an unwanted growth, a useless makeweight, an annoying corn, disfiguring her womanly nature. . . . Women's intellectual work is essentially a banal, often absurd compensation for the intellectual woman's innate insufficiency of femininity. There is always a more or less hidden element of hysteria even in her purely professional opinions and convictions. . . . The 'false woman' cannot be [Pushkin's] 'wonderful moment' that lights the spark of inspiration for an individual's creative fire . . . her existence in no way contributes to real creativity, without which a person's life loses all meaning.[16]

If we sift out all the rhetoric from these statements, we are left with one very simple thought: women's mission is to serve as the source of human inspiration and creativity. The overt misogyny of this professional psychotherapist is, of course, disturbing enough; but one cannot help but laugh at the poverty of his ideas about the human being and creativity.

It is surprising that although such views on women are generally accepted in Soviet sex psychology, the impression is given that scarcely any of these 'professionals' suspect that they merely echo the ideas of Sigmund Freud, as outlined in his article 'Anatomy is Destiny'. According to Freud, the differences in male and female anatomy form two specific characteristics (fundamental for the development of the female psyche) – the castration complex and penis envy. These complexes, in Freud's opinion, determine three possible ways in which the female psyche can develop: one leads to suppression of sexual impulses and therefore to neuroses; the second leads to women modifying their personalities in the male image. This is characterized by manlike aspirations to be creative, have strong social interests and be active in public affairs, etc.; and the third leads to normal femininity, which Freud understands as achieving a desire to possess the object of their envy, through marriage and childbirth. In other words, for Freud, the symbol of full human value is a certain specific male organ, and the lack of this in women, which in his opinion inevitably causes envy, predetermines the three types of female personality and destiny: hysteria, mannishness and 'normal' femininity (which is realized in the bedroom).[17]

These views have been subjected to criticism by psychoanalysts (Hannah Arendt, Karen Horney et al.) and within the framework of psychoanalytical feminism. Soviet psychologists' simplistic perceptions and attempts at transplanting on to our soil ideas about what constitutes a 'normal' woman testify more to their own ideology than to their scientific objectivity.

Another deeply rooted sexist tendency characteristic of our mass media is their transmission of ideas about women as obviously inferior, second-rate and defective human beings. For instance, in answer to a question about why there were no women on the political television programme '9th Studio', the presenter, Leonid Zorin, gave the 'witty' reply that since this was a programme for intelligent people talking about intelligent things, there was simply nothing for charming women to do. On one side of its 'family page', the newspaper *Nedelya* offered a description of a new game parents could play with their children to train powers of observation. The piece was called: 'Daddy and his Son are Clever' (although the game did not have any sexual dimension at all). On the other side of the page were cooking recipes under the heading 'For You, Ladies'. And in this same paper a psychologist giving advice on how to settle family rows characterizes women as chatterboxes, troublemakers, gossips, telltales and slatterns, while she represents men as nice, rather absent-minded fellows, worn out by work and their wives.[18] Women, it seems, are more suitable for the demonstration of negative human qualities: in order to teach tact and delicacy in family relationships a relevant example is a troublemaking wife;[19] a pretty but empty-headed woman demonstrates the need to observe traffic safety rules in a traffic police advertisement.

The poet Yuri Kuznetsov, writing in *Literaturnaya Gazeta*, declares: 'Women are doers, not creators. Women have not created a single great work. . . . In poetry, women introduced nuances of a female mood that arose from the mess and chance whims of their personal lives . . . no motif of a humanistic or even national nature has ever sounded in their verses.'[20]

In addition to the tactic of ignoring women's positive qualities, another method is employed to give a negative assessment to those qualities historically ascribed to women (the clearest example here is emotionalism). There is a very obvious double standard in judging emotionalism: where the family is concerned, female emotionalism is presented as something good; in other areas of life it is seen as a shortcoming.

The mass media often use the tactic of keeping women in the background (when authors or reporters are men, and women are in attendance as typists or receptionists and 'adorn' the screen with their presence). Women are virtually absent from the mass media (apart from specifically women's pages and programmes, the overwhelming majority of reports, news, photographs, articles and topics in practically all newspapers and TV programmes are about men); women are remembered on International Women's Day. If there is a report about some woman scientist or deputy, it is presented as if they were talking about a yeti.

Traditional public opinion polls for 'Person of the Year' put forward only leading male personalities; women figure in a quite different questionnaire under the heading 'Woman of the Year'. We have only to recall that the biggest compliment our men can make to a woman is to tell

her that she has something extra, apart from the purely feminine –
something that all 'normal' people have, like a 'man's brain'.

The poet Kuznetsov does not resort to allegories to assert his ideas: he
straightforwardly declares that 'if man is a unit, then woman is a
fraction'.[21] Or take the deputy head of labour resources and employment
at the USSR State Committee for Labour, Ye. Afanasyev, who once
stated bluntly: 'Enterprises . . . are striving to be profitable, but we are
asking them to hire young people, women with children, amnestied
ex-convicts. In my opinion,' he continued, 'the local Soviets should allow
enterprises to raise their profitability by relieving them of the
responsibility to find jobs for teenagers and women.'[22] Notice that it is not
a question of women's qualifications or vocational training. Our
'comrade boss' does not want women around, full stop. And he has no
compunction in putting women on the same level as prisoners released
under amnesty. And although this particular official no longer holds his
position and the USSR no longer exists, the ideology is still in place and
still operating . . .

The fourth masculinist tendency in our mass media is not only the
ascription of negative characteristics to women, but the creation of a
sharply negative stereotyped image: women as the embodiment of all that
is dirty and disgusting. This tendency is partly a natural progression from
the former – viewing women as second-rate beings is easier and more
convenient if they are essentially bad and dirty – and in part reinforces the
former tendency. The poet I have already mentioned several times, Yury
Kuznetsov, maintains that if men think of God and godly things, then
women think only of base and depraved things.

In 1988, when I had just begun work on this topic, I did an analysis of
that year's publications devoted to the image of women (not 'women's'
issues, but simply their image). It turned out that in the vast majority of
these publications, women were depicted in an extremely negative way –
as prostitutes, drug addicts, alcoholics and 'cuckoos' (that is, women who
abandon their babies in the maternity hospital). Another example: a
piece about AIDS begins with a reminder to readers about 'high-risk
groups' – and prostitutes are almost always at the top of the list. AIDS is
often identified with them (for instance, health education posters put out
by the Ministry of Health consist entirely of pictures of a seductive
woman – or parts of her body – and the words: 'Fear AIDS!' Moreover,
even when the talk is of prostitution or giving up babies for adoption as a
widespread phenomenon, no one ever mentions the social causes or male
behaviour in these situations. Thus, talk about negative social phenomena is replaced by the idea of individual guilt and the amorality of
women as such. Women alone are held responsible for amoral acts
involving two people – only women are usually blamed for prostitution

(even though it is demand that gives rise to supply). And when commentators talk of 'cuckoos', they never mention the men involved, as if men had had nothing to do with the problem. The double standards in respect of men and women may be observed not only in statements like 'you won't find bad men in the company of a good woman', but also in the fact that, for the same misdemeanours, women are subjected to harsher social sanctions. I believe that this attitude can be traced back to Christian ideas about original sin, in which it was supposedly the initiative of Eve which caused the downfall of Adam, which in turn led to sinfulness in the whole of humankind. It is paradoxical that such echoes of traditional Christian views should be discovered in our atheistic consciousness.

Sometimes the misogyny of our society can be discerned in situations that bear no relation to women at all. In *Moscow News*, for example, I once came across a small piece about KGB phone-tapping, which stated: 'and all the telephone operators employed in tapping our phones are women'. Everybody knows that to say that the KGB is bad simply on the grounds that all its officers and generals are men is absurd; but to draw a link between the obscene unconstitutionalism of phone-tapping and the telephone operators' sex is perfectly all right . . . The utter nonsense of the notoriously misogynistic Yevgeniya Albats in *Moscow News* does not offend the editorial board's taste because the abasement of women and everything female has become normal for this country. Outlining our unhappy future, Albats writes: 'The authorities will try to prevent a social explosion . . . by further limiting the sale of alcoholic drinks. WOMEN will be the main driving force behind the riots; consequently, these will immediately become very AGGRESSIVE' [author's emphasis]. In a country where it is men who get drunk in vast numbers, why would restrictions on the sale of vodka provoke women to riot and act aggressively? But it is perfectly acceptable for such nonsense to appear in a popular newspaper.

The so-called 'beauty contests' are particularly responsible for the increase in pornography, in the sense that they create an atmosphere of obscenity, degradation and sexualization around women. What has it got to do with beauty when half-naked women are measured and compared according to the size of their breasts, ankles, waists – and even sometimes checked as to whether they are virgins – by men, 'smartly dressed' for the occasion in evening dress? The amorality of such contests is made worse by the fact that they are being popularized as if they were a way of expressing admiration for female beauty in a country where the majority of women have no chance of having a healthy body: their bodies are disfigured from youth by poor diet, heavy work, too many abortions, brutal births and the never-ending heavy shopping-bags. In how many households, I wonder, do women get home after work at the factory, carrying the usual bags of food bought after standing in queues for hours, not surprisingly after all that not looking like the beauties on the TV screens, only to have to put up with their husbands' vulgar jokes and comments about their looks?

Scorn and contempt for women, an abasement of women which at the same time makes them feel guilty about everything that they do, how they look and everything that happens to them – this is the attitude that is constantly reinforced in the public consciousness. It is openly supported and transmitted by this country's mass media. These tendencies have become stronger in recent times. The amoral, antisocial and destructive thrust of these tendencies is there for all to see. Genuine humanization and democratization of society requires that the curse that has ruled women for centuries be overcome, and the whole of society and culture be liberated from sexism and masculinist ideology.

Notes

1. V. Rasputin, 'Cherchez la Femme', *Nash Sovremennik*, no. 3, 1990, p. 169.
2. L. Vasilyeva, 'The Living Soul of Woman', *Pravda*, 4 March 1987.
3. L. Kovalenko, 'Women's Lofty and Wonderful Mission', *The Education of Schoolchildren*, no. 1, 1986, pp. 66–8.
4. *Pravda*, 21 November 1989.
5. *Sudarushka*, no. 2, 1991, p. 10.
6. One cannot help recalling here Adolf Hitler's 'ideology of the three Ks' for women – 'Kinder, Küche, Kirche'.
7. The very concept of a law-based state is as yet semi-barbaric in this country: even our most progressive statesmen seem to think that it can be created merely by drawing up a lot of good laws. Nobody raises the question of whether these laws are being implemented or observed. It is apparently for this reason that sexism is gaining ground through replicating the ideology of woman's mission in life. And the fact that this takes place in a country which signed the United Nations Convention on overcoming all forms of discrimination against women raises no objections from anybody.
8. K. Rash, 'More Precious than Any Kingdom', *Pravda*, 22 February 1989.
9. 'Against Matriarchate', *Kuranty*, 27 March 1991.
10. V. Rasputin, 'Cherchez la Femme', pp. 168–72.
11. The results of a sociological survey into people's voting intentions in parliamentary elections showed that most of those questioned thought that the most important parameter in the questionnaire (which included age, sex, party affiliation, nationality, family situation) was the candidate's sex – and, naturally, it had to be male. *Argumenty i Fakty*, no. 43, 1987.
12. An analysis of managerial and administrative redundancies, carried out by the Centre for Gender Studies at the Russian Academy of Sciences' Institute for Socio-Economic Population Studies, revealed that 80% of those made redundant in 1990 were women.
13. L. Vasilyeva, 'The Living Soul of Woman', *Pravda*, 4 March 1987.
14. V. Rasputin, 'Cherchez la Femme'.
15. *Sotsiologicheskiye Issledovaniya*, no. 4, 1987, p. 83.
16. A. Shchogolyev, 'Lozhnaya Zhenshchina', *Leningradsky Universitet*, 16 March, 23 March and 13 April 1990.
17. S. Freud, 'The Dissolution of the Oedipus Complex', *Standard Edition of the complete psychological works of S. Freud*, vol. 19 (London 1964), pp. 170–92. S. Freud, 'Femininity', in *New Lectures on Psychoanalysis* (New York 1933), pp. 170–85.

18. *Beata Busheleva, 'Nye nanesi obidy', Pravda*, 1 November 1989.
19. S. Ya. Doletski, 'Umeniye byt' shchastlivym', *Nedelya*, no. 17, 1987, p. 8.
20. Yuri Kuznetsov, 'Pod zhenskim znakom', *Literaturnaya Gazeta*, 11 November 1987, p. 5.
21. Yuri Kuznetsov, 'Pod zhenskim znakom'.
22. Ye. Afanasyev, 'Bez raboty sredi morya raboty', *Argumenty i Fakty*, no. 45, 1989, p. 4.

10

The Lesbian Subculture: The Historical Roots of Lesbianism in the Former USSR

Olga Zhuk

A lesbian subculture simply did not exist in the former USSR in the sense that it did in the West. This is mainly because it was invisible. There were no clubs, bars, cafés nor, indeed, any specific behaviour patterns. In the last two years, mixed homosexual and lesbian organizations have appeared in the major cities of the Russian Federation; there is a lesbian club in Estonia, mixed discos in Moscow and St Petersburg. There has been an upsurge in lesbian culture and art, too, but none of this has radically altered the situation, nor could it have been expected to.

This essay does not claim to be a definitive investigation into the origins of something as complex and diverse as lesbian subculture in the former USSR. It merely attempts to define its place within a specific historical context. There is very little literature on this subject. For many decades lesbianism and homosexuality were taboo themes for Soviet science and the media. These topics were analysed exclusively in medical literature[1] and then from a very different standpoint than that of contemporary West European or American science. That is, homosexuality and lesbianism were treated as a deviation from the sexual norm, as a perversion or an illness. The situation has improved slightly over the last few years; books written from a more modern standpoint have appeared, which examine the question of homosexuality in an objective and unprejudiced way.

Among these is an academic book based on research by a well-known Soviet aestheticist and sexologist Igor Kon, 'Introduction to Sexology',[2] which is the study of sexual cultures, and, in a totally different genre, an essay by the Russian author Tatiana Suvorova and her German colleague, Adrianne Gaigess.[3]

It was only during perestroika that it became possible to publish these two works, though even then there were obstacles. The authors chose

146

different genres, set different goals and wrote for different readerships. Kon's work investigates the historical and cultural preconditions for the emergence of a mythology around lesbianism, but does not deal with the present situation. Suvorova and Gaigess give a good picture of the present-day scene, but their essay deals more with the moral issues.

The lesbian subculture in Russia and the former Soviet Union finds representation only in Western studies, e.g., in books and articles by the leading American Slavonic scholar, Simon Karlinsky, in particular his work on Tsvetayeva;[4] Vladimir Kozlovsky's[5] dictionary devoted to criminal and camp subculture; the works of the first Soviet feminists (now living abroad), Yulia Voznesenskaya[6] and Tatiana Mamonova.[7] Simon Karlinsky's well-documented books and articles are concerned more with concepts than with problems. Vladimir Kozlovsky is more interested in the philological and etymological aspect of the homosexual, principally male, subculture.

Yulia Voznesenskaya and Tatiana Mamonova wrote virtually the only authentic work about Soviet reality and therefore attempted to answer a number of questions about the position of women in Russia. Their book contains a great deal of new and interesting material, but the wide range of issues covered deprives their work of a certain depth of analysis and makes it difficult to draw general conclusions.

A definite lesbian subculture existed in pre-revolutionary Russia at the turn of the century and for the subsequent three decades. It had its own individual spiritual mythology, aesthetics, culture and art.

Pre-revolutionary Russian lesbian literature includes such well-known names as Zinaida Gippius, Lidia Zinovieva-Annibal, Yevdokiya Na-grodskaya, Lidia Charskaya, Marina Tsvetayeva and Sofia Parnok (of all the aforementioned writers she was to some extent the arbiter of lesbian artistic tastes in post-revolutionary Russia too).[8] These writers are all very different in their talents, world view, and in the way they approach the lesbian theme, yet all of them together comprise an artistic stratum that we can certainly refer to as a Russian lesbian subculture. And this applies not only to their works, but also to their artistic image and the literary and artistic world in which many of them played an important role at the beginning of the twentieth century. We can therefore say that by 1917 a lesbian subculture had undoubtedly taken shape in Russia. It continued until the early 1930s when almost all the spiritual traditions of the past underwent transformation; the old relations collapsed, spiritual continuity disappeared for ever, leaving behind only fragmentary and local centres of culture. A new kind of person, a new system of values and a new type of relationship began to take shape within the lesbian subculture.

The old romantic image of two female friends – the 'elder' and the 'younger'[9] – was replaced by a faithful replica of heterosexual role relations, 'he' and 'she', due to the change in historical and cultural mythologies. Tsvetayeva's ambiguous, charming creature 'not woman nor boy. But something stronger than me' (M. Tsvetayeva, 'Podruga', no. 10), 'The tenderness of a woman, the boldness of a boy' ('Podruga', no. 9), which was appreciated precisely 'For that wonderful irony, that you are not he' ('Podruga', no. 1) gave way during the thirties and later to an odd sort of woman, trying hard to be like a man. The fictional element of masquerade was replaced by socialist realism's duplication of the surrounding banal and tedious world of simple and clear relationships – 'he' and 'she'. The new 'aesthetics' were not peculiar to Soviet society, but could be observed in Western Europe and America during the post-war years. But in the USSR, due to the particular way in which society developed within the system of concentration camps and their exact reflection 'outside', the new aesthetics acquired special features, which again not only had its place in the lesbian subculture, but also helped to shape it and give it its particular character.

Totalitarianism had a particular effect on people's state of mind in society, where the main problems, not least of which were sexual problems, were deliberately made taboo. Much was due to the fact that Soviet culture was new, as indeed were Russian history and nationhood, compared with Western Europe. And like any new formation, it was characterized by rather strong polarization, which in the homosexual subculture found its expression in certain traditions, rituals and ceremonies. Totalitarian conformity in questions of activeness or passiveness, the fixed nature of role functions and sexual conduct led to a caste system in the subculture along the lines of ancient cultures.

Until the beginning of the Second World War, female prison camps were sited next to male camps: living quarters were separate but men and women worked alongside each other. And although it was not encouraged – in some cases it was even punished by the camp administration – inmates of different sexes did sometimes engage in sexual relations. This did not, however, prevent the growth of homosexual relations, which were also banned. In the Stalinist camps it was of course the criminal milieu that made the running. It was here that homosexual relations of a definite type were formed, and these have remained practically unchanged until now. Stark delimitation of the sexual, psychological and hierarchical functions of the active and passive partners are most characteristic of male camps, where the active partner, according to the camp's own 'table of ranks', does not consider himself a homosexual, and the passive partner is usually humiliated – 'abused', and may be subjected to all sorts of indignities.[10] In the female 'zone'[11] the hierarchical pyramid and 'moral code' is entirely different. Unlike the male 'zone', lesbianism is not forced, but voluntary. The partners are 'socially' equal, though the sexual behaviour of each of the partners – of each of the 'halves' – is from the outset predetermined and monofunctional.

Now let us look at the reasons for the origin and development of female homosexuality in camp conditions. During the post-war decades the practice has been to segregate the sexes, which deprived inmates of any choice from among the opposite sex. Thus the question of sexual orientation was determined right from the outset – if there was to be any sexual activity at all, it would have to be exclusively homosexual.

Most first-time female offenders have no earlier lesbian experience. They fall under the influence of more experienced inmates who have been in prison and camps for years. These women, who have usually been convicted more than once, offer a set pattern of sexual relationships: the active partner – *kobyol* (butch) – and the passive one – *kovyryalka* (femme).[12]

Girls brought to young offenders' colonies often have no sexual experience at all or have had nothing more than childhood relations with inexperienced boys of their own age. Yet, because they have been brought up in heterosexual society, they have a clearly defined psychological orientation towards family relations. Under the influence of criminal stereotypes, this orientation becomes grossly deformed and leads to changes in role functions. Pathological disturbances lead to savage occurrences, such as rape – the so-called 'uncorking' of virginity with a spoon.[13] New *kobly*[14] practise mainly on *malolyetki* (young girls), and it is the *kobly* who, having passed through a young offenders' colony, then go on to dictate their particular style of sexual behaviour in the adult 'zone'. This tends to be imposed on everybody, even on 'professional' lesbians with experience of such relationships in the outside world, as a result of free choice.

Kobly behave like men both socially and in their intimate lives. The *kovyryalka* does everything for the *kobyol* – washes her clothes, prepares food, etc. The social behavioural role of the *kobyol* and *kovyryalka* are a distorted reflection of the patriarchal and strictly regulated structure of heterosexual Soviet families, where women, in this case the *kovyryalki*, are assigned a secondary, subordinate role.

In intimate relations the role conduct of *kobly* is an attempt to imitate men. All that is feminine is suppressed and concealed, and so the *kobyol* does not get fully undressed and does not allow her genitals to be touched. The sexual act is also carried out along male lines. In contrast to patriarchal Soviet male chauvinists, the *kobly* care about the sexual satisfaction of their partners, and perhaps it is due to this quality that they have achieved such popularity among a certain group of women who value the traditional sexual act. *Kobly* enjoy a number of privileges – their 'other halves' not only solve all their domestic problems for them, but sometimes even do their work quota as well. Clearly it is advantageous to be a *kobyol*, so even women without transsexual leanings tend to change into *kobly* at the earliest opportunity.

Women need spiritual warmth more than men, but their behaviour conforms to the usual psychosexual stereotypes. By posing as substitute men, the *kobly* offer the essentially familiar type of relationship. Initially, this is what women expect of them. But in many cases they begin to find that something is lacking; they want to feel the fullness of lesbian relations. In this case the relationship is not merely one of physical satisfaction but the full range of lesbian psychological experience. Cases of passionate love are widely known, where one of the 'halves' serving a shorter sentence deliberately breaks some administrative regulation not long before she is due to be released, so as to stay in the colony with the partner she loves.

The entire system of female corrective labour colonies was infused with lesbian passions. Drama-filled true stories, cast in the form of romantic legends and tales, described unfaithful wives of camp administrators in love with *kobly*, with all the soulful passion of lonely hearts stifled by the boredom and monotony of everyday existence.

Prevailing opinion in penitentiary conditions was primitive and naïve in the extreme.[15] So even if their views on intimacy in relationships were not lesbian, *kobly* were unable to transgress the many taboos and were forced to conform to generally accepted norms of behaviour.

Soviet reality was in many ways a copy of the criminal underworld and it is no coincidence that we find an extension of the 'zone' family outside among the working class, especially among its lumpen elements. Some of these women experienced camp life and follow their own sexual inclinations once they are free. But the psychosexual type of relationships, of the kind we see in the camps, is not only due to the direct influence of the 'zone'. Its roots go much deeper – they are to be found in the patriarchal and archaic nature of many of our traditions which is why this type of relationship often tends to be stable. The difference between the 'zone' and freedom is simply that there is a choice. And how is this choice exercised by lesbian-inclined girls from the working class? Their stories are so alike that in the minds of our researchers they have long since become one large epic comprising many similar plots with slight differences. Before meeting her *kobyol*, a girl from this background – even if in childhood or early youth she has experienced lesbian feelings – will long since have got rid of them as a result of heterosexual society's clear orientation towards marriage and childbirth. But life will have turned out considerably more complicated and different from her romantic, rose-coloured picture of a fairy-tale prince and pure, noble love. Her first experience of love will often leave her with feelings of disgust and despair. The man has turned out to be boorish and unfaithful, and their drunken intimacy has resulted in unexpected and unwanted conception. Then follows abortion, separation, loneliness and heartache. And then a *kobyol* or kind-hearted girlfriend comes on the scene. From confidante she soon becomes 'admirer'. With her *kobyol* it is easier, more comfortable – and her female stereotype as a girl remains the same. The *kobyol* starts to court her: she brings her flowers, invites her to a restaurant and so on. The new 'suitor' is affectionate, well-mannered and loving. In intimate relations she tries to give her pleasure. No wonder that the girl starts to feel love for her. Besides, since there is no possibility of children, she does not fear an unwanted pregnancy. Couples who have been together for many years may break up, but the girl's circle of reference will now only be lesbian. The sexual scenario changes over the years and becomes exclusively homosexual. Partners tend to be chosen for their similarity to the first lesbian love. Maternal instincts become more marked with age, the woman starts to want a child (if she did not already have one from her unsuccessful affair or marriage). So she has a child, using a man simply as a stud, and continues to live with her female lover, bringing up the child jointly.

In most cases couples like these share common property and run the house together. The structure of family and daily life differs little from the average Soviet heterosexual family; work, shops, visits with friends at weekends, but the surrounding world, apart from those close to them, is unaware of the true nature of the relationship. If the *kobyol* uses the masculine in referring to herself, the couple can often deceive neighbours, and sometimes even parents. Or in other cases, those around them often suspect nothing, assuming that it is simply two lonely women 'surviving' our harsh reality together.

The older generation of women in technical professions and to a lesser extent in the arts, who live together call one another 'sisters'. In most cases the spiritual bond 'mother–daughter', 'older sister and younger sister', is in effect violated. It is preserved formally in the use of the term 'sisters', which, to some extent, serves as a continuation of centuries-long traditions. But the desire to hide their relations from those around them is usually damaging to people and human relationships. Carefully conceal-ing their love, living in perpetual fear of being found out, inwardly split in two, they become hostile in their relations with the heterosexual world, which, naturally, responds in similar fashion. In this milieu one often comes across couples deprived of any homosexual circle of reference, women who do not have great experience of lesbian relationships and who do not identify themselves with lesbians, and who in fact get upset at the very use of the word and would never themselves say it aloud.

There are always two related reasons for homophobia, like other forms of xenophobia – the intolerance of society towards minorities and deviations from the accepted norm, and the aggressiveness or vulnerability of those who are discriminated against. These are expressed in the ugly forms of repression that we come across in modern society. It is like the executioner and his victim. Thus, because of society's negative attitude towards homosexuals and lesbians, and the guarded, at times openly hostile attitude of homosexuals and lesbians towards society, they often do acquire certain unattractive features and behaviour that most ordinary people think characteristic of people with homosexual orientation. Men, as a rule, tend to become timid, pathologically reticent; women can seem cowed, unattractive, sometimes paying no attention to their outward appearance. Many women not brave enough to stand up to society's homophobia and philistine ignorance become prey to public opinion, unwittingly influenced by the viewpoint prevalent in our male-centred, patriarchal consciousness – that women are driven into becoming lesbians because they are unattractive to men. So they often do turn into those ageing and resentful 'old maids', pictured in the fevered imagination of the Soviet philistine.

Some intellectuals of the older generation hold to the persuasive, but surely long outdated, view that Russia and Russian history have a different cultural and spiritual tradition from the West. Apart from the short period following the Revolution of 1905 and the outbreak of World War I and the flashes of keen interest in problems of sexuality at the very beginning of the Bolshevik period – when it was considered one of the ways of combating the 'old sanctimonious and hypocritical bourgeois morality' – the theme of intimacy has consistently been taboo in Russia. Following Russian national traditions, the Russian mentality and the Russian Orthodox influence, Russia is emerging today on to a new, different road, on which there is room both for the development of science and of sexuality, a civilized, not sanctimoniously hypocritical attitude towards sexual relations, including homosexual relations. If Russia goes along this road, then in a few decades the historical roots of lesbianism in Russia and the former USSR, in the form in which they exist today, will simply be a subject for study, and the lesbian subculture will acquire the great spiritual traditions of the past – the spiritual mythology of Ancient Greece – and the best achievements of modern West European society.

Notes

1. Cf. *Individual Sexual Pathology*, ed. G. Vasilchenko, in 2 vols (Moscow 1983); A. Svyadoshch, *Female Sexual Pathology* (Moscow 1974).
2. I. Kon, *Vvedenie v Seksologiyu* (Moscow 1989).

3. A. Gaigess and T. Suvorova, 'Lyubov' vne plana' (Moscow. *Sobesednik*, 1990).

4. S. Karlinsky, *Marina Tsvetayeva* (Cambridge 1986); S. Karlinsky, 'Russia's Gay Literature and Culture: the importance of the October Revolution'. And in the book: 'Hidden from History: Reclaiming the Gay and Lesbian Past.' New York. New American Library, 1989, pp. 347–65.

5. V. Kozlovski, *Argo russkoi gomoseksual'noi subkultury*. Benson. Chalidze Publications, 1986.

6. Yu. Voznesenskaya, *The Women's Decameron*. Boston Atlantic Monthly Press, 1986.

7. T. Mamonova, *Women and Russia. Feminist Writings from the Soviet Union*. Boston Beacon Press, 1984.

8. S. Parnok, *Sobraniye stikhotvorenii. Vstupitel'naya stat'ya, podgotovka teksta i primechanii* by Sofia Polyakova. Ardis/Ann Arbor, 1979. S. Polyakova, *Nyezakatnye ony dni: Tsvetayeva i Parnok*. Ardis, 1983.

9. Cf. M. Tsvetayeva, 'Podruga'. In: S. Polyakova, *Nyezakatnye ony dni: Tsvetayeva i Parnok* (Ardis, 1983). And M. Tsvetayeva, 'Pis'mo k Amazonke', *Zvezda*, 1990, no. 2, pp. 183–91.

10. Cf. L. Samoilov, 'Puteshestviye v perevernuty mir', *Neva*, 1989, no. 4, pp. 150–64.

11. *Translator's note*: 'Zone' is the word used popularly to mean detention and labour camps.

12. *Translator's note*: *kobyol*: a variant of the word *kobyel'*, which means a male dog. *Kovyryalka* is formed from the word *kovyryat'* – to poke around, pick at.

13. Cf. I. Leshchiner, 'Devochki v robakh.' *Yunost'*, 1989, no. 4, pp. 50–51.

14. *Translator's note*: *kobly*: plural of *kobyol*.

15. Cf.: L. Samoilov, 'Puteshestviye v perevernuty mir', *Neva*, 1989, no. 4, pp. 150–64.

11

Feminism in Russia: Debates from the Past

Svetlana Aivazova

Russia at the end of the eighteenth century lagged behind the rest of Europe, but the most enlightened groups of Russian society took a keen interest in what was happening elsewhere in Europe, while developing their own ideas independently. The emergence of a new attitude towards women in Western society, the birth of a new feminist consciousness, the advent of a new type of woman – all signs of society's emancipation did not go unnoticed in Russia. The same process had already begun in Russia. We do not have to go very far to find examples. That brilliant expert on the history of his time, Alexander Pushkin, repeatedly speaks of these new developments. One has only to look at his notes entitled 'Table Talk', for example, where he writes:

> Is it not ridiculous that women, who impress us with their quick comprehension and their subtle feelings and reason, are considered inferior beings as compared with us! This is particularly odd in Russia, where Catherine II reigned and where in general women are more enlightened, read more and follow European trends more closely than we proud ones, God knows why.[1]

Pushkin himself, in both his life and work, followed 'European trends'. We have only to recall, for example, his famous poem 'Gypsies'. Pushkin scholars long ago correctly pointed out how Pushkin's ideas in this poem correspond with those of French philosopher Jean-Jacques Rousseau, founder of the theory of 'natural law'. But there is one important difference they have failed to recognize. According to Rousseau, only members of the stronger sex should enjoy the full range of rights and freedoms: he never overcame his mistrust of female abilities. Pushkin's hero Aleko is conceived in the image of Rousseau's 'natural' man: he seeks liberty and free love – but he alone has the right to these. He kills the woman who has dared to live and feel the way he does. In Rousseau's view, she could not be allowed such freedoms. But Pushkin himself has a different view: the old gypsy tells Aleko that Zemfira is free, that she is in charge of her own life and her love, as all free people are. Pushkin's view was that it is either one thing or the other – either natural law for all, which includes women, or both men and women should submit to authority. Pushkin's poem is clear evidence of the emancipation process that was just beginning among the most enlightened groups in Russian society.

Not only was Pushkin ahead of his time in his views on women's right to freedom, but he also describes how women were themselves changing and acquiring a new awareness. His short story 'Roslavlyov' relates how on the eve of Napoleon's invasion Moscow high society was delighted to meet one of the greatest celebrities of the time, the French writer and thinker Madame de Staël. Why delighted? Because she was a woman who had dared to challenge Napoleon Bonaparte, the fearsome subjugator of Europe, of whom she was an enemy. She was forced to flee, but wherever Napoleon's troops were, she could find no safe haven. He pursued her through Europe, but finally she reached Moscow, where she was fêted. Pushkin himself was an ardent admirer of de Staël and shared many of her views. She was a convinced advocate of English constitutional monarchy, and had tried during the 1789 French Revolution to turn history in the same direction in her own country. Pushkin's heroine, a young, aristocratic Russian girl, was also 'in love with the famous woman, as kind as she was great'. It was not the traditional female virtues that the young Russian noblewoman found so fascinating in Madame de Staël. She was won over by her amazing ability to 'influence public opinion', by her 'bold mind and soul' and her 'patriotism' in the loftiest sense of the word. These can all be viewed as indications of the new female consciousness.

A decade later, the behaviour of Russian women confirmed what Pushkin had been so quick to grasp – a new female individuality was being born in Russia. The fateful year of 1825 had arrived.[2] Of course, women did not join their husbands and brothers in Senate Square,[3] but they did show their understanding and support throughout the terrible days of reprisals. The most loyal set off to join their menfolk in the grim conditions of Siberian penal servitude; those who stayed behind kept their memory alive. This required courage and a new civic conscience. In his memoir *My Past and Thoughts* Aleksandr Herzen recalled the high morals, even heroism, that these women displayed and reflected: 'Female evolution is altogether a mystery: at first it's all nothing, just dressing up and dances, playful gossip and reading novels, eyes brimming with tears – and all of a sudden you find this gigantic will, mature thoughts and a colossal brain. The young girl carried away by passions has disappeared and we see in her place Théroigne de Méricourt, beauty of the tribunes, who can move the popular masses'.[4] In *My Past and Thoughts* Herzen describes his meeting with one of these new Russian women, whom he calls 'gentle Charlotte Corday' or 'Charlotte Corday from Oryol' because of her fighting spirit and fervent faith in her mission to influence her country's destiny.[5]

Judging by Herzen's memoirs, the leading Russians of his time already knew about the impassioned women involved in West European revolutions, in particular the French Revolution. This awareness took the shape of a series of symbolic images, each of which represented a particular type of political behaviour or a specific social and political position. His generation – that of the revolutionary democrats of the 1860s – was schooled in this system. In the words of Herzen's friend and colleague Nikolai Ogaryov: 'the young generation inherited a feeling of political freedom with a certain European flavour, but with the presentiment that something was also about to happen in Russia.'[6] This inherited feeling of political freedom took for granted that the liberation of Russian society from the feudal autocratic yoke was unthinkable without emancipation from society's patriarchal ways and traditions. Emancipation of women was seen as the guarantee of genuine equal rights and freedom.

Nikolai Chernyshevski, a prominent influence among progressive youth of the 1860s, expressed this mood better than anyone in his novel *What Is To Be Done?*. When he describes the new relations between men and women, and between the 'new' people, Chernyshevski refers allegorically to the experience of the French revolution and its ideas. A mysterious 'radiant beauty' appears in the famous 'fourth dream' of the novel's heroine, Vera Pavlovna. Before teaching Vera the new principles for life, the radiant beauty reveals the riddle of her origin: 'Men were becoming wiser, women were more and more certain that they were equal to men – then I was born. It was not long ago.'[7] To people of that time it was obvious that the 'radiant beauty' was a symbol of the freedom and equality that the French Revolution had proclaimed, and at the same time a symbol of the new woman. Any doubts the reader may have are dispelled later in the novel when one reads what the 'radiant beauty' thinks about the future reign of freedom and justice that she advocates:

> I have discovered something new in me . . . and that is equal rights between those who love each other, an equal relationship between them as people. . . . When a man recognizes a woman's right to be his equal, he ceases to look on her as his property. . . . This equality gives me the feeling of freedom, without which I would not exist.[8]

These could have been the words of the French advocate of women's liberation, Olympia de Gouges, or her compatriot, Théroigne de Méricourt, that 'beauty of the tribunes', or the 1789 leader of the Parisian poor – Claire Lacombe. Chernyshevski's romantic allegory reminds us of all these women. It is interesting that whereas the slogans of these early champions of women's liberation met with fierce resistance from the male section of Western Europe's democratic movement, in mid-nineteenth-century Russia the opposite was the case. Chernyshevski's novel shows that for the Russian revolutionary democrats, the aim of the fight for emancipation was to create the most favourable social conditions for the complete development of a woman's personality and abilities. They wanted their campaign to bring about radical changes in social relations and humanize relations between men and women.

Though not a great work of art, Chernyshevski's novel caused a stir in Russia's political and ideological life. He ensured that emancipation became one of the most important topics of public debate. Virtually all major Russian thinkers therefore felt compelled to respond. Dostoyevsky, Tolstoy, Solovyov, Berdyayev, Fyodorov and Rozanov all interpreted it in their own way. While one would come out in defence of age-old patriarchal principles, another would talk of eternal feminine qualities and the human soul or of the equal value of Sophia (Wisdom) and Logos (Reason). Representatives of the Silver Age of Russian philosophy went further and talked of the mystery of the sexes, the mystery of life, death, love and the transient significance of the patriarchal division of social roles into 'male' and 'female'. Some even argued that the perfect individual was ultimately androgynous in nature. Nikolai Berdyayev, one who put forward such a concept, writes:

> The approach of a new world epoch is preceded by profound upheavals in the nature of sexuality. The new person is above all a being of transfigured sex, recalling the androgynous image and likeness of God, which has become distorted by the separation into male and female in the human race. The mystery of the human being is tied to the mystery of the androgyne.[9]

It is important to note that the key point in this discussion was the emancipation of each individual 'from the enslavement of constraining objectivity' and from 'ancestral clan power over all', which was patriarchal in form. Berdyayev also emphasized that the patriarchal family represented a tyranny much more dreadful than that of the state:

> The hierarchic, authoritarian family mistreats and maims the human personality. The profound significance of the emancipation movement which abhors this type of family is the struggle for the dignity of the human personality.[10]

It is interesting that these ivory tower philosophers, for whom emancipation was an important topic, regarded Chernyshevski as their direct predecessor. Berdyayev himself referred to this: 'Chernyshevski's *What Is To Be Done?* is a lacklustre work of art. . . . But from the social and ethical point of view, I totally agree with Chernyshevski and have the greatest respect for him. Chernyshevski is utterly correct in his humanistic championing of freedom for human feelings. . . . His book, vilified by rightist circles, contains a strong ascetic element and great purity. . . . This nihilist and utilitarian genuinely advocated that women's free development was sacred.'[11]

Russia in the late nineteenth century was riven by political and ideological battles. Historians and political figures harked back to the Chernyshevski tradition in their discussion of the nascent women's movement and emancipation which seemed to point towards an era in which a new kind of individual would exist. But there were very different opinions as to what the new individual would be like and what the consequences would be for the world. Liberal individualists and Marxist collectivists stood at opposite ends of the spectrum. For the liberals, emancipation was a social and cultural phenomenon; while Marxists insisted that its emergence was socially and economically determined. Liberals viewed emancipation as a unique process that shaped the individual and enabled self-realization; whereas the Marxists reduced emancipation solely to the 'woman question' and made its solution dependent on radical social changes alone and, in the final analysis, on the triumph of the proletariat. V. Khvostov, a Moscow University history professor, A. Sologub-Chebotarevskaya, who researched cultural questions, and Ye. Shchepkina, a historian and liberal activist of the women's movement, all supported the social and cultural approach in their studies.

V. Khvostov analysed the concept of emancipation throughout the development of civilization, and was convinced that the emergence of the women's movement marked a turning point in the history of humankind. The 'age of predominance of physical strength' was coming to an end, he wrote. 'A feeling of altruism is gradually becoming predominant in our culture, and spiritual strength is starting to be valued more highly than physical force.'[12] Woman, who embodied these spiritual and altruistic principles, was now in the forefront of history. Khvostov viewed equal rights for women as part of the overall demands for human rights and dignity of the individual. He was convinced that these demands marked the transition to a genuine democracy, which was unthinkable without women being fully involved in public life. Khvostov believed that the idea of equal rights for women had been disseminated in the eighteenth century primarily through the influence of Enlightenment philosophers. This was inevitable because, paradoxical though it may seem, women predominated in the fashionable high-society salons. 'In these salons ladies engage most successfully in politics and strive to have their say in public affairs. It was under the influence of such salons that public figures of the time like Mesdames Necker, Rolan and de Staël took up politics. Women took a great interest in the modern philosophy of the French encyclopedistes and contributed in no small way to disseminating those new ideas, although the attitude of the encyclopedistes themselves towards such female activities was far from sympathetic.[13]

Anastasia Sologub-Chebotarevskaya greatly admired the culture and ideas of the eighteenth century. She called it the 'age which saw the greatest development of personality', when subversively attractive theories of visionary freethinkers abounded and the individual and his or her rights were highly regarded and respected. It was this century that had placed human rights at the top of its agenda and pushed women onto the historical stage.[14] Sologub-Chebotarevskaya considered the well-educated society hostesses of the Paris salons to be women of a new type – women interested in public and political affairs. They were turning their drawing rooms into a 'laboratory of public scrutiny in the realms of politics, literature and the arts', where 'they in their own way were preparing for revolution'.[15]

Shchepkina agreed with the general view that the first 'eruption of aspirations to liberation' in women came as a result of the ideas of the Enlightenment, which had been a gradual liberating force in society. However, Shchepkina was the first historian to acquaint the Russian reader with the biographies and opinions of the illustrious equal rights campaigners Olympia de Gouges, Théroigne de Mericourt and Claire Lacombe. Olympia de Gouges has the honour of being the foremother of feminism: she penned the 'Declaration of the Rights of Women and Female Citizens' demanding the civic recognition of women. Théroigne de Méricourt was an example of a woman who took part in the revolutionary movement as a political leader and 'comrade to the men', an equal among equals, representing her 'Women's Party'.[16] Shchepkina's heroines are dedicated to revolution. They champion 'respect for the natural rights of the individual and humanism'. They uphold the idea of revolution, seeing it principally as a process which would 're-educate the nation morally' and implement the principles of Paine's *Declaration of the Rights of Man*.

The entire social and cultural approach to emancipation and the women's movement was subjected to harsh criticism by the Marxists, who had become firmly established in the revolutionary movement at the beginning of the twentieth century. They considered themselves the true heirs of the revolutionary democrats of the 1860s and paid close attention to all ideas of revolution and emancipation. Alexandra Kollontai, the Bolshevik activist no less famous than Shchepkina's heroines, became the mouthpiece for their ideas. She was famed as a fiery orator and theorist, who had the ability to expound in simple language on the theories of Marxist classics on the question of emancipation, which was considered a women's question. Kollontai showed convincingly how the 'woman question' was caused solely by social and economic development – or rather, by capitalist economic development, which brought women into the production process. She argued that it was a progressive step for women to work outside the home, since it enabled women to free themselves of economic dependence on their husbands, leave behind petty domestic concerns and be full members of society. But, she argued, in the initial phase of capitalist relations women were exploited as hired labourers, therefore their liberation was inextricably linked with the liberation of the proletariat, and the woman question was simply one form of the proletarian class struggle. Kollontai maintained that talk of the Enlightenment's influence, the moral re-education of society and re-education of women, or application of the principles of the *Declaration of the Rights of Man* were nothing more than 'bourgeois feminism'.

Kollontai tried to prove that the social and cultural approach to emancipation and the women's movement was a distortion of the history of the woman question. She believed it failed to take into account the new 'economic basis that puts women – as a labour force – on an equal footing with men'. Advocates of the social and cultural approach, Kollontai claimed, were guided solely by 'intellectual conclusions, arising from their declared position on human rights'.[17]

Kollontai not only rejected such liberal interpretations of emancipation; in a sense, she rejected history itself. She therefore revised history by declaring that feminists' actions during the bourgeois revolution had been 'premature', since economic relations at that time were still not ripe for the recognition of equal rights for women, as 'the broad masses of women had not yet been drawn into capitalist production'. Or, as she writes elsewhere: 'The question of equal rights for women . . . did not arise from the relations that were being formed as the bourgeois class consolidated its supremacy.' Kollontai was convinced that the real heroines of the new era were not those first feminists – as, say, Shchepkina would have it – but the 'anonymous female masses', who selflessly fought for the rights of the entire 'downtrodden, hungry and ragged working people'. Such women thus 'did more for the principle of equal rights for women than even the most outstanding speeches of individual, but lone, champions of bourgeois feminism.' After the 1917 revolution Kollontai stressed that only 'the proletarian revolution in Russia, by concentrating all its strength on creating a new economic order, is at the same time solving . . . the great, insoluble problems of the French Revolution: equality, fraternity and equal rights between the sexes'.[18]

Those who advocated a social and economic solution of the woman question thus replaced the concept of emancipation with the 'woman question'; and they replaced the concept of female personality with the female masses. This substitution of terms explains the subsequent history of emancipation and the women's movement in Russia. At the height of the dispute between liberals and Marxists in the first decade of the twentieth century, the women's movement in Russia was rapidly gaining strength. Women's newspapers and magazines had a mass circulation, among them popular titles like *Zhenski vestnik* (Women's Herald), *Zhenskoye Dyelo* (Women's Business). There were active organizations such as the Women's Mutual Charity Society of Russia, the Union of Equal Women and the Women's Progressive Party. The Bolsheviks fought these for influence over the female masses – and won.

When the Bolsheviks came to power their first decrees granted women in the new country of Soviets the full extent of legal rights and freedoms. But at the same time they banned the activity of all independent women's organizations, thus for many years putting an end to the independent women's movement. The new authorities took full responsibility for teaching women about the new society and their new rights and obligations, and set their best cadres to this work. In their struggle to emancipate society, Alexandra Kollontai, Inessa Armand and Nadezhda Krupskaya contemplated another revolution – a revolution in domestic life. Their plan was for the state to set up a large network of public dining-rooms, laundries, nurseries and other public facilities, in order to free Soviet women from their domestic worries and the burden of housework. Women, thus emancipated, were expected in turn to engage in socially useful work. Kollontai openly declared that the new society would need to 'forge an army of women workers and peasants from the female labour reserves'. This directive, together with the revolution in domestic life, was replaced by Stalin's blunt slogan: 'We'll free the peasant women by putting them to work.'

And so there came into being female work brigades, the stakhanovite movement, the first women tractor-drivers, weaver heroines and builders of Komsomolsk-on-Amur. This was accomplished by one order after another in the praesidiums of meetings and congresses. These were the focal points of a widespread campaign to solve the woman question and the issue of Soviet women's work and domestic life. Finally, in 1936, Stalin's Constitution ceremoniously proclaimed that this question had been resolved, a task of enormous historical importance had been carried out and genuine equal rights for women had been ensured. Since that time, this assertion has become firmly entrenched in all resolutions, official speeches, scholarly works and school textbooks. The truth was that women, 'emancipated' in this easy way, found it difficult to cope with their double burden – at work and in the home. They had not been relieved of the worry of how to earn their daily bread, nor freed from fears for their children left without supervision. These concerns were simply dismissed as 'trivial' details belonging to women's private lives. No wonder our women today have a real aversion to the words 'emancipation', 'feminism' and 'women's movement'. Many women also wonder what is meant by 'liberation from the power of men', when no such power exists.

The mysterious disappearance of the individual and the human being – both men and women – is the main result of the 'solution' to the historic task of achieving equal rights for women in Russia. This is the sum total of the debates about emancipation and the women's movement that Russian society conducted throughout the nineteenth century right up to October 1917.

Is this peculiar achievement really the only possible one? I think not. The democratic changes in our society, however slow-moving they may be, are nevertheless raising the question of freedom and equal rights, and the liberation of every person from the 'enslavement of constraining objectivity'. Unfortunately, at present such ideas of liberation are in danger of being overwhelmed not merely by prevailing patriarchal attitudes but also by materialistic values and crude consumerism. Despite their dissimilarity – or perhaps because of it – Pushkin, Chernyshevski, Solovyov, Berdyayev and Rozanov are in fact more interesting and more relevant than some of our own contemporaries. They speak of what is most important at the present time – the need to revive the individual and personal dignity – for both men and women. We are also seeing the rebirth of feminism in our society, but so far it is regarded more as a problem than as a challenge.

Notes

1. A.S. Pushkin, *Works*, vol. 7 (Moscow 1962), p. 215.
2. *Translator's note*: In December 1825 there was an uprising of army officers, known as the Decembrists, which was bloodily suppressed by Tsar Nicholas I. Decembrist leaders were either executed or exiled to Siberia.
3. *Translator's note*: In St Petersburg, where the Decembrist uprising took place.
4. A.I. Herzen, *Byloye i dumy*, Part I (Moscow 1969), p. 347.
5. *Ibid.*, Part II, p. 252.
6. N.P. Ogaryov, *Izbrannoye* (Moscow 1983), p. 354.
7. N.G. Chernyshevski, *Chto delat'?* (Moscow 1957), p. 276.
8. *Ibid.*, pp. 278–9.
9. N.A. Berdyayev, *Smysl tvorchestva* (Moscow 1989), p. 418.
10. N.A. Berdyayev, 'On Enslavement and Freedom of the Human Being', in *Philosophy of Love*, vol. 2 (Moscow 1990), p. 407.
11. *Ibid.*, p. 416.
12. V. Khvostov, *Zhenshchina v obnovlennoi kul'ture* (Moscow 1917), p. 8.

13. V. Khvostov, *Uchastiye zhenshchiny v umstvennoi kul'ture Chelovechestva* (Moscow 1914), p. 15.

14. A. Sologub-Chebotarevskaya, *Zhenshchina nakanune revolyutsii 1789 g.* (St Petersburg [Petrograd] 1922), pp. 26, 34, 56, 73.

15. *Ibid.*, pp. 86, 89.

16. Ye. Shchepkina, *Zhenskoye dvizheniye v gody frantsuzkoi revolyutsii* (St Petersburg [Petrograd] 1921), pp. 28, 36.

17. A.M. Kollontai, Foreword to Ye. Shchepkina, *Zhenskoye dvizheniye v gody frantsuzkoi revolyutsii* (St Petersburg [Petrograd] 1921).

18. *Ibid.*

A Feminist Critique of Policy, Legislation and Social Consciousness in Post-socialist Russia

Anastasia Posadskaya

Over the last twenty-five years, the women's movement in the West has successfully overturned, or at least called into question, many persistent stereotypes concerning the position of women in society. One such stereotype is that 'women's' issues will automatically be solved when society has created the requisite economic and social conditions. In my view, experience has demonstrated that only an independent strategy – one worked out *by* women, not *for* them – can truly transform gender relations. Otherwise we shall merely see a move from one form of patriarchy to another.

We in this country can now look at our experience in solving the 'woman question' not only during the period of 'actually existing socialism' but also during the perestroika years.

Whenever I address Western readers, I feel I must clarify the meaning of the concepts used. When I speak of socialism, I am not referring to the theoretical construct that may correspond to the Marxist, social-democratic or some other socialist tradition. I am talking about *real* socialism, a specific historical period in the life of the state that until recently was called the USSR. With the virtual political disintegration of the USSR into separate independent states, I think it can be said that perestroika's formal temporal setting was April 1985 to December 1991, at which time the main building destined for reconstruction – the USSR – ceased to exist as a single political entity.

The events of the last eight years have radically transformed the economic, political and cultural paradigm of the peoples inhabiting this country. The political transformation of a one-party totalitarian system,

164

as it passed through the stage of glasnost, has resulted in the formation of a multi-party system and the rudiments of a civil society. However, it has become abundantly clear that the democratization of society has turned out to be a male project in which women are assigned the role of objects, not subjects, of social reforms, although this may not always be obvious.

The experience has raised a number of questions. Why is it that over half of Russia's population is not taking an active part in Russia's opportunity for democracy? What are the prospects for feminism in present-day Russia? What changes are there in policy on women and in the state bodies responsible for implementing this policy? In what way is society's image of women changing? Who is today's 'new woman'? Is she unemployed or an entrepreneur; custodian of the family or an escort-girl for the new Russian businessman; young 'model' or domestic servant in the homes of the new middle class? This chapter attempts to draw a picture of women's situation in the new Russia.

Women and Politics

Gender relations have a certain structure that permeates all spheres of social life, breeding sex inequality. It is this structure, acting as an invisible gender barrier, that an individual has to overcome on the road towards any kind of self-fulfilment.

That is why, for example, the outwardly 'sexless' strategy for transition to a market economy has different consequences for men and women. If it continues, the situation is fraught with danger of social unrest. In the same way, granting women 'equal' voting rights (abolishing quotas for women) has meant a sharp fall in the representation of women in the power structures. This is mainly due to the fact that former policy not only failed to overcome, but to a certain extent even reinforced, the gender barrier for women who sought a political career, because it discredited the image of the female politician.

Research has shown (see the draft outline for the State Programme for Improving the Position of Women and Protection of the Family, Motherhood and Childhood [1990], Women in Modern Society [1991]) that socialism did not succeed in overcoming the patriarchal nature of gender relations; rather, it reduplicated them at the level of society as a whole. The gender dimension of the social reforms begun in 1985 remained virtually unnoticed until 1989. This year can be considered something of a watershed: quotas for women's representation in the country's parliament were partially lifted, thus halving the number of women represented there. It became clear that the 'successes of the socialist state in achieving real social equality of the sexes' had been largely symbolic.

We are therefore faced with a situation where it is essential to elaborate a special policy aimed at achieving sex equality. However, the fact that the ideology and practice of social equality became discredited during the period of state socialism puts into jeopardy the success of any social policy aimed at egalitarianism. At the level of political decision-making, this is expressed in the freezing of social programmes and the merely rhetorical nature of such programmes; in transferring to local authorities the functions of social provision for the population; in abandoning the practice of positive discrimination for certain sections of the population (workers, collective farmworkers, women, youth, etc.) by means of quotas of seats in parliament and the administration. As a result, both old and newly formed social structures engender the patriarchal type of gender relations, in which women and everything female is subordinate, derivative, specific and secondary to everything male. What are the historical and political roots of the present situation?

The feminist tradition that had existed in Russia was interrupted by the socialist revolution. The revolution had its own conception of how to solve the 'woman question', which was not to treat this problem separately from the overall problem of social reform. The main components of this socialist strategy are well known: drawing large numbers of women into social production; the so-called socialist transformation of everyday life, the accent being on developing this area; emphasis on the social upbringing of children; propaganda about new relations between the sexes.

Alexandra Kollontai was an outstanding propagandist of this strategy.[1] But the Bolshevik leadership did not give equal attention to each of the planks of this policy during the process of socialist reconstruction of society. Most attention was in fact given to drawing women en masse into social production[2] while other components of this policy – such as the sort of work women do and to what extent they are involved in decision-making, or developing services or propagating new relations between the sexes – were not properly implemented. As regards the universal democratic aspirations of equality of men and women before the law, the unequal status of women in conjugal and family legislation had already been put right during the brief rule of the Provisional Government (February–October 1917) and by the first Soviet Constitution of 1918.

The Russian feminists at the turn of the century – the *ravnopravki*, or equal rights girls, as they called themselves – were eliminated from the history and memory of future generations by the Bolshevik era. The October coup of 1917 initiated the rapid legalization of sexual equality, and the Communist Party itself conducted an active policy among women right up to the beginning of the 1930s. But once the Party declared in Stalin's 1936 Constitution that equality between men and women had been achieved in the country, it closed discussion of the woman question, putting a stop to any interpretations that might have been at variance with the 'spirit of great achievements'.

At that point a period of what I call 'symbolic equality' began. The gender dimension of social existence was, as it were, transferred to a kingdom of distorted mirrors: on the one hand there was the successful façade, which had a life of its own; on the other, 'beyond the looking-glass', actual gender relations existed, but remained outside society's field of vision.

The sole feminist attempt at criticizing this 'beyond-the-mirror land', undertaken by the authors of *Woman and Russia* in the late seventies, ended, as we know, with their expulsion from the country.

The early perestroika years witnessed a revision of socialism's social doctrine: less radical on the part of Party functionaries whose intention was to 'improve' socialism; more radical on the part of the newly emerged democratic opposition. In relation to the idea of how to solve the woman question, the ruling party put forward the well-known theory expressed by Mikhail Gorbachev in his book *Perestroika*.[3] First came the usual list of 'achievements' in solving the woman question:

> We are proud of what the Soviet government has given women: the same right to work as men, equal pay for equal work, and social security. Women have been given every opportunity to receive an education, to have a career, and to participate in social and political activities. (p. 117)

Then the Party advances a 'new', perestroika interpretation of the woman question. In the words of its General Secretary:

> But during our difficult and heroic history, we failed to pay attention to women's specific rights and needs arising from their role as mother and homemaker, and their indispensable educational function as regards children. Engaged in scientific research, working on construction sites, in industry and the service sector, and involved in creative activities, women no longer have enough time to perform their everyday duties at home – housework, raising children and the creation of a good family atmosphere. We have discovered that many of our problems – in children's and young people's behaviour, in our morals, culture and even industry – are partially caused by the weakening of family ties and a slack attitude to family responsibilities. (p. 117)

Then comes what amounts to a revision of the concept of sex equality – one of the fundamental ideological planks in the doctrine of the entire preceding socialist period:

> This is a paradoxical result of our sincere and politically justified desire to make women equal with men in everything. Now, in the course of perestroika,

we have begun to overcome this shortcoming. That is why we are now holding heated debates in the press, in public organizations, at work and at home, about the question of what we should do to make it possible for women *to return to their purely womanly mission.* (p. 117, my italics)

What is interesting in this excerpt is that the Party claims as its own achievement the media campaign to 'return women to their real mission' – i.e., to return them to the home.

Thus, the role of women in perestroika was defined: 'Further democratization of society, which is the pivot and guarantor of perestroika, is impossible without enhancing the role of women, without their active and *specifically female* involvement, and without their commitment to all *our* reform efforts', and in this sense it was maintained that 'women's role in our society will steadily grow' (p. 118, my italics). But the Party reserved for itself the right to define the 'specific nature of female involvement'.

It is telling that this stand by what was the ruling party at the time was not subjected to any serious criticism in the pages of the democratic press. It met with a stormy reaction from international women's organizations, which as usual caught the Soviet Women's Committee off guard, so that it had to pester its academic consultants to find a democratically acceptable interpretation of this unacceptable affirmation by the ruling party's leader.

But if the Party's criticism of socialism from within at least contemplated a 'female dimension' to the ongoing social transformations, Gorbachev's pronouncement was never assessed at all, nor was any stand on this question expressed during all the democratic and radical criticism of the totalitarian state and how it could be transformed. What is this? An oversight owing to political inexperience, or a definite position that considers it unacceptable to single out the rights of individual social groups from the overall fight for democratic freedoms? I think to a certain extent both factors played a part. It became clear during the first *almost*-free elections to the USSR Supreme Soviet in spring 1989 that both Party candidates and democrats in fact held the same position on the 'woman question': women must be helped to take part in perestroika in their own specific way – by seeing to the family, children and domestic matters. Even if any candidate did have a 'women's' programme, this usually amounted to promises to shorten their working day, win further entitlements for women and so on. Today we can say that this was the only promise the deputies have kept: women are not only having their working day shortened, but are seeing it eliminated altogether, since 70–80 per cent of those currently registered as unemployed are women.

The 1990 elections to republican and local government bodies showed with utmost clarity that the new authorities would in fact shape their policies without the participation of women. In the republics, only 3–7 per cent of women were elected to parliament. The reasons for this situation are, I believe, rooted in the preceding period. The quota system discredited the image of the female politician: women deputies tended to be either textile-workers who knew nothing about politics, or 'iron' ladies from the *apparat*. It is not surprising, then, that 'being a woman' was often sufficient reason to be crossed off people's ballot papers, no matter what their pre-election programmes had been like.

Now that the multi-party system has gained momentum, the situation in future elections might be even worse: after all, there are practically no women in the more politicized parties and organizations, and independent women's organizations are still weak. The Soviet Women's Committee, which has changed its name but remains the same bureaucratic institution as before (in January 1992 it was renamed the Union of Russian Women), is not an organization capable of promoting a new type of woman politician. That is why the slogan of the First Independent Women's Forum, 'Democracy without Women is not Democracy', will probably remain topical for a long time to come.

After decades of political silence the independent women's movement in Russia is an attempt by women to speak out in their own voice: on their own behalf, concerning those problems that women themselves consider the most important. This, it seems to me, is the essence and significance of contemporary Russian feminism, even if women themselves are not familiar with the word.

The revival of feminism in Russia is not, in my opinion, a reaction against the attempt to return women to the home. We know that there have been such attempts before, even in the Soviet period (during the NEP period, the post-war years and the 1965 economic reforms), but these did not lead to a rebirth of feminism.

In my view, feminism is re-emerging in Russia because real socialism showed that attempting liberation of the sex without liberation of personality was completely utopian, while the years of perestroika prove that the reverse – liberation of personality without liberation of the sex – is doomed to failure. That is why Russian feminism's main mission today, in my opinion, is to bring about a synthesis of the two emancipations: emancipation of the personality *and* emancipation of the sex.

Which way are things moving at present? What is the position of women in the new labour market? What changes can be discerned in special legislation concerning the position of women? What gender stereotypes exist in the family?

Women in the Labour Market

The increasingly radical market economy reforms have revealed gender asymmetry. It is women, especially women with higher education, who comprise the majority of the officially registered unemployed, while the new economic structures (joint enterprises, cooperatives, private firms, etc.) employ women in a very narrow range of jobs (secretaries, consultants, low-paid service staff). Another tendency is that men are more likely to leave their jobs in the low-paid state sector and move into the socially more prestigious private sector. Women make up a tiny minority of those sent on retraining courses.

The very concept of a labour market was not recognized in law until 1991, when Parliament passed the Employment of the Population Act of the Russian Federation. This act manifests an essentially new approach to the definition of employment as compared with the socialist period: employment in state enterprises is described as a right, not a duty, and the law does not include an obligation to work. The Act legalized employment patterns such as a shorter working day and flexible hours. The various enterprises, whether they are state-owned, private, collectively owned, leased, joint-stock companies, etc., are put on an equal footing in regard to the status of workers and staff employed. The status of unemployed person and the conditions and procedure for granting unemployment benefits are also defined.

The employment centres that have been opened in accordance with this law have revealed with utmost clarity that 70–80 per cent of all unemployed people are women, and that up to 75 per cent of these have higher or specialized secondary education. At the same time 85 per cent of vacancies are for blue-collar workers. There is an enormous discrepancy between supply and demand for labour-power. Moreover, the situation is soon expected to worsen considerably, since in Moscow alone some two hundred thousand people stood to lose their jobs in 1992 due to conversion, one hundred and forty thousand through abolition of departments and one hundred thousand in the course of privatization and liquidation of enterprises.

One of the most serious problems on the labour market is unemployment among women between the ages of 50 and 53: it is too early for them to qualify for their pension (even the special early pension the Employment Law introduced for women who are made redundant begins only at age 53, and only if there is no possibility of their being offered other work) and it is too late for them to retrain. It is practically impossible to live on unemployment benefit. Unfortunately, there is no special programme for social and vocational rehabilitation for women of this age-group. These women are in what can only be called a desperate situation.

Young women fare no better on the labour market. Commercial advertisements in the papers often show young men declaring: 'Business is not for women'. This is precisely how one of the most successful businessmen, the young millionaire Genrikh Sterligov, sees the place of women in this new sector: 'I see women in business in one role alone – as an elegant secretary who brings me coffee.' The 'Alisa' stock exchange, of which he is director, placed an advertisement for a company manager – 'man, 35 max, with higher education' – and for a secretary – 'girl, 25 max, with English language and computer skills, uniform – miniskirt'. It is widespread practice in advertisements to indicate the preferred sex. Reading job or training course announcements, young women have the following choices: governess, secretary (the training programme will certainly include a course on 'image' and 'shaping'), the new 'profession' of model, show-girl (often with dubious offers of work abroad), sewing-machine operator or house-painter. Most of the courses offered are commercially run, and young women have to pay several thousand roubles in order to acquire one of these occupations. And whereas enterprises most often pay for men to take commercial training courses, women usually have to pay for such courses out of their own pockets.

The cause of this sorry state of affairs for women in the labour market is often attributed to the fact that women were supposedly ill-prepared to move into the new private sector. The data of our sociological research carried out in Taganrog (south Russia) in 1989 show that when the policy encouraging different forms of ownership first began (cooperatives, self-employment etc.) men were almost as mistrustful as women in their attitude to these. (See Table 1.) Therefore the limited possibilities available for women to be absorbed into the new economic structures cannot be attributed to their low level of potential social mobility. In fact, it is only slightly lower than for men: both men and women are somewhat mistrustful of the prospect of working in conditions of economic independence, which entails risk. During the period following our research, when the private sector really began to develop, women were left in the position of economic outsiders. The reasons for this must be sought in the social organization of female labour, not in women's lack of inclination to change. Unfortunately, at the present time the Russian

Table 1   Attitude to Work in Cooperatives (% of state-sector employees)

	Men	Women
Would agree immediately	12.7	9.2
Would agree only as a second job	18.7	15.3
Would refuse	68.4	76.6

government does not have any special programme directed towards incorporating women into the new firms and enterprises, which makes the problem of women and unemployment one of the most urgent of all women's issues.

The Other Side of the Coin: Men and Parenthood

When we speak of gender relations as a hidden, but nevertheless real component of all social processes, we primarily have in mind those aspects of women's activities that society does not see and therefore underrates. There is, however, another component of gender relations which, as a rule, similarly remains out of sight, and this is the problem of fathers shirking their role in the family, and the absence of social support for those men who are family-oriented. In order to highlight this aspect of gender relations, in 1989–90 we carried out a sociological survey in Taganrog. We attempted to obtain replies to the following questions:

- Is the combination of work and motherhood (parenthood) a purely 'women's' problem?
- Is it right to orient the policy of 'family assistance' principally towards women? What does society think of 'assistance for fathers', to enable men to combine fatherhood and work? What does divorce mean for the wife and for the husband?
- Do both men and women have a high opinion of family values and domestic work?

Research on female labour carried out during the Soviet period usually indicates that such labour has a specific character owing to the fact that women fulfil several roles: mother, housewife, and worker in state-owned industry.[4] Researchers cite data showing that women would prefer a shorter working day, or that they would prefer to devote all their time to family responsibilities. The suggestion is to 'let women choose' whether to work more at home or at work, i.e., to offer various 'non-standard' work schedules: partial working day, flexible hours, work at home, etc.

In our survey we asked respondents whether they would like to change their work schedule. And we asked not only women, but men, too. Our findings indicated that not only 23 per cent of women, but also 13.9 per cent of men would like to transfer to non-standard work schedules. In addition, 3.5 per cent of men and 2 per cent of women are unable to work a full day even though they would like to. It is interesting that among those we questioned 10.2 per cent of women and 4.4 per cent of men were

Table 2   Work Preferences of Men and Women, Given Sufficient
Prosperity (%)

	Men	Women
Devote time solely to family and running the house	13.0	37.0
Dedicate oneself entirely to one's work	25.6	10.1
Work less both at job and at home; have more time for self-improvement	5.8	6.3
Work at home, so as to spend more time with family	3.0	8.2
Share time equally between work and family	44.1	31.8
Other preference	1.4	1.3
Cannot say	6.8	4.9

not working full-time, which is considerably higher than the official level
of one per cent for the country as a whole. Women's desire for a
'non-standard' working schedule tends to be attributed to their family
responsibilities. But how can the same desire on the part of men be
explained? To shed light on this problem, we asked the 'classic' question
which in sociological surveys in our country is normally only put to
women and which forms the basis for the conclusion that many women
work outside the home only for financial reasons. We asked men and
women about their preferences in hypothetical circumstances of sufficient material prosperity. (See Table 2.)

The data obtained reveal that 13 per cent of men who 'go to work only
out of economic necessity' (as against women's 37 per cent), which is a
substantial proportion. It is noteworthy that only 25.6 per cent of men
would apparently prefer to devote themselves entirely to their work,
compared with 10 per cent of women. The biggest group of men (44.1 per
cent) constituted those who wanted to divide their time equally between
work and family; among women this group constituted 31.8 per cent. In
all, 65.9 per cent of men preferred some form of reduction in, or
termination of, their workload; among women this proportion was 83.3
per cent.

The so-called overemployment in the state sector is thus by no means
solely a women's issue. Both sexes experience a strong, unsatisfied desire
for self-fulfilment outside the workplace. And if this desire by women
receives even symbolic support from the state (the right to a shorter
working day, leave for working mothers, etc.), then for men there is no
similar 'pro-family' policy. On the contrary, the traditional stereotype

Table 3   Frequency of Overtime (%)

	Men	Women
Every week	21.2	6.8
Several times a month	20.0	11.5
Several times a quarter	11.04	9.15
Hardly ever	47.8	72.56

whereby the man is seen as the primary breadwinner in the family forces him to look for additional work and agree to overtime to a much greater extent than women. (See Table 3.)

We discovered overall an extremely high level of family orientation in both women and men. Some 84 per cent of men and 85.9 per cent of women questioned did not agree with the statement 'People today do not have to start a family'; only 7.8 per cent of men and 6.9 per cent of women agreed.

Soviet and foreign researchers dedicate much space to discussions about the social nature of domestic work and how it is valued. Researchers in our country often emphasize that housework should be recognized as socially essential and payment for it should be guaranteed.[5] In the West, one movement actively campaigns for wages for housework. It is interesting that both men and women in our survey highly value household labour. Among women questioned, 88.9 per cent thought that labour in the home was just as important as labour in the workplace and the vast majority of the men questioned – 87.6 per cent – held this opinion.

It seems to me that it is not so much a question of whether housework is remunerated or not, as the fact that it is precisely in this area that there is most gender asymmetry. In our research, we singled out thirteen basic types of domestic work. The analysis showed that twelve of these contained a marked gender disproportion and, moreover, that eleven were usually done by women. Only one type of work – flat renovations – is clearly a 'man's job'. We also discovered that only one activity was truly egalitarian – work in the dacha garden. Most of the answers about equally shared work were for activities like playing with the children, taking them out for walks and other child-oriented activities. It is interesting that the estimates of both men and women differ, each sex claiming it does more in one activity or another. As for decision-making within the family, the situation is the exact opposite of what happens in the workplace. It is mainly women who decide how to spend holidays and days off, how to furnish the flat, about buying the house, car or furniture, and who controls household income and expenditure, though it is true that there was also quite a high proportion of egalitarian answers (50–60 per cent).

One could draw the conclusion that it is basically women in the family who work in and manage the home, whereas men are only in charge of the car – if, of course, there is one.

The data obtained can obviously be interpreted in different ways. In our opinion, gender asymmetry in the area of decision-making in the family is not so much connected with the fact that women have to do more housework as with the fact that they also do valuable work outside the home. The following correlation can be observed: the greater men's involvement in work in the home, the more egalitarian will be the decision-making.

It seems, therefore, that there are two possible scenarios for changes to gender relations in the family:

(1) Reducing the level of women's employment at the workplace, which would lower the proportion of the family budget coming from women's wages. There would thus be a decrease in the kinds of work done equally by both sexes in the home, as the area of female work expands. And there would be fewer decisions taken equally by both sexes due to an increase in male decision-making.

(2) Increasing the amount of domestic work men do (possibly by means of a relative or absolute reduction in their workplace employment). Female labour in the family would thus diminish and the area of joint decision-making would increase correspondingly.

The first scenario reinforces gender asymmetry in the sphere of the family; the second forms an egalitarian (i.e., gender-neutral) family structure.

Both men and women, in my opinion, lose out as a result of gender asymmetry in the family, men perhaps most of all. This hypothesis is clearly illustrated in the case of family break-ups, when the man experiences the full force of gender stereotypes. In our country over seven hundred thousand marriages with young children break up every year. We all know that in the vast majority of cases the child remains with the mother, no matter what particular special relationship might exist between father and child in a given family. After divorce, the father's role is reduced in most cases to that of maintenance-payer. It is not surprising that our survey revealed a big difference in the viewpoints of divorced men and women as to whether they had had disagreements about whom the child should live with: 18.1 per cent of men but only 5 per cent of women reported having had such differences. This question could only be

Table 4   Should Benefits be Given to Fathers Fulfilling Parental Obligations?
(% of positive responses)

Benefit	Men	Women
Right to take leave to look after child, due to family situation	13.2	15.8
Right to take 5-day paid leave while wife is in maternity home	34.1	32.7
Right to take annual leave for birth of child	48.4	47.8
Right to shorter working day or flexible hours	28.4	26.0
Other entitlements	4.3	4.2

resolved, not on the basis of gender stereotypes but on the possibilities, needs and real participation of each of the parents, if there was an egalitarian structure of gender relationships, and that includes gender relationships within the family.

One of the conditions for this scenario to be realized is that a policy of equal opportunities for men and women must exist in all walks of life. This policy means establishing a legal and institutionalized mechanism to create conditions for self-fulfilment of men and women in those areas where gender asymmetry exists: the private sphere for men, and the public sphere for women. But how will society react to such a policy? Are our men and women ready to accept that not only the mother, but also the father should receive certain legal and social benefits for parenthood? We can see from the data in Table 4 that a considerable number of respondents supported fathers' rights to entitlements, and that the opinion of women on the whole coincided with that of men. It is interesting that more of the male than female respondents support the right of fathers to a shorter working day. Women's conservatism can apparently be explained by their doubts as to whether, if fathers were to enjoy a shorter working day, they would spend more time on domestic chores.

The actual experience of legalization of fathers' leave in our country and abroad has shown, however, that it takes more than a single legal judgment to enable fathers to make use of this right in any significant numbers. Intensive social and cultural work is required to create a favourable framework for this to happen, among fathers, mothers, managers and the population at large. Otherwise, this progressive legal ruling will remain a mere façade concealing gender inequality.

It is interesting that organizations defending the rights of divorced fathers have sprung up in Moscow in recent years – Mapulechki and the

Union for the Protection of Childhood and Fatherhood. Unfortunately, these fathers are not calling for a change in the traditional patriarchal structure of the family during the time before its break-up, when their real contribution to the upbringing and care of the child could also transform gender relations after the family's break-up. Rather, these fathers prefer to fight for the right for fathers, not mothers, to keep the children after the break-up of the family – i.e., for fathers to decide the matter. The problem of fathers after divorce is thus being openly discussed in society, but within the framework of the patriarchal gender relations in the family. Yet our survey showed that there are a number of men who are prepared for relations of partnership in the family, which means after divorce too. But the question remains an open one: Is society prepared for this?

Legislation on Women during the Perestroika Period: Integration or Exclusion?

Of all resolutions in this field during the perestroika period, two documents can be singled out: The USSR Supreme Soviet resolution of 10 April 1990, 'On Urgent Measures to Improve the Position of Women and to Safeguard Maternity and Childhood', and that of the USSR Council of Ministers of 2 August 1990: 'On Supplementary Measures Guaranteeing Social Protection of Families with Children in View of the Transition to a Regulated Market Economy'. These resolutions turned out to be the only possible minimal part of the State Programme for Improving the Position of Women, and Protection of the Family, Motherhood and Childhood, which had been drafted but never put into practice.

The first special feature of these resolutions is that they include the traditional range of Soviet legislation on the position of women: women's working conditions, measures relating to birth and early childcare, entitlements at work for women with family responsibilities, special assistance to poor families with children. Let us look at these measures from the point of view of their gender consequences.

Women's working conditions

Working conditions represent a traditional area for regulation of female labour typical of Soviet legislation. It includes such measures as the banning of night shifts for women, prohibition of labour in harmful working conditions, restrictions on lifting and carrying heavy loads, additional remuneration for work in conditions that do not meet labour protection regulations and standards (wage bonuses, shorter working day, supplementary leave, early retirement, etc.). This approach, oriented mainly towards either prohibitive measures or various compensatory payments and entitlements, was proven to be if not actually negative, then largely ineffective during the years of the Soviet regime, since it creates strong economic vested interests in keeping such jobs on the part of both management and women workers.

So, from the 1930s onward, the state's labour ministry, together with the trades unions, drafted lists of jobs from which female labour was totally banned, and these became firmly entrenched. However, quite large numbers of women still continue to perform these jobs (about 8,000 at the present time). In addition, over 4 million women work in conditions that do not meet labour protection regulations and standards. And women are often forced to make do with insufficient compensation, since the management imposes a 'risk fee'. Some 44 per cent of women in industry do heavy work in conditions that are injurious to their health.

Clearly, if a truly effective means of solving this problem is to be found, new approaches are needed to motivate plants to abolish shop-floor conditions that are injurious to health (for these, of course, are just as injurious to men), and, conversely, to stimulate women to improve their skills and thus enable them to find more highly paid work that would not be at the price of their own health.

How do recently passed resolutions look in this light? Unfortunately, it has once again been decided to engage in the extremely expensive procedure of drafting a new list of jobs prohibited for women. The proposal, moreover, includes drafting a list of *recommended* jobs for teenagers and women of childbearing age.

The latter decision, despite its obvious ineffectiveness, was passed during the transition period to market relations (when competition is increasing on the new labour market), and could have most negative consequences for the position of women on the labour market. The programme for removing women from jobs injurious to their health could turn out to be a way of removing them from jobs altogether.

Labour entitlements for women with family responsibilities

The overall tendency in legislation is to give women more and more labour entitlements for fulfilment of family responsibilities. But these measures often have a purely ideological significance, since there is no mechanism for putting them into effect. These entitlements include the right to a shorter working day, flexible hours, additional days off for family matters and additional holidays for working mothers. These entitlements depend on the number of children below the legally stipulated age.

The entitlement to a shorter working day deserves special attention, in my view, from the standpoint of gender analysis. The very concept of a shorter working day in the post-socialist context has an interesting gender interpretation.

During the period of state socialism, full employment, or a full working day, was the absolute norm, violation of which was a criminal matter. In practice, of course, it was a rule that was often simply a formal proclamation, since there existed hidden unemployment in the workplace. Nevertheless, any formal departure from this rule was looked on as a deviation, as something abnormal. The symbolic right of women to a shorter working day has resulted in a particular gender pattern, which has made women's labour an area of special relations that differs from the norm and has turned women themselves into a specific, 'irrational' kind of labour-force. Conversely, society perceives the male labour-force to be the normal, 'correct', rational form of manpower.

A similar interpretation, in my view, might be applied to other measures of the labour legislation that are protectionist in relation to women, including the ban on night shifts. On the one hand, the ban once again is purely symbolic, since more women work night shifts than do men. On the other hand, the fact that they are 'exempt' even if only at an ideological level, engenders the kind of gender relations in the workplace where women are assigned a special status, 'protected' by the state.

During the transition to market relations this entitlement, despite the fact that at present managements not only can but are obliged to give women the chance to work a shorter day or flexible hours upon request, is largely symbolic, since a private firm can always decline to hire women, whose labour becomes more expensive with such regulation.

On the other hand, once enterprises are truly economically independent, they are far more interested in making effective use of their labour-force – i.e., in giving some of their workers the opportunity to work reduced shifts.

Maternity (parental) leave

Maternity leave for childcare, as a continuation of pregnancy and birth leave, was first introduced in the mid 1950s. The practice of legal registration of parenthood by women dates from this time. Fatherhood was not given commensurate legal status. Thus a separate pattern of opportunities began to take shape for men and for women, both from the legal point of view and from the standpoint of society's expectations as to who is chiefly responsible for raising and looking after children.

In the 1960s, during the period of economic reform, there was a tendency towards lengthening maternity leave and improving its social benefits (allowances). Some demographers and economists proposed introducing payments equivalent to the minimum wage, and extending maternity leave right up to school age. They also proposed that where there were three or more children in the family, the mother should be completely freed of the obligation of working outside the home, advocating that commensurate payments be made for household work and that years devoted to looking after children should be counted as part of a woman's overall work record.[6] For economic reasons these proposals were never put into practice, although the tendency towards lengthening maternity leave continued in the 1970s and 1980s.

The first years of social change were accompanied by increased calls to extend maternity leave considerably and to raise the maternity allowance as a possible way of reducing female unemployment in view of impending mass redundancies.[7] It is important to note that the main motivation of this strategy is economic; the interests of women are merely instrumental. The interests of women also serve as the means whereby demographers have called for a big reduction in the employment of women with children, since they are concerned by the decline in birthrate that characterizes the population in the European part of the country, a decline which is usually ascribed to the fact that women are working outside the home.[8]

On the whole, the USSR Supreme Soviet Resolution of 10 April 1990 also lends support to the aim of reducing women's employment by means of extended maternity leave. At present, the leave's overall length is three years, of which eighteen weeks are partially paid. It is stipulated that when the mother's leave expires, she is to be given the opportunity to resume her previous job. Unfortunately, in practice this right is often unfeasible in current circumstances, when many factories are closing down or changing their status. The procedure for payment of leave has also changed: before it was paid as a fixed allowance but now the amount is equivalent to the minimum wage and varies according to the level of inflation. For the first time, those parents without seniority have been given the right to an allowance worth 50 per cent of the official minimum wage. This is an important change given the new market conditions (although, unfortunately, regular publication of official minimum wage level figures is not yet standard practice).

This resolution contains another change, in my opinion, one of fundamental importance (and I believe that recommendations by the staff of the Moscow Centre for Gender Studies played a role in this). Leave now is not maternal, but parental, for it can be extended not only to mothers but also to fathers and to grandmothers or grandfathers too.

However, it would appear that once again the achievement is more symbolic than real. We obviously cannot expect men to make use of parental leave on an equal footing with women when the average female wage is two-thirds of the male wage. Traditional gender stereotypes form another obstacle, which create a negative public opinion of equality-minded fathers. In my opinion, the introduction of parental leave must be accompanied by an integral strategy of positive actions. It would be useful to set up a special independent body to oversee the implementation of equal opportunities for men and women (along the lines of the Swedish or Finnish ombudsman). It might be expedient to make a certain proportion of parental leave obligatory for fathers. All these measures may, however, turn out to be ineffective in a situation where patriarchal stereotypes are increasingly propagated, which is a characteristic feature of our post-socialist reality. Support is therefore needed for those representatives of the mass media that come out in favour of forming gender relations of equality.

It should be noted that the extension of maternal (parental) leave coincided with the formation of market relations. Enterprises have therefore either tried to close the nurseries and crêches they used to fund, especially those for children under three, or have raised fees so high that it becomes financially impossible for families, especially one-parent families, to use them. Thus once again women find themselves without a choice. In the past they were denied the possibility of *not* working; now, on the contrary, sometimes the only possibility they have is to stay at home and look after the children. So in practice, prolonged maternity leave limits the framework of opportunities for women, and becomes a means whereby women are excluded from the public sphere and isolated within the private sphere.

Amendments to the special maternity legislation made during the recent period of social transformations have on the whole continued the tendencies already observed in the preceding period, when legislation directed at equality was little more than a norm proclaimed in the constitution, which had no effective means of implementation and which allowed a number of coexistent measures reinforcing conventional gender relations. Most of the changes in the sphere of special legislation proceed from an inadequate understanding of what women's problems are. They are directed not at integrating women into the social reform process, but rather at excluding them from this process.

No legislative measures have been enacted to increase both the numbers and calibre of women taking part in decision-making processes, nor to eliminate discriminatory wage differentials between the various sectors of industry, widening opportunities for vocational training and inclusion of women in retraining programmes. In fact, current legislation facilitates women's exodus from, rather than their incorporation into, the labour-force. The law introduces and propagates division into male and female spheres, both within the workplace and between public and private spheres. The female sphere is categorized as different, specific, irrational, a deviation from the norm. The male sphere is the norm, that of order and rationality.

The protectionist nature of the law regulating women's working conditions, on the one hand, is of a purely symbolic nature (since it does not bring about real practical improvements) and on the other hand, it propagates the notion that the female labour-force is highly specific, requires special conditions, and is therefore more expensive. This becomes particularly important in a situation where a labour market is taking shape, and when women, thanks to their 'specificity', are forced into a special, marginal area of the labour market. By offering women 'entitlements', the law is in fact making women dependent on the state's potential for charity (which, as we know, is severely limited), and holding them back from striving for self-determination and autonomy. For the role of the law to change, we need to elaborate a strategy within which the law would play the role of a factor contributing towards the creation of gender-neutral structures.

I should like to end this article with some words of hope. Despite all the burdens of life in Russia today, I should like to believe that what is taking place *might* nevertheless represent some movement towards the liberation of women. But today, as never before, how long this change will take depends on us. Independence, Solidarity, Integration – that is the thrust of our movement today.

Notes

1. See A. Kollontai, *Sotsialnye osnovy resheniya zhenskogo voprosa* (Moscow 1928).

2. See N. Zakharova, A.I. Posadskaya and N.M. Rimashevskaya, 'Kak my reshayem zhenskiy vopros?', *Kommunist*, no. 4, 1989.

3. M.S. Gorbachev, *Perestroika i novoye myshleniye* (Moscow 1988); translated as *Perestroika: New Thinking for Our Country and the World* (London 1987). Page references to this work follow in brackets in the text.

4. See the works of N.M. Shishkan, T.M. Yuk, E.Ye. Novikova, T.N. Sidorova and G.P. Sergeyeva, among others, in this respect.

5. For example, the work of Z. Yuk and T. Sidorova.

6. See, among others, the work of A. Vermishevk and B.Ts. Urlanis, 'Demografichesckiye protsessy i demograficheskaya politika', in *Problema povysheniya effektivnosti ispol'zovaniya rabochei sily v SSSR* (Moscow 1983).

7. See V.G. Kostakov, 'Osnovnye tendentsii i problemy zanyatosti naseleniya', in *Naseleniye SSSR za 70 lyet* (Moscow 1988).

8. See A.I. Antonov, *Sotsiologiya rozhdayemosti* (Moscow 1980); and V.A. Borisov, *Perspektivy rozhdayemosti* (Moscow 1976).

APPENDIX
Self-Portrait of a Russian Feminist

An Interview with Anastasia Posadskaya

What sort of family do you come from? How did you become what you are now?

I was born in 1958 and grew up in Moscow as the daughter of a single mother, who was a pharmacist. In my childhood, my maternal grand-mother and grandfather lived with us. He was Lithuanian, and she was Jewish. My mother was their only child, as I was hers – we were two generations of single daughters.

What about your father?

We never lived with him – my parents were not married. My father was from a German aristocratic family in Gatchina. His parents had emigrated during the Revolution, and as the son of a baron he had a very difficult life. He organized amateur concerts, which were very common at the time, but because of his background he could never get a permanent job in Moscow. He was a Christian, and I was called after his mother, who was Ukrainian. So I am quite an ethnic mixture. But my parents never lived together.

Why not?

When they met, my father was married. His wife was very ill, and he couldn't leave her. When she died, he wanted to live with us, but my mother would not accept this. Her own situation was very difficult: she was living with me and her two parents in a single room in a communal flat. My grandparents hated him. He was twenty-nine years older than her – the same age as my grandfather – so one would expect them to be prejudiced against him. The neighbours, of course, gossiped about the whole story. So my parents never really had a satisfactory place to meet, or live together. My mother could more or less cope with this before I was born, but by the time I arrived I think she was just very tired, and decided she could not keep up the relationship amid so much uncertainty and hostility, but must devote all her energies to me.

What happened to him?

This is a sad story. He was very much alone, and had no other children. He had two elder sisters who were both blind, whom he went to look after in Gorky. There he died in 1970, when I was 12. Later, when I went to look for his grave, I couldn't find it. I never knew my father when I was a child, and still know very little about his life, which is a great loss for me. I realized this when I was 18, and friends of his came to me and told me that before he died he had asked them to give me his letters to my mother. He wanted me to see what their love had been for seven years before I was born. When I read these letters, I was very moved – I not only felt close to him, but also that many aspects of my own character come from him.

What was the background of your mother's family?

After my grandfather died, I discovered a notebook in which he had written a short autobiography. You can imagine how excited I was when I came upon it. But when I read it I was very disappointed – worse than that, really depressed. Because it was clear that this was not something written from the heart, but as a precaution in case he was arrested. It was a terrible document. It just detailed all the activities that would show him to be an obedient and dedicated member of the Party – his record in the Red Army, his role in the mobilization for this or that official campaign, and so on. Not one personal word. My mother told me that he had been expelled from the Party at one time, but was reinstated. He had many books at home, a lot of them from the 1930s. But if their authors had later been prosecuted and condemned as enemies of the people, he would cross out their names. For example, we had the third edition of Lenin's *Collected Works* at home, of 1927–29. That is where I for the first time came across criticisms of Lenin, because it contained comments from Axelrod and others on his ideas about imperialism, for instance; also objections to his polemical style against opponents. I was obviously fascinated, and looked to see who had edited the volume. The three editors were Bukharin, Skvortsov-Stepanov and Molotov – but my grandfather had carefully deleted Bukharin's name. This is highly symbolic. It was always very difficult in my family to learn the truth about the past, and this is quite typical for my generation. There are many blank areas in my grandfather's life.

Is that all you know about him?

Not quite, because by chance a family photograph from his childhood survived – I don't know how, because all other traces of his pre-revolutionary past disappeared. When I saw this photograph, it was absolutely clear that this was a rich family. His mother and grandmother – who was Polish – are in long, elegant dresses and his own baby clothes are very fetching, including pretty shoes on his feet – this at a time when peasants wore straw sandals, at best. But in his autobiography my grandfather described himself as a boy from a poor peasant family, who were still virtually serfs.

Do you know more about your grandmother?

Yes, although she too was afraid. The fear of the knock on the door at night made people adopt a psychological strategy of forgetting the past. It was like a kind of amnesia: they genuinely forgot the past. I believe that my grandmother truly no longer remembered the names of all her brothers, for example. When she was very old, I would insist to her: 'Grandmother, after you go I will have no one else from whom I can learn about the family who brought you up. They do not deserve this. Please try to recall at least some of their names.' In the end, in the last year of her life, when she was too weak to resist and fight me off any longer, something did open up in her head, though many things were still lost. She told me that her grandfather had been a bookish man in a small town in Belarus, held in honour by its inhabitants, who had devoted his life to learning. But her mother had been a disobedient daughter in the family, disavowed by her father, because she had rejected her religious upbringing and married unwisely. Many of her relatives had emigrated to America. Now, about a year ago the Moscow press started to give a lot of coverage to a big Hasidic campaign from the United States to recover the collection of a famous rabbi from Lyubavichi in Byelorussia called Ber-Schneerson which was confiscated during the Revolution and ended up in the Lenin Library. They want the books back for the Hasidic community in America. Well, my grandmother told me her grandfather was called Boris Schneerson, which I suppose might be a Russian transformation of the Jewish name. I have no idea whether they were the same person, although obviously I'm curious. This kind of mystery about origins is very common in Russia today.

What about your grandmother herself?

She was in fact an important influence on me. For she had managed to come up from Ukraine and graduate from Moscow University, in the

Department of Chemistry. Her knowledge of various foreign languages made a great impression on me, and I was determined to follow her path and go to the University. My mother, who is now a pensioner, had trained at the Institute of Pharmacy. I wanted from the start to achieve something in a research field. So from my schooldays onwards, my ambition was always to study at Moscow University.

Was that straightforward?

By no means. My idea was to apply to the Department of Philosophy. I had many questions about the society I lived in, and thought philosophy would help me answer them. In my last year at school I won a prize for an essay in the subject, and so I was told I might get support from the department since they already knew I could do something in the field. But the father of my boyfriend at the time, a man I very much respected, said to me: 'A woman philosopher? I've never heard of anything so silly.' This was quite a blow – I was very discouraged. So I decided that, if not Philosophy, perhaps the Department of Economics would let me in, and I could study some philosophy on the side. So I studied for the economics examination. But that too was far from easy. For, by the mid 1970s the Economics Department at the University was deeply corrupt. The children of our political leaders and of others in power were virtually assured entry, and of course I was nobody from this point of view. We had a saying, in fact, that the competition for places was between parents rather than students. I invested an enormous amount of time and effort in preparing for the exams, while my mother took on a menial job to pay for additional training for me. But I failed in the first year. This was the time of deepest frustration for me: I had always wanted to do everything very fast, and in fact even finished school in nine years rather than ten. I was suicidal for a period. I would never want to live through a year like 1974 again, when my grandfather also died. The following year, however, I did get a place at University.

What kind of economics courses did Moscow University give at the time?

Political economy, mostly devoted to studying *Capital* and other Marxist texts. The compulsory subjects were very restrictive, with only a limited choice of optional courses. We read a little Smith and Ricardo, and Keynes, in Russian translations. But there were some interesting courses, under the rubric of critiques of bourgeois theories.

What was your experience at the University?

I started out in the evening department, which of course is the least popular. But after a year of good marks, I was able to transfer to the day department – because some of the students who were admitted just because of their parents' position, without any real qualifications, dropped out. This was a common pattern if you were a student without connections: in fact it was just about the only way to get into the day department. Now, every year we had to write papers and I wrote all of my papers on topics that were more or less directly to do with women – as treated in the classics of Marxism–Leninism, naturally. So I was reading Bebel and the like. My final dissertation was on the social, economic and demographic aspects of women's employment in the United States – since I wanted to practise my English and was interested in what was going on there. Of course, that raised in my mind certain comparative questions – it made me think about the economic situation of women in the USSR.

Meanwhile I had a daughter, which meant that I stayed at home for a year, before graduating in 1981; soon afterwards I got divorced from my first husband, and moved back to our family flat, where there were now just the four generations of women. However, when I took my final examinations, the results were good: a red diploma, as we called it – more or less a *summa cum laude*. But it only led to more frustration.

What sort of frustration?

Well, I hoped and expected to be able to pursue postgraduate work. But when I applied to various institutes of the Academy of Sciences to do so, as a woman with a child I met with unabashed discrimination. The matter was not even given some indirect gloss. I was simply told: 'Don't bother to apply, you will not pass the exams. Forget about your red diploma – give us a young man with any kind of diploma.' So I realized I had no chance. When I failed to get into the University in 1974, people said to me: 'Anastasia, why are you even trying to get into that sink?', and I would reply: 'What are you saying? We live in a socialist country; there may be some exceptions to fairness, but why should I be one of them?' By 1981 I was not so naïve, and I understood that if people in authority said I would not get a place, there were mechanisms to ensure I did not.

Did you have any recourse against this kind of rejection?

What I wanted to do was to write a doctorate on women's employment in the USSR. I immediately ran into this blatant contradiction. Everyone said to me that the problem of women's equality with men had been solved long ago in the USSR, and no one was interested in me as a woman researcher, still less as one working on women's questions. I knew I was being discriminated against as a woman, only to hear that discrimination had ceased to be a problem. In desperation, I wrote to my departmental supervisor, who was then working for ILO in Geneva, to ask advice. This supervisor was a woman – I think that thirty years earlier it had actually been easier for a woman to follow a career in the University than it was now – and she told me to get in touch with an elderly professor, Mikhail Sonin, who had once done work in the field I was interested in. He read my dissertation, and told me: 'Anastasia, you want to pursue a very unpopular subject, but I believe it is still topical, and will agree to supervise you. But please bear in mind that you will also have to do something for me. I shall need you to translate some English books.' This was very characteristic of the time. I couldn't criticize him, because on the whole he was nice to me and without his recommendation I would have had no chance in the exams, which I now was able to sit in order to obtain a place at the Institute of Economics at the Academy. Even so, if I had got a single mark that was lower than the highest grade, I would not have made it. Nevertheless, if you had a professor behind you, psychologically you felt safer. So I am grateful to him. Unfortunately he died three years later, so I couldn't defend my thesis while he was alive, which led to problems for me.

You could start work on it when you entered the Insitute?

Yes, but I was assigned to the section whose field was 'economic reproduction' – nothing to do with childbearing, as the associations of the term in the West lead people to think, but with reproduction as understood in Marx's schemas in *Capital*. There I was told that women's employment as such was not a topic of interest; I could only study it as part of the general condition of the labour-force. So the working title of my thesis had to be 'Socioeconomic Issues of Women's Contribution to the Labour-Force and the Intensification of the Economy'. In those days, we had to stitch onto whatever we were doing references to economic intensification or reform – today, of course, it is the same with marketization. The section was headed by a Professor Notkin – famous because he had been criticized by Stalin in his last writing – whom we saw as an antique and who was rather suspicious of women's issues. But my topic was approved, and I completed my work on it by 1984. But when Professor Sonin died, it became very clear that no one else was willing to supervise me, and so I had to postpone the defence of my thesis.

By now Brezhnev was dead. Did the subsequent interregnum make any difference to conditions affecting you?

After Brezhnev, we did expect better times. But I was looking for a job, and still encountering the same kind of discrimination. I wanted to continue research on women, but this option was closed to me. There was not one department in the Academy of Sciences to which I could apply – no one wanted to include me in their programmes. So I thought I would try to become an assistant to a professor in political economy, since by now there was somewhat more scope to teach what one wanted, or at least nobody would really check what one was saying to students. This proved a depressing business. I applied to innumerable institutes. They all said: 'We are happy to take you as a part-timer, paid on an hourly basis for the time you work; but the work is not guaranteed, and is for half a year only.' What this meant was earning about 420 roubles, which is practically nothing. But it was my only option. For these were still Soviet conditions, in which no one was supposed to be unemployed: not to have a job was something extremely suspicious. I knew of nobody without one, so even this kind of employment was better than nothing; I conducted seminars in political economy at a couple of industrial institutes. They at least gave me a kind of status, and I would try to hide the fact that I was only part-time. The only advantage of the situation was that I was left with a lot of free time for reading. Eventually, I did well at both institutions, because by now – this was an innovation – students were supposed to evaluate their teachers' work, and I got good reports. But I was very unhappy that I was nevertheless still not invited to apply for a full-time post. The only reason given was that I was not a member of the Party – for every candidate for the job had to be approved by the local Party committee and by the regional Party committee. That situation lasted for three years, up to 1988.

Right through the zenith of perestroika?

Yes, as late as that. But finally the changes in the country transformed my personal situation. In June 1988 I was simultaneously offered a job as Assistant Professor in Political Economy at the Aeronautical Institute, and a research position in the newly created Institute of Socioeconomic Studies of Population in the Academy of Sciences. I chose the latter, because with it my dream came true: the director invited me to work on women's issues.

How did the Institute come into existence? Who was the director?

The idea of an institute for demographic studies was an old one, which I think went back to the 1960s. But it had always been blocked in the Academy. Now the new political conditions created an opening for it. There was a lot of competition to head it. The appointment went to a woman who had been working in the Central Economic and Mathematical Institute on family income distribution, with a lot of survey experience: Natalya Rimashevskaya. I had met her some months earlier and she had made it clear that she wanted new people involved in the new unit. She was a contemporary and friend of Gorbachev at the Law School in the fifties, which gave her some protection in the new Institute. For you have to understand how isolated women in her position are. There is still only one other woman heading a research institute in Moscow: Tatiana

Zaslavskaya at the Russian Centre for Public Opinion Polls, which is partly a trade-union affair. So there has been a lot of opposition to Rimashevskaya in the Academy, and many attempts to remove her. Academicians who didn't know my convictions would often say to me: 'Why don't you come and work in my Institute? I don't know how you can stand this old woman. What's she doing in the Academy anyway? She should be at home looking after her grandchildren.' This is the atmosphere that exists.

What direction did your work take at the Institute?

I was heavily engaged from the start in the surveys it undertook. It took me some time to establish myself in the new setting, in which, for example, there were many formalities to fulfil before I could finally defend my thesis, which I did in 1989. But by now the context of my work had changed quite radically. For in 1988, before the Institute was set up, I had the great good fortune to meet three women who had a feminist background – something that I lacked. One of them, Natalya Zakharova, worked with Rimashevskaya in the Mathematical Institute; another, Olga Voronina, had a job in the Institute of Philosophy at the Academy, while the third, Valentina Konstantinova, was employed – very unhappily – in the Social Science Academy of the Central Committee. Two of them had written their theses on Western feminism – of course, as 'critiques' of ideas they actually found very appealing. This was a tradition quite unknown to me: I had never connected my approach to the problems of women's employment in the USSR with it. So it was through my discussions with them that I started to read this literature, and realized how close it was to my concerns. This was the first time I started to identify myself as a feminist. I was tremendously exhilarated by this new intellectual environment. We began to meet informally, calling our tiny group of four Lotus – the League for Emancipation from Sexual Stereotypes – and dreamed of some kind of a Centre where our central commitment would be work on women, rather than having to tack it on as a subsidiary to other obligations.

Could you bring this new orientation to bear on your work at the Institute?

Yes. Immediately I got there I realized that something had changed at the top. This was a structure in which a lot of information we had never had before was coming down from above, and in which we could provide feedback in the form of comments, consultative reports, and so on. In August 1988, an emissary from the Council of Ministers of the USSR told us that a new section on women was being created inside the Council, and that we were invited to submit whatever ideas we had – 'as crazy as you like' – about how to change the current situation for women. You must understand what an enormous difference this made to me. For years I had been sitting alone in my room, thinking to myself in despair: 'What am I doing? No one has the slightest interest in my ideas except my husband' – I was remarried by then – 'and he only shows it to give me some sense of self-respect.' Now all my thoughts suddenly seemed of value. This was a wonderful time for me, and I was very much inspired. Our little group produced a position paper, which aroused interest, and when *Kommunist* – the theoretical organ of the Central Committee of the CPSU – asked our director for something on women, she sent them our report. This was a time when Otto Lacis was the editor; Gaidar was also working there. They took the decision to print it, so on 8 March 1989 – Women's Day – *Kommunist* published the report.

What were the reactions to its appearance – something like a feminist manifesto in the official journal of the ruling party?

Well, the first thing that happened was that Mayeva, the woman who had been put in charge of the Council Ministers' Department of Women, told us she was very interested in cooperation. Then, a month later, the first partially free elections to the Congress of Soviets were held. Quite a number of women from the old Soviet Women's Committee got seats through the quota reserved for public organizations. This was a bad system, of course, but the results were quite good for us, because these deputies promptly set up commissions on women, maternity and children, and started to press for new legislative programmes. In response – because of the article, and our contacts with the Council of Ministers – the government asked us to produce a position paper. Towards the end of 1989 we used this opportunity to request a special Centre for Gender Studies with five researchers. We were in luck: the president of the Academy, Marchuk, gave us the five positions, the Council of Ministers a telephone line, and Rimashevskaya an office. So by the spring of 1990 I found myself in the new Centre, together with the others from the Lotus group – except for Natalya Zakharova, who was now working with the UN in Vienna. Since then we have gradually built up the Centre; today it has a staff of fifteen – ten full-time and five part-time researchers.

Why did you invent a new Russian word – 'Gendernii' – to name the Institute?

I know, some of my friends told me it was barbarous. But our problem was that the Russian word for 'sex' – *pol* – is in our culture too associated with the physical acts, and we lack a term that is distinct from it, which you have in English. So we had to import 'gender'.

How important is Rimashevskaya's protection of the Centre, as the director of the Institute to which it is attached?

Her position is an important guarantee for us. But I think that by now it might in any case be difficult to remove us, because of our standing within the Academy – and outside it – as an independent authority. Any new government, and we can expect a good many, will know that the Centre for Gender Studies produces work that is not designed to conform to the wishes of whomever is in power.

Who are the officials responsible for policy on women's issues in the Yeltsin regime?

The Minister in charge of Social Protection is Ella Pamfilova, who was a deputy in the Soviet Congress. She was made a token co-chair of the committee set up to investigate Party privileges – Primakov was also on it. But she proved not to be docile, and many officials lost their dachas because of her. It was perhaps for this reason that Yeltsin appointed Pamfilova to her present post. But the Ministry is not effective – she has so few resources there. Yeltsin's state adviser on women's questions, Yekaterina Lakhova, may well be more powerful. She is a former gynaecologist who was part of his Sverdlovsk team, then a deputy in the Russian Parliament who acted as a confidante during his presidential campaign. Her influence comes partly from Yeltsin's own style as a politician. Gorbachev, when he was asked if he consulted his wife on major political issues, very sincerely – but perhaps unwisely – said yes. Yeltsin most definitely says no, never. Lakhova is there to give a feminine dimension to the new government.

What is her stance?

She is not a token woman. Lakhova is very hostile to the old Soviet Women's Committee, now renamed the Union of Russian Women, which still continues to function from its headquarters in a magnificent manor house once visited by Pushkin, though now confining itself mainly to organizing business courses for women, so they can raise some money, now that Party subsidies have ceased. We cannot work with them either. Lakhova understands that Russia needs some kind of official programme for women that goes beyond pious enthusiasm for democracy in general. She has recently commissioned the Centre to produce a report on women's situation in Russia today, which will allow us access to data that we otherwise could not obtain. So although Lakhova is no feminist, her role so far has been relatively positive.

What is the situation in the mass media – do you receive sympathetic coverage? How much space is there in the press and on television for the expression of feminist viewpoints?

This is a very tricky area for us. One danger is a tendency in the media to use feminism as just another sensation, in the same way that they treat an issue like homosexuality – as something marginal and exotic, but disreputable. They have no concern whatsoever for the people involved, in either case. Journalists come to us and say: 'When are you going to have your feminist forum?' We say: 'Some women do identify themselves as feminists, but the forum is going to be for independent women.' I try to keep a distance from them. Every time they ran an interview, it always turned up with some title like 'Our Feminists Claim Gorbachev is Bad'. I really hate this way of scandalizing the issue.

Aren't there women journalists who are better than this?

Yes, there are some who are sympathetic. But it is very difficult to place an anti-patriarchal article in the press. Women journalists who tried to write about the independent women's forum found it impossible to get anything in the democratic newspapers. The men who control these have a consistent attitude. They tell one: 'What are you talking about, my dear? Why does a pretty young person like you want to be politically active, to do professional work? Aren't you tired of all that? Look at our Soviet women: they do not look like women any more. You can't want them only to work. Please, do something else.' Of course, if anyone takes this line, they are happy to publish it.

Is this true of the 'quality' press as well, or principally of the popular newspapers?

There is no difference at all. In 1989, I gave a big article on the situation of women in Russia to *Moscow News*, the leading paper of liberal intellectuals. It discussed the way that the media regularly represented women, not as the victims of social evils in our society, but as their cause. In one part, I noted that it was the case that men, too, suffered from the discrimination operating against women in the public sphere, since one result of it is a kind of discrimination against them in the private sphere, when women keep the children in 99 per cent of cases of divorce, and very often men are denied any access to them. However, I pointed out that this stemmed from the usual situation that preceded divorce: the husbands play no role in the house or in looking after the children. If only men would understand the logic of the situation, I observed, perhaps we might see a movement for men's liberation too. What did Yegor Yakovlev, the celebrated editor of *Moscow News*, do? He simply cut the whole article, except for the line about men's liberation! That is typical of the democratic press.

What was the attitude of the Communist press at the time?

I have to admit that, ironically, it was sometimes better. For example, *Pravda* gave considerable coverage to the Independent Women's Forum, and published fairly accommodating interviews with me and also with Olga Lipovskaya, another feminist. *Moskvichka*, their women's weekly in Moscow, also gave a lot of space to serious women's issues. But, of course, they were also insisting that the Soviet Women's Committee did such valuable work, along the lines of 'Look, we are active too.' They grasped the fact that women are a significant group in the population, whom it was important to control. This, of course, is a widespread attitude. When I remarked that the democrats were losing women, Boris Kagarlitsky – on the Far Left – was very offended, and said to me: 'Okay, if we are losing women, why don't you write something on women for our Party of Labour?' But the fact is there are very few women in that party, and therefore really no one to address; and besides, we did not want to write on women for them – this should be the task of women inside the party. In the new elections that are coming, we may see a different attitude among the various political forces, when they realize they have to fight for the cause of women. So far their approaches have simply been manipulative.

What about television, especially since the end of the USSR?

Back in 1989, I was invited to appear on *Vzglyad*, one of the most popular current affairs programmes, hosted by Listev. The interview was cut savagely. Then two other feminists were invited. They recorded interviews, and some time later were rung up and told: 'Watch your TV tonight, because you are on the programme today.' In fact the interviews were never screened – they must have been withdrawn at the last minute. In January 1993, in the new Russia, Listev phoned me saying he was running a new programme called *Tema*, which was going to discuss the problem of fathers struggling for the right to see their children after a divorce. He asked me to appear – 'Everyone will blame women, you know, and we want someone who will put in a good word for them.' I agreed on the understanding that a colleague at the Centre was invited too. What happened in the studio? She was allowed to say only a few words, before two prominent men, Zhukovitsky and Kabakov, held forth for about half an hour each. When I protested at the discrimination against her, Listev just cut me off, saying 'Excuse me, please', and continued in the same way. On his script, which I could see, he didn't even have my name: I was entered simply as 'A Feminist'. What were these men saying? Were they fighting for their right to do some work in the house? Not at all. They simply wanted a prior claim over the children in cases of divorce – though, of course, if men don't want the children, let them stay with their mothers. That was it. Another speaker declared that Soviet women had been the hedgehogs of Stalin in the family – the word is *yozh*, close to Yezhov[1] – controlling their husbands and preventing them from overthrowing the regime. Ninety per cent of what I said was cut when the show was aired, making the rest incomprehensible. But this comparison with the hedgehogs was left in.

What is the reality behind this agitation over fathers' rights?

Formally, of course, the partners in a marriage are supposed to have equal rights and responsibilities in bringing up their children. But in a divorce, the courts will assign the charge to one parent, who is always the woman. There are cases, like my own, in which the parents consensually agree all the arrangements – financial, residential, custodial – between themselves. But unfortunately in the majority of divorces women prefer to get court guarantees of alimony. This often comes as a shock to the fathers, whose response tends to be: 'Well, if you want to make everything so formal, you'll get only what I'm legally obliged to provide; but I would have been much more generous if we'd decided things between ourselves.' This is another way for men to blame women. It is entirely understandable that most women go to the courts, because their wages are so low, and the men make such a minimal contribution to the running of the household, that they want to guarantee the right to at least 25 per cent of the man's salary. Of course, men have their way of opting out of their obligations: they often have other jobs besides their official ones, but they make over only a proportion of their primary income. Many don't pay the alimony at all; although in the last three years we have gained an alimony fund, and the militia will search for defaulters, who have to pay back much more if they are caught. Where men perhaps do worst out of a divorce is in housing, where the courts will often assign them to a room in a communal flat. But housing is so terribly short, and now so impossibly expensive, that divorce is becoming for both parties an increasingly tragic affair. Every third marriage breaks up. But women initiate 60 per cent of the divorces. That gives you an idea of the suffering they go through.

Under perestroika, the authorities started for the first time to become very concerned by the consequences of what was happening to family patterns in the USSR: the level of alcoholism, the drop in the birth rate, the fall in life expectancy. Demographic questions became public issues in a new way. How has this interacted with work on women's problems?

In Russia today, demographers form a very conservative lobby – but one with real influence, because they are dealing with genuine problems. It is their solutions that are regressive. I watched this development closely, because I specialized in demography in the economics department when I was in Moscow University. Those currently the leading figures were my teachers then – professors like Antonov and Borisov. Even at the time, I felt there was something odd in the conclusions they drew from their studies. Their message was that unless the state took special measures, the Soviet population would dwindle: what was needed was an official policy aimed at support for an ideal model of a three- or four-child family.

That is very high.

Yes, it is. Their argument was that if policy was officially oriented to a family of two children, couples would have only one – people will always have fewer than they are urged to. So if they are told to have three or four, then at least they might have two. This kind of thinking made me very angry. What about those who cannot have even one, or do not want two, or actually want ten? – such people were not to be considered by the state. The idea of an active demographic policy originated in the 1970s – I think it was the 24th Party Congress that put it on the agenda. I can remember the air of self-congratulation in the department at the news – the word went out: 'We have succeeded.' So, longer and partly paid maternity leave, and other measures, were introduced. But the effects of these were only temporary: after one or two years the birth rate reverted to the same level again. The only change they produced was to bring forward the age at which people had children, not to increase the number.

What is the situation now?

Today, the demographers are very active indeed – much more directly so than ever before. They submitted a major position paper to the Soviet Congress, supported by doctors and paediatricians, arguing that mothers should not work, that women should stay at home and have more children, that this was the only way to improve the disastrous health record of the nation, and so on. We submitted our own paper, with a quite contrary diagnosis, and there was a major debate in the Congress and in its Commission on Women. Despite all their lobbying, it was our report that prevailed. But they were better than us in seeing where power was shifting, and so they quickly transferred the whole issue to the Russian Parliament. There they have now prepared a draft law on the family which declares that traditional values need to be revived, and that children must be brought up in families, ignoring pre-school facilities as if they were harmful or non-existent. Lakhova, I may say, doesn't see how dangerous this draft law is. In fact, she organized the discussion of it in the Parliament. We have told her that if she comes to us for anything after this law is adopted, she will have a hard time of it.

Presumably there is another motivation for the draft law as well: a bid to retire as many women from the labour market as possible, at a time when unemployment is bound to soar – a pattern that is marked in much of Eastern Europe now?

Exactly. In 1990 we made a study of the huge Kamaz complex that produces heavy trucks in Tataria, which employs about 140,000 workers in some twenty plants. Interviewing the manager in charge of the finances of the whole enterprise, I was astonished to learn that, for six years, it paid 100 roubles to a number of women with children, just to stay at home – not a bad sum at the time; indeed, more than the state maternity grant. 'We spend millions of roubles on this programme', he told me. 'How much do you spend on retraining them when they come back to work?', I asked. He looked thoroughly uncomfortable, as if I had said something improper. 'Why should we spend money on that? I have no idea; maybe the personnel department knows.' I replied: 'All right, but you must have some policy on the question.' Then he said: 'Yes, a very simple one: our aim is that there should be no women in production.' In spite of my considerable experience, I was truly shocked. Managers at lower levels of the enterprise explained that – as they put it – they had more and more difficulty keeping women because of male competition in the work brigades, which now included some performance-related earnings. 'No one wants women in the brigades, they have all these benefits and time off: the social funds of the firm should be spent on something else.' When we looked at the figures the pattern of dismissals in 1989 and 1990 was clear: the number of women in work was falling, by several thousand. Interestingly enough, however, in 1991 the proportion of women in the firm recovered to its previous 50 per cent level. The reason is that Kamaz is still a state enterprise, whose room for wage increases is limited; so men have started to desert it to set up their own little businesses, or to find jobs in cooperatives or joint ventures. So the Kamaz management has had to keep more women than they want – for the time being. But the trend is absolutely clear. At all levels of the occupational structure, the position of women is going to get worse.

In the private sphere, what are the stress lines in the pattern of relations between the sexes? The material and cultural conditions in which affective life is led have long differed in obvious ways from those in the West – with

an official ideology of egalitarianism and puritanism, much less space for
privacy, a good deal of brutalization, yet within a strong Russian romantic
tradition. How far are things changing in this area?

It is a bit difficult to answer that, partly because I am insufficiently familiar with Western patterns, and partly because the subject doesn't lend
itself easily to investigation, especially in our culture. A Finnish sociolo-
gist, who took part in our study of Kamaz, tried to distribute a questionnaire to women there about their sexual experience, including any
harassment. Their reaction was to laugh, or throw the questionnaire
away. They would come to me and say, 'Oh, what a strange woman that
is! Should I really write about such intimate matters?' Recently, a Dutch
student has been doing some visual anthropology in this field. I found
several women for her, whom she interviews very carefully – but only
after about five sessions does she broach this subject. So there is a lot we
don't know. But we can say that some things have improved, at least in
the cities. I was the daughter of a single mother, and I can remember how
difficult this was for her. Also for me – being asked every day, 'Where is
your father?', and seeing the smiles and nudges. Now this happens much
less. There are many women who decide to have children on their own,
and bring them up on their own. That represents a certain progress. On
the other hand, there are many continuing forms of humiliation of, and
injury to, women. According to the latest statistics, about six million
people live in dormitories. When I was a student I heard terrible stories
about these from girls who had to live in them, for the lack of parents to
protect them. Recently, during the work in Tataria, I was invited to give a
talk at an institute in the city of Yelabuga, not far from Naberezhniye
Chelny where Marina Tsvetayeva committed suicide. Afterwards, the
girls invited me to their dormitory. I noticed that the doors to most of the
rooms had their locks torn out – of course, everything in the building was
in a dreadful condition. When I asked, 'Why don't you have locks?', they
looked at each other and replied: 'Do you really think it's possible to have
a lock here?' Men – sometimes students, sometimes others – simply force
their way in. Rape is a daily occurrence. The girls often come from villages, to which they do not want to go back; they cannot rent a room; they
cannot drop out of the Institute, because they have nowhere else to go. So
they just have to live with it. Many get married very young just to escape
from the constant danger of sexual violence. To try to stop this violence,
some enterprise managements have gone to the lengths of banning sexual
relations of any kind in the dormitory buildings, with security checks on
anyone coming in or out – people have to climb out through windows to
see a partner, and risk punishment if they're caught; couples are obliged
to separate at eleven o'clock, and so on. We have many institutions in our

society where sexual life is barbarous. This is not to speak of the effects of alcoholism – which is a form of national escapism – on men's behaviour in marriage, which leads to a great deal of violence too.

Is this the main problem affecting women in this area today?

In the public sphere, the greatest threat to women in Russia today is unemployment. But in the private sphere, it is violence. In this respect, I have to admit that I feel more secure as a woman when I am in the West than in Russia. Of course, there is a difference in the academic and professional worlds; there is less direct brutality. But from my own experience I can tell you that, regrettably, in every case where I worked under the supervision of a man, there was always some occasion where he tried to take advantage of me – usually, it is true, leaving himself an escape route, by subsequently pretending it was a joke. So, believe me, I am happy to have Rimashevskaya as a director.

What has been the impact of Western sexual culture in contemporary Russian society, which in many ways represents a sharp break with the official – however hypocritical – puritanism of the past?

Yes, there was always a gulf between the prim codes proclaimed by the regime and the realities of everyday life. People got used to a double standard, and of course this bred cynicism. This was a very unhealthy situation, in which society became accustomed to live out a part of its life like a secret, hidden from public sight. Now this clandestineness is no longer necessary. One result is a big demand for pornographic materials, imported or imitated from the West. I view this as a kind of childhood disease, that adults get over. You can be given medicines to avoid these diseases as a child, but then you become dependent on them afterwards. This was the kind of role played by state censorship in this field. Now we are having to acquire an internal immunity. I think this is starting already. At the beginning, I could see among the men around me a lot of excitement at these changes. My former husband, for example, with whom I keep good relations, announced to me that he had bought an erotic magazine. Naturally, I regard this kind of material as a bad use of women's bodies, one that objectifies them in the wrong way. But I didn't criticize him, because that was his choice. But now I can see that he has calmed down – like many of his generation, who are now in their forties.

How does the revival of traditional Russian values consort with this liberalization – but also commercialization?

Well, the old role models persist alongside it. The romantic ideals of women with which we were brought up were a mixture of elements from the past: the refined Turgenev girl, more or less aristocratic; the bolder salon type, rather more modern, but still with a special feminine charm; and so forth. It certainly didn't include artists like Popova or Grigorieva, still less the feminists Kuskova or Filosofova, who were quite unknown – there was zero influence from avant-garde models of the early part of the century. Now these traditional stereotypes retain a lot of power, especially among the more conservative men. I remember a highly regarded architect presenting to a foundation a plan for the revival of various old cities in Russia. I submitted some suggestions for integrating women in these development projects, emphasizing the importance for them of values of sexual equality and emancipation. To my amazement, he looked at me when I had finished and said: 'You know, Anastasia, all the best men in Russia took their brides from the provinces.' That was the sum of what had passed through his head! This was supposedly an intellectual, and actually quite a decent person. Others – from newspaper editors in Moscow to small-town notables, of whom I've met a good many – are much more aggressive. They tell one bluntly: 'You will spoil our women. They are already spoilt by socialism, and you want to continue that. No thanks.'

What about the younger generation – is there a new teenage culture?

In every country of the world, teenagers are preoccupied with sex – they want to find out about it as much as they can. In my time, we learnt not from parents, but from friends who were a bit older. Today teenagers can buy a lot of literature about it, most of it unfortunately of bad quality. They can find it difficult to distinguish between what is pornographic and what is informative, and what they are able to obtain is usually restrictive in its own way too. There is nothing about homosexuality, for example. Still, you could say there is some advance here. On the one hand, another feature of this more Westernized culture that is taking hold is the imposition of new physical norms: the beautiful, long-legged woman and the strong, ultra-masculine man. The result, I think, is that many feel distress because they are aware they are not like that – that the norm can't be made to fit their own image of themselves. So, for them, growing up is perhaps both easier and more complicated than it was for us. In our time, the visual ideal was not so all-important. Here Communist puritanism did have some kind of egalitarian effect – not too much, but still it did make the whole issue of the physical image less important between the sexes.

Does the politics of gender have any echo in this new generation?

I think it may do. I hope so. I never thought my daughter, who is fourteen, was particularly influenced by what I do. But I remember discussing with her the problem of whether a woman could run for the position of president in Russia. Maybe she had read something I'd written on the subject, I don't know, but six weeks ago she decided to interview her schoolmates on this point. She also included questions like, 'What do you think of the transition to the market economy – will it help you?', and so on. Then she wrote up the results as an article and, it's funny, this will be published by two newspapers and maybe even broadcast on the radio, on the 8th of March, which is Women's Day. Of course, it is not a scientific sample, but the results were interesting. The boys proved to be absolutely cynical about politics, without having any interest in them – they could express no real opinions about what a market economy would be like, for instance. The girls were very advanced: their answers were consistently impressive. On the final question, which was about the presidency, all the boys said it was a man's position and should not be occupied by a woman. The girls were much more egalitarian. Their view was that any person, regardless of sex, could occupy the post, provided they possessed the right personal qualities.

One of the paradoxes of the contemporary scene in Russia – also Eastern Europe – seems to lie here. Both at the official and the popular level there is an overwhelming fixation – a longing admiration, and desire for imitation – on the West as the capitalist Eden. Yet the West is also the culture that has generated modern feminism, and now more and more frequently produces leading women politicians – Thatcher or Cresson or Brundtland. How does Westernizing fantasy cope with this?

The attraction of the West is still quite new, and is based on ignorance. There is a kind of overexcitement that fails to notice much, except the features that take its fancy. In this vision, Western women are illustrated mainly by the seductive figures of the fashion models in *Burda*, the German photo magazine that now publishes in a Russian edition. They represent the opposite of the emancipation that ruined our women. Of course, feminism exists in the West, but it is confined to a crazy minority that has no influence – this is more or less the outlook at the moment. However, common realities are going to change this outlook.

Note

1. Nikolai Ivanovich Yezhov, State Security Minister 1936–8; responsible for mass repressions.

Notes on the Contributors

Svetlana Aivazova has a PhD in History, and is a senior researcher at the Institute of Comparative Political Sciences. She is a specialist on the history and theory of Russian and Western women's movements. She runs the F-1 Club, whose members include sociologists, historians, journalists and writers interested in the theme of women in Russian culture.

Zoya Khotkina has a PhD in Economics, and is a senior researcher at the Gender Centre. She has worked on labour resources for the Russian State Employment Committee (Goskomtrud), and is the author of numerous research papers on socio-economic problems of female employment. She coordinated the project 'Producers and consumers of statistical data on women' jointly with the United Nations statistics department. She is mainly concerned with the socio-economic and psychological aspects of women's careers.

Tatiana Klimenkova has a PhD in Philosophy, and is a senior researcher at the Russian Academy of Sciences Institute of Philosophy. She is the author of numerous papers on feminist theory and patriarchalism. She is particularly interested in issues of gender and culture, and has organized theoretical seminars on gender studies.

Valentina Konstantinova has a PhD in History, and is senior researcher at the Gender Centre. Her doctoral thesis was on the contemporary British feminist movement. A co-founder of the Lotus group; her research concerns women in the new political parties and movements of present-day Russia.

Olga Lipovskaya is a journalist and translator who has chaired the St

202

Petersburg Centre for Gender Problems since April 1993. She is the author of several articles on feminism, on women's rights during democratization, and on the new women's organizations published both in the Russian press and abroad.

Yelena Mazentseva is a researcher at the Gender Centre. She has taken part in sociological research. She is the author of a report for the World Health Organization on social aspects of men's and women's health. She is at present doing research into the links between health and occupation and women's employment problems.

Anastasia Posadskaya has a PhD in Economics from Moscow University. She has undertaken sociological research into women's employment and other issues at KamAZ plant, and in the town of Taganrog. One of the four founder members of Lotus – the League for Emancipation from Sexual Stereotypes – she has headed the Moscow Centre for Gender Studies at the Russian Academy of Sciences' Institute for Research into Socio-Economic Problems of the Population since 1989.

Olga Voronina has a PhD in Philosophy, and is a senior researcher at the Russian Academy of Sciences. One of the co-founders of the Lotus group, she is the author of many papers on the position of women in Russia and the Former Soviet Union and Western feminism. Specializes in the image of women in the mass media and their status in the public consciousness.

Olga Zhuk, also from St Petersburg, is a cinema historian, author of articles on cinematographic arts in Russian journals. She specializes in homosexuality and lesbianism in Russia, and is co-author of films on this theme. Currently she edits a gay cultural magazine, and is writing a book on Russia's lesbian subculture.